QUARRY BANK

PAST & PRESENT

NED WILLIAMS AND MEMBERS OF THE MOUNT PLEASANT LOCAL HISTORY GROUP

Olive Allchurch, Oswald Biddle, Marie Billingham, Mary Brookes, Carol Cobb, Bessie Cranton, Gladys Davies, Horace Dunn, Vera and Bram Dunn, Ira and Sandra Hampton, John James, Raymond Lilley, Gary and Sheila Marshall, Eddie and Pat Mattocks, Joyce and Lorraine Parkes, Joan Pearson, Doris Peat, Walter Perks, Margaret Priest, Charmayne Redding, Patrick and Sylvia Shaw, Colin Southall, Fred Tipton

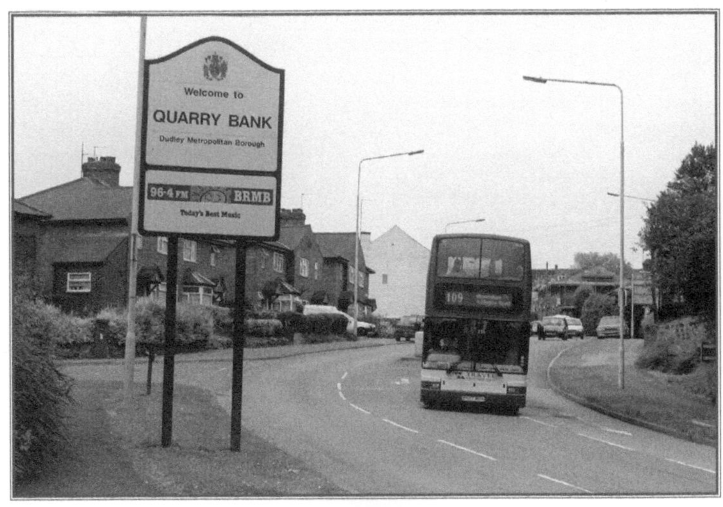

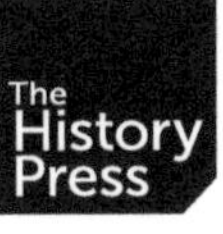

First published in 2003 by
Sutton Publishing

Reprinted 2016 by
The History Press
The Mill, Brimscombe Port, Stroud,
Gloucestershire, GL5 2QG
www.thehistorypress.co.uk

Copyright © Ned Williams, and members
of the Mount Pleasant Local History
Group, 2003 , 2016

Title page photograph: Welcome to Quarry
Bank.

British Library Cataloguing in Publication Data
A catalogue record for this book is available from the
British Library.

ISBN 978-0-7509-3715-3

Typeset in 10.5/13.5 Photina.
Typesetting and origination by
Sutton Publishing Limited.
Printed and bound in England..

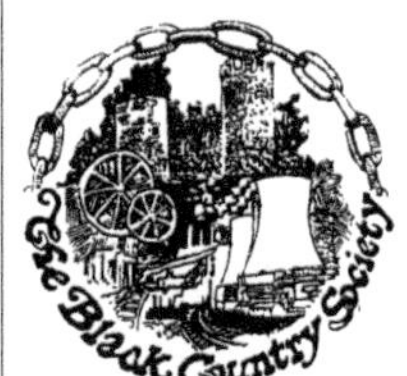

THE BLACK COUNTRY SOCIETY

The Black Country Society is proud to be associated with **The History Press** of Stroud. In 1994 the society was invited to collaborate in what has proved to be a highly successful publishing partnership, namely the extension of the *Britain in Old Photographs* series into the Black Country. In this joint venture the Black Country Society has played an important role in establishing and developing a major contribution to the region's photographic archives by encouraging society members to compile books of photographs on the area or town in which they live.

The first book in the Black Country series was *Wednesbury in Old Photographs* by Ian Bott, launched by Lord Archer of Sandwell in November 1994. Since then over 70 Black Country titles have been published. The total number of photographs contained in these books is in excess of 13,000, suggesting that the whole collection is probably the largest regional photographic survey of its type in any part of the country to date.

The society, which now has over 2,500 members worldwide, organises a yearly programme of activities. There are six venues in the Black Country where evening meetings are held on a monthly basis from September to April. In the summer months, there are fortnightly guided evening walks in the Black Country and its green borderland, and there is also a full programme of excursions further afield by car. Details of all these activities are to be found on the society's website, **www.blackcountrysociety.co.uk**, and in *The Blackcountryman*, the quarterly magazine that is distributed to all members.

PO Box 71 · Kingswinford · West Midlands DY6 9YN

CONTENTS

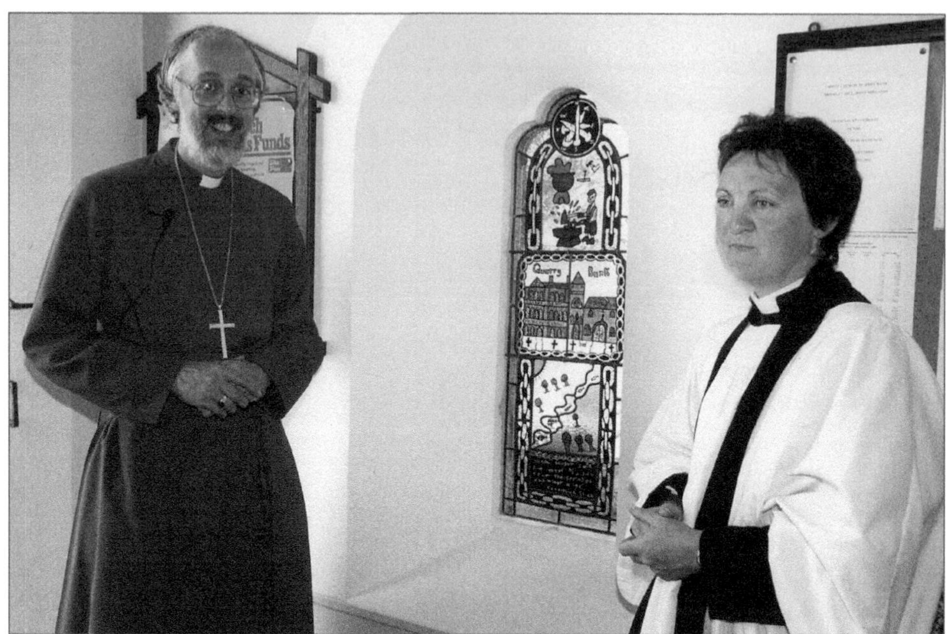

On 16 July 2003 a new window was dedicated in Christ Church, Quarry Bank. The late Nancy Marchant, a lifelong member of the church, had left a bequest to sponsor this window, and its design was the work of local children at Quarry Bank Primary School. *Above*: Bishop David Walker, Bishop of Dudley, and the Vicar of Christ Church, the Revd Caroline Windley, admire the window shortly after its dedication. *Right*: Jamie Field, from Quarry Bank Primary School Year Six, represents his school colleagues, who had worked on the design of the window, guided by the artist Keith Brettle. The window is intended to celebrate the past, present and future of Quarry Bank. (*John James*)

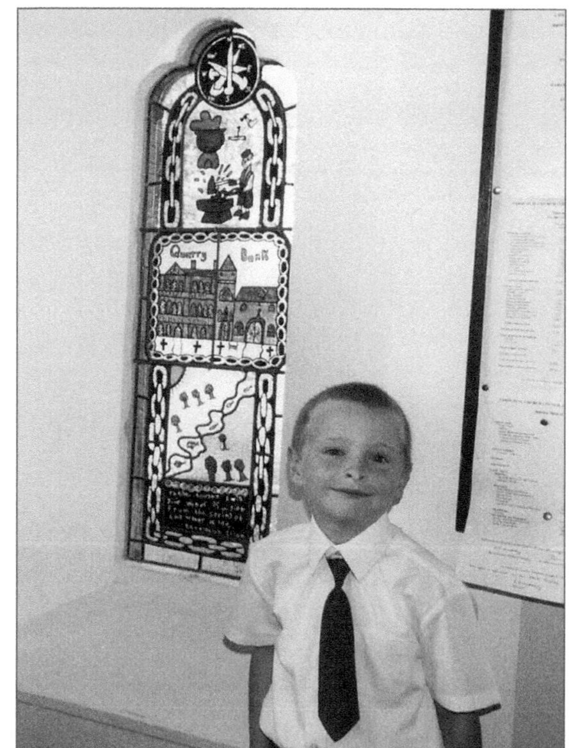

INTRODUCTION

Quarry Bank enjoyed a brief period of running its own affairs and having its existence acknowledged by the organisation of local government. From 1897 until 1934 Quarry Bank was an independent township, or 'Urban District', in the southernmost part of South Staffordshire. Since then it has been absorbed by Brierley Hill, and then by Dudley. But anyone who knows the Black Country will be familiar with the independence and strong sense of local identity that persists on a local level whatever the organisation of local government might decree. Quarry Bank is very real, very alive, and still has its own distinctive quality. As an acknowledge-ment of this, Dudley MBC has, in recent years, erected large signs at the borders exclaiming 'Welcome to Quarry Bank'.

In September 1997 the Mount Pleasant Local History Group began meeting on Friday afternoons at Mount Pleasant Primary School. In theory, our focus was just on the Mount Pleasant part of Quarry Bank, and its school. In practice, people were drawn to the group from all over Quarry Bank, and part of the excitement of being part of this group comes from the realisation that Quarry Bank may be small, but it can be endlessly divided into even smaller parts that have their own identity and history. Quarry Bank is quite a complex jigsaw puzzle, and we are still discovering the pieces, let alone trying to put the picture together!

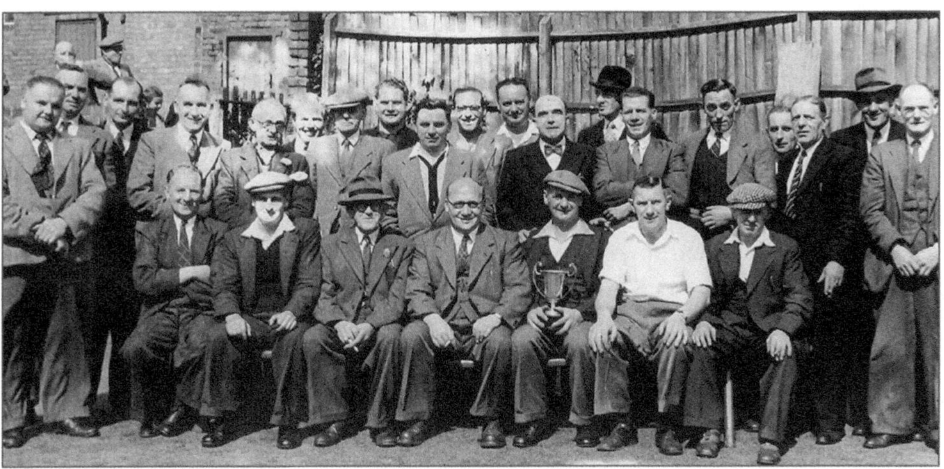

The Bowls Team at The White Horse, New Street, Quarry Bank, *c.*1948. One link between the past and the present is that a bowls team and bowling green still exist at The White Horse. But fashions change and the landscape changes. The bricks and mortar of a Quarry Bank that created a late-Victorian and Edwardian urban landscape still exist in part, but a new Quarry Bank dominated by housing of the second half of the twentieth century has emerged. (*The White Horse Collection*)

The History Group has produced three other publications prior to this one. The first was produced to celebrate an important anniversary for Mount Pleasant Primary School and was called 110 Not Out. The second was Quarry Bank in Old Photographs, the third was What's Happened to Quarry Bank? We have never stopped asking that question and we have returned to Sutton Publishing to present another selection of photographs in which we hope to link the past and present in Quarry Bank.

Quarry Bank's past is linked to mining, to nail- and chain-making and to the hollow-ware trade. Until the middle of the twentieth century the areas of Quarry Bank not used by industry or housing were semi-rural open space of a type that gave the Black Country quite a distinctive quality when compared with other industrialised or urbanised regions. Today that has changed and much of Quarry Bank seems residential with a small commercial central area. But Quarry Bank is not a bland piece of 'unified suburbia', because each section of Quarry Bank has its own story to tell.

The History Group has recently been preoccupied with the residential development of the area between Caledonia and the Amblecote Road. At other times we might lose ourselves in the mysteries of Birch Coppice, or Dunns Bank. We have tried to look at farms in Quarry Bank, while at the same time acquainting ourselves with the story of the local crisp factory. Everywhere we look there seems to be masses of local history that can vanish without being recorded. Now the pace of change has become so fast that we can barely keep up with recording the present so that future generations will be able to enjoy Quarry Bank's story!

As we finish assembling the pages of this book we already know that there is lots more to find out about Quarry Bank, and lots more to put on the record with books such as this one.

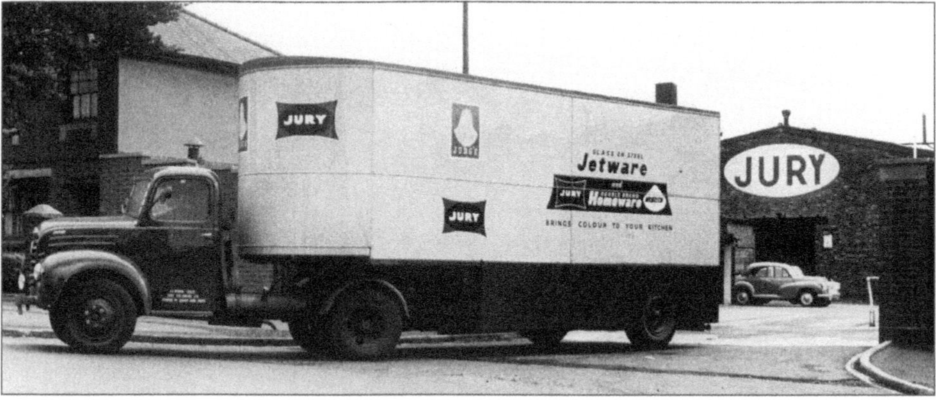

Another load of Quarry Bank-made products leaves the Jury Hollow-Ware Works factory in Thorns Road to be sold and exported worldwide, c.1960. Today, forty years later, local industry and its products do not seem to play such an important part in our sense of local identity. (*Marie Willetts*)

CHAPTER ONE

THE QUARRY BANK LANDSCAPE

The appearance of Quarry Bank is determined by two things: physical geography and urban development. A fairly high ridge, followed by the Amblecote Road, reaches the crossroads in the centre of Quarry Bank and then rapidly descends 'the bank' down to the floor of the valley of the River Stour. The descent follows the High Street down to Cradley Forge, and down Thorns Road to the boundary with Lye. In the other direction the lofty heights of Quarry Bank descend into the valley of the Black Brook and its tributaries: the Tipsyford Brook and the Mousesweet.

The surface of this 'up-and-down' landscape was frequently mined and quarried, for coal and fireclays, but gradually a scattered collection of small hamlets grew up and began to think of themselves as a village. The names of these hamlets have survived in the names still used to describe the subdivisions of Quarry Bank – Dunns Bank, Caledonia, Birch Coppice, The Thorns, Mount Pleasant, etc. – but by the middle of the nineteenth century the Anglican Church acknowledged that all these settlements added up to a 'parish', and by the 1890s the merging structures of local government recognised Quarry Bank as an 'Urban District'.

The twentieth century saw the High Street develop as the focal point of this township, and housing spread across the district in a succession of waves of development, surrounding small pockets of industry. The Stevens Park and some remarkable pockets of surviving 'open space' add some greenery to the bricks and mortar of Quarry Bank. Today the township is remarkable for its visual diversity, its striking views and its many surprises – especially when explored on foot.

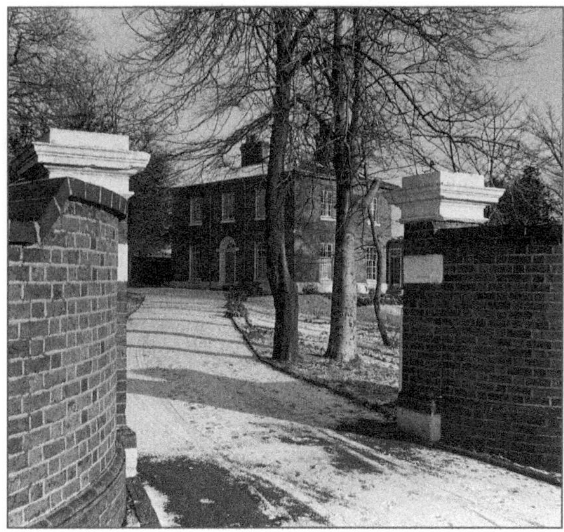

The vicarage, at the back of Christ Church, is generally thought to pre-date the church and still looks rather like an earlier manor house from this entrance in Maugham Street. (*Dave Whyley*)

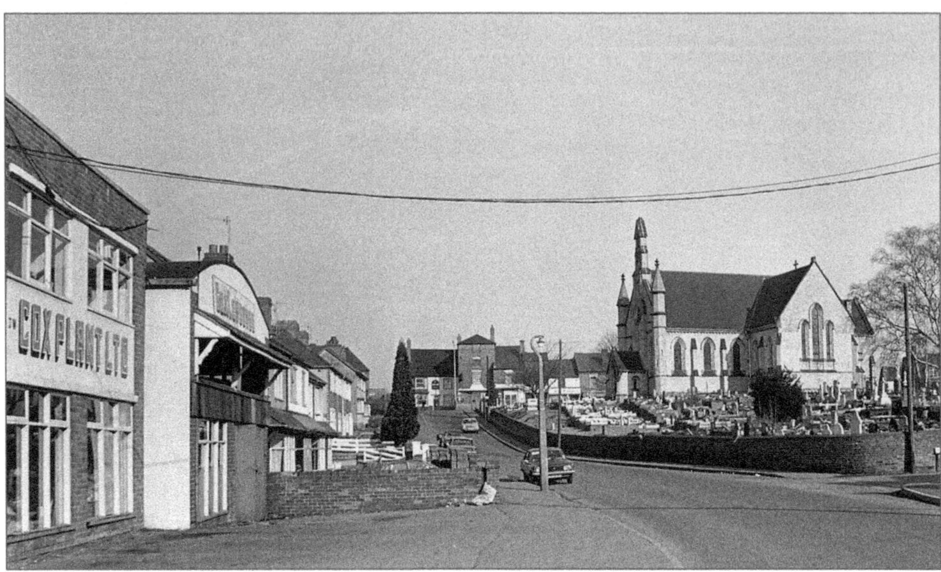

The church dominates the skyline in the centre of Quarry Bank, particularly when seen from what is now known as Park Road. The Royal Oak forms a backdrop to this part of the High Street, but the pub has now gone and modern shops have replaced the ones seen here. On the left is the headquarters of Percy Cox's building company and plant-hire business, but this is now replaced with housing. (*Dave Whyley*)

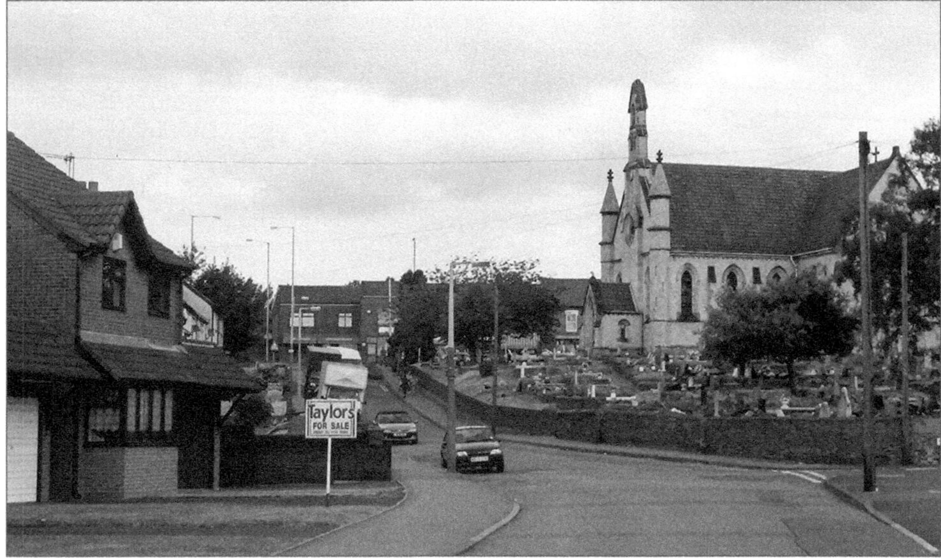

Apart from the loss of the Royal Oak in the background, and Percy Cox's in the foreground, the view from Park Road has remained much the same over the years. Until the opening of the park, this stretch of road was regarded as the top of Bower Lane – a route from Quarry Bank to Cradley. (*Ned Williams*)

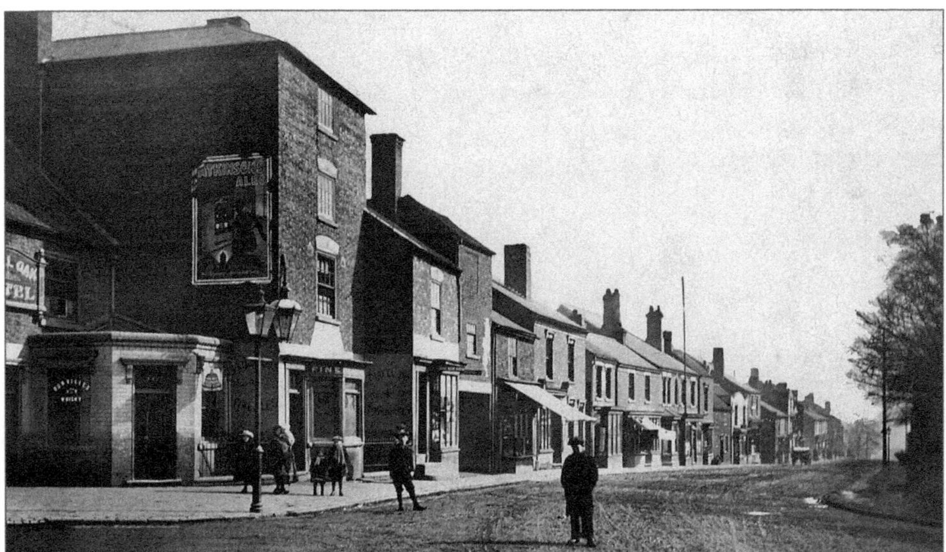

This John Price postcard presents a classic view of Quarry Bank High Street in Edwardian times. Out of the picture to the right is the parish church, on the left is the Royal Oak – behind which Pat Collins annually presented a few fairground amusements as a 'Quarry Bank Wake'. Shops then line the High Street until it dips out of sight and begins its descent into the Stour Valley. (*Ken Rock*)

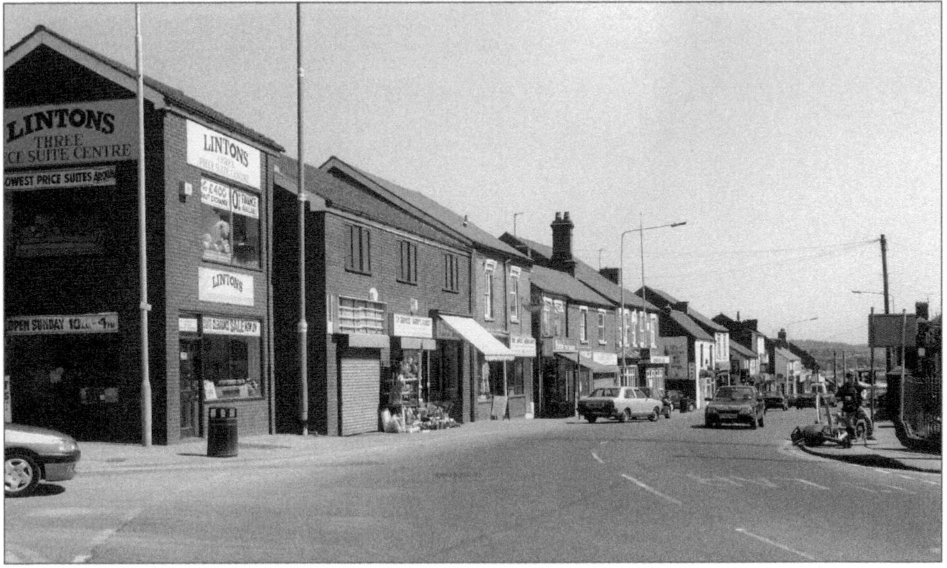

The Royal Oak and adjoining shops have been replaced with modern buildings, but the High Street still has the same feel about it as in this picture taken 1 May 1998. Traffic is now very heavy and retailing has struggled to survive, but the High Street still plays an important part in the life of Quarry Bank. (*Ned Williams*)

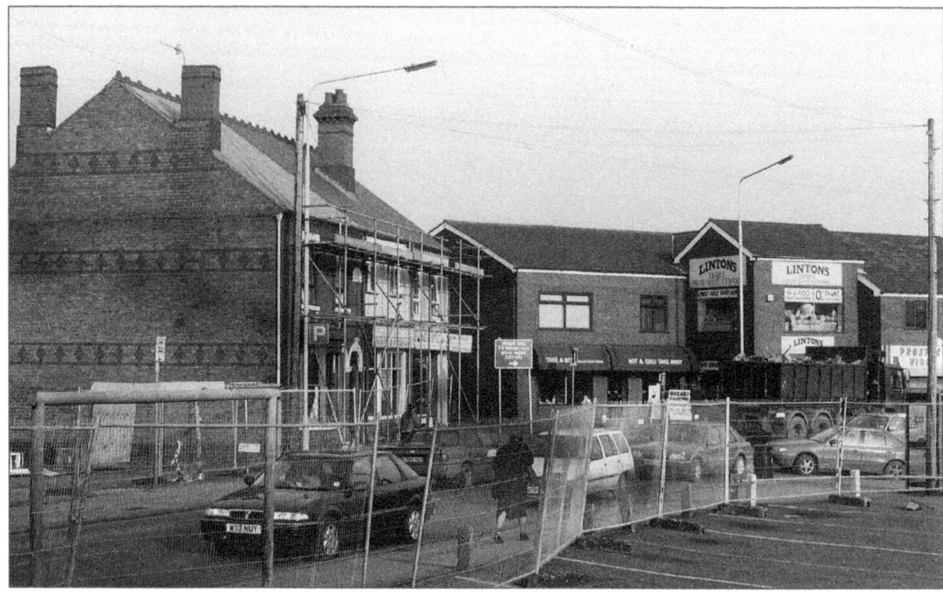

Above: Quarry Bank High Street being realigned on 23 January 1998. Salisbury House (of 1892 vintage), on the left, is being demolished in the process. In recent years the High Street has struggled to survive and the spread of shops has contracted at both ends in the process, the shops now 'starting' beyond Oak Street. *Below:* Mary's Fashion (just out of sight on the right-hand side of the above picture) has been in business for over forty years, proved by the fact that Mary Stevens can be seen standing in the same doorway in 2002 (left) and 1962 (right). (*Ned Williams*)

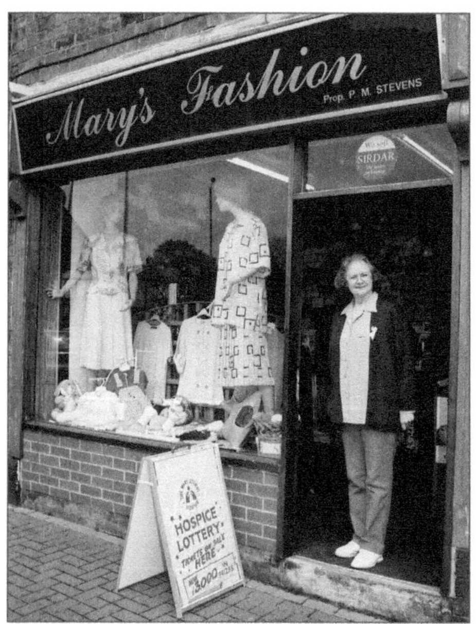

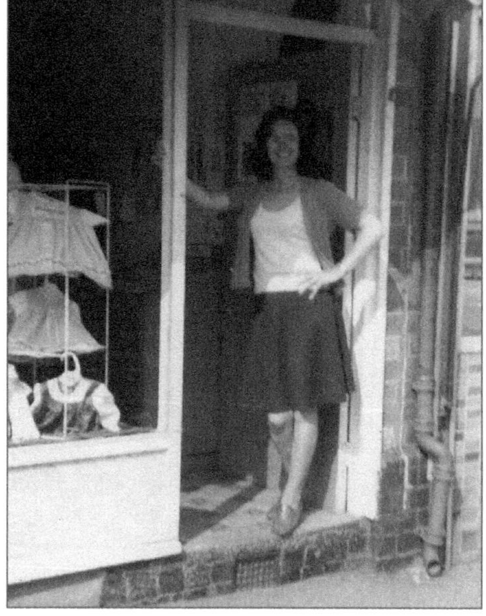

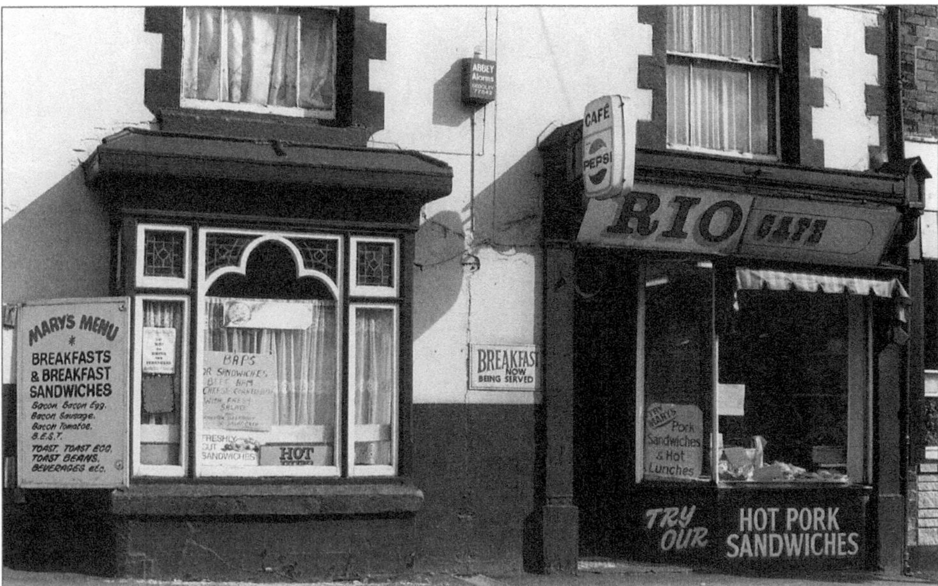

The Rio Cafe in Quarry Bank High Street, 1989. Today the premises are known as The Saucy Sausage and the premises next door have become The Li Garden – a Chinese take-away. (*Ned Williams*)

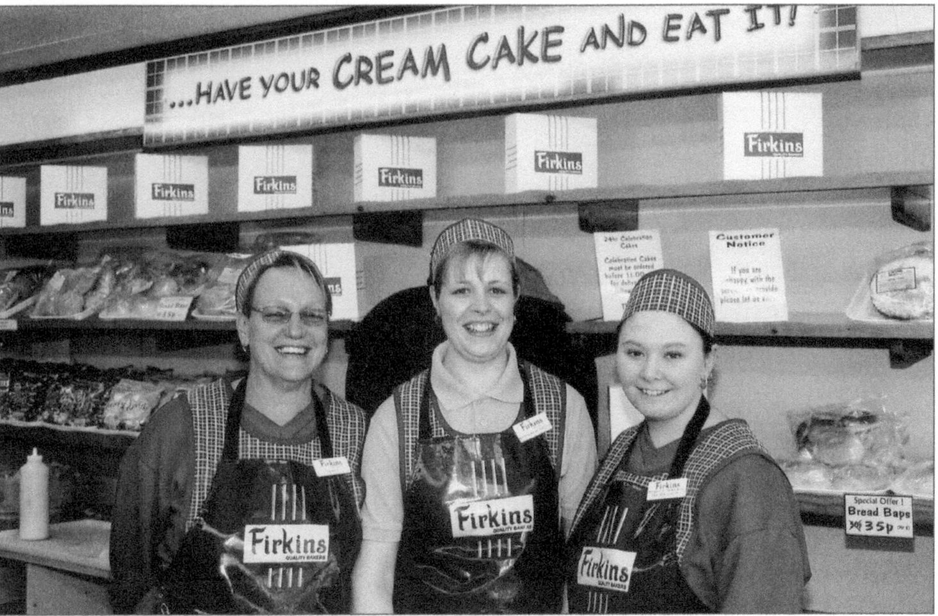

J.H. Paskin's General Drapery at 27 High Street became Robinson's Bakery and is now Firkins. Today the manageress, Donna Evans-Hadley, and her staff, Janet Holt and Rebecca Pickett, sell bread, cakes, pastries and sandwiches from this busy shop. (*Ned Williams*)

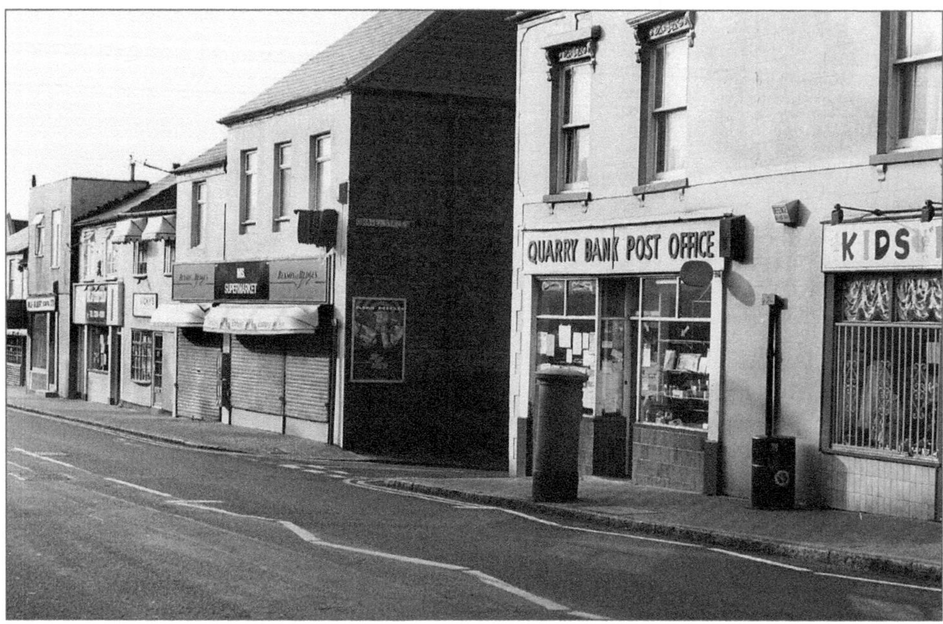

Quarry Bank post office, 14 July 1994. This photograph was taken just as the post office was about to be moved to the other side of the High Street. On the far side of Chapel Street is the shop once occupied by the Quarry Bank Branch of Dudley Cooperative Society. (*John James*)

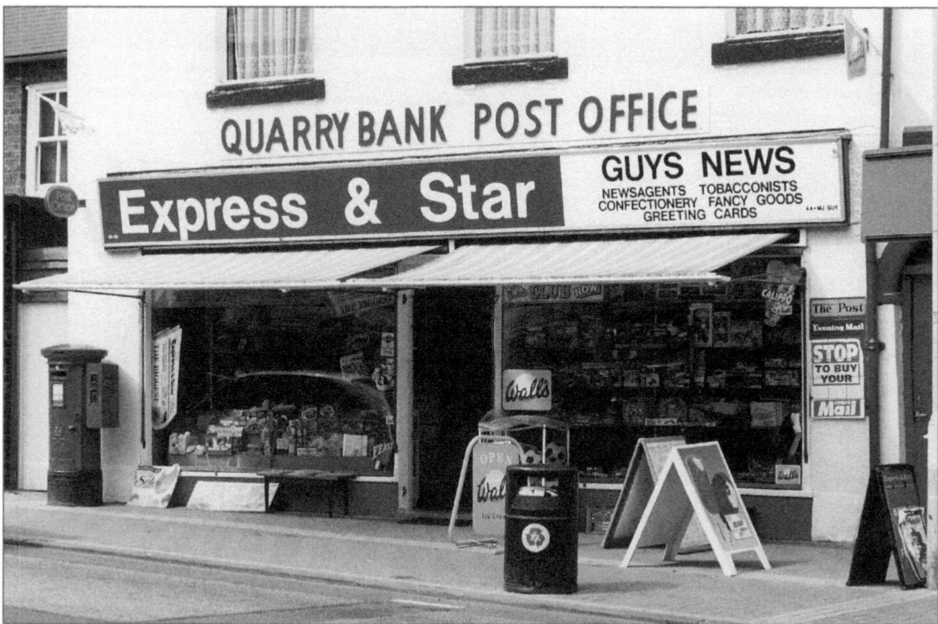

By 1 August 1994 Quarry Bank post office was open on the other side of the High Street. It is still there today, but Guys News has become a Spar shop. (*John James*)

Mark Johnson and Sharon Bagley now run Betty Stitch Kits in Quarry Bank High Street. They started the business in Halesowen and then moved to this shop, formerly occupied by Creations, but known to many Quarry Bank folk as Kendall's shop. (See *Quarry Bank in Old Photographs*, page 18.)

After two years, in June 2002, soon after these pictures were taken, they moved a few doors down the High Street to no. 51 on the corner of Victoria Road (once again moving into premises vacated by Creations.)

Offering a specialist needlecraft and picture-framing business, they serve an area much larger than Quarry Bank, and now have a much more spacious showroom, in which to serve customers from as far away as South Birmingham.

Retailing in Quarry Bank High Street has seen many changes, and specialist shops may help it survive. (*Ned Williams*)

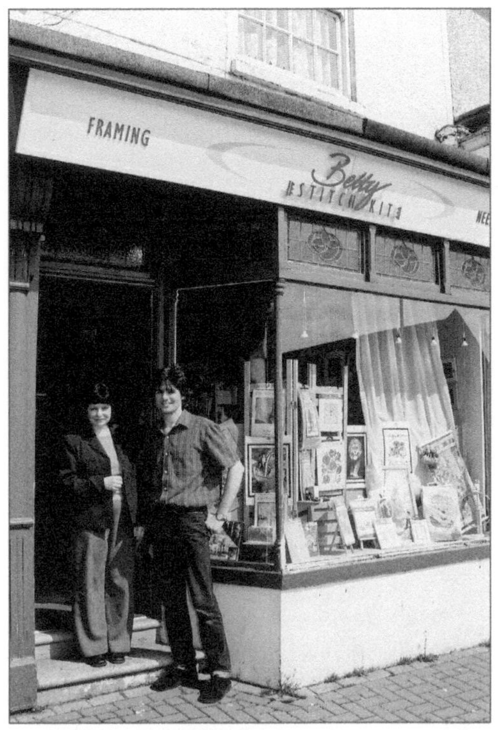

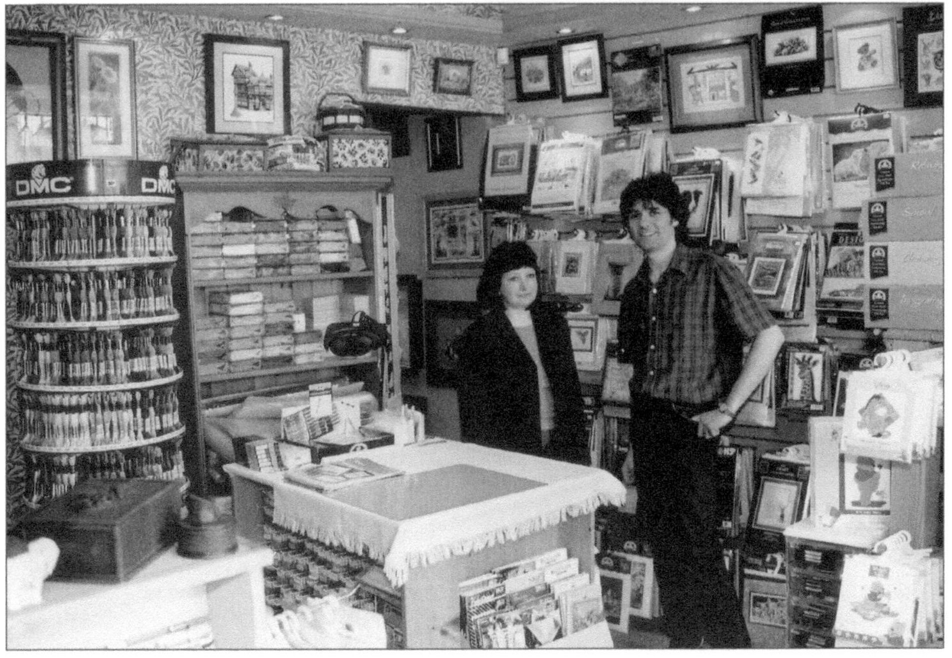

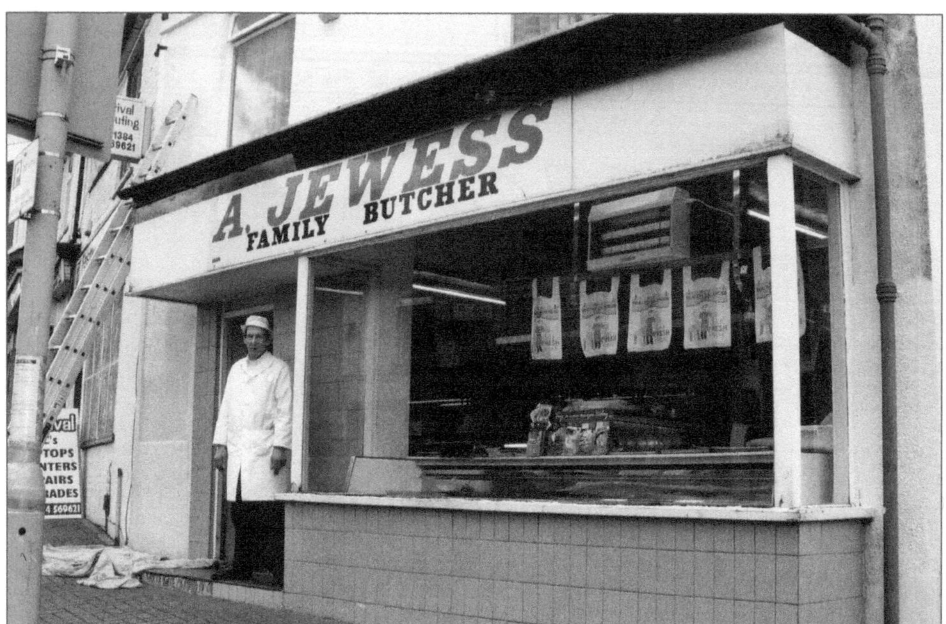

This butcher's shop, once Grove's, now Jewess's, marks an invisible boundary between Upper and Lower High Street. A large tree once stood outside the shop also marking the boundary. The front of the shop is at an angle to the pavement, and evidence suggests that the shop was built before the more linear development of the High Street above this point. (*Ned Williams*)

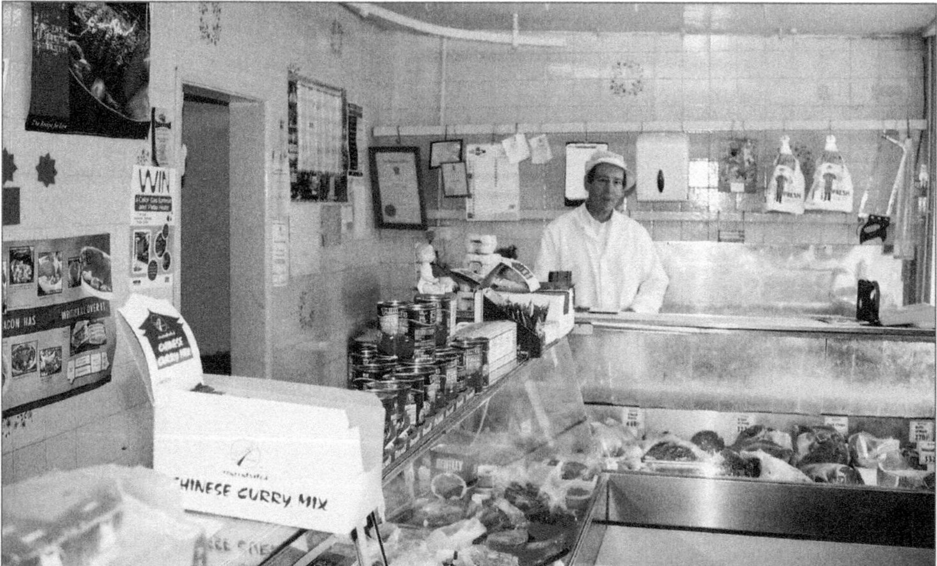

Anthony Jewess welcomes customers to his High Street shop in July 2002. He has deeds that show that the shop was built in 1868 for Joseph Burley, a butcher based in Cradley Heath. It was later owned by a Mr Paskin, and then the Grove family. (*Ned Williams*)

Right: Mrs Elizabeth Batham, widow of Jabez Batham, a chain-maker. She previously kept a small shop at 30 Stour Hill, until taking on these premises at 157 High Street. She ran the drapery business until her death on 19 February 1942. (*MPLHG*)

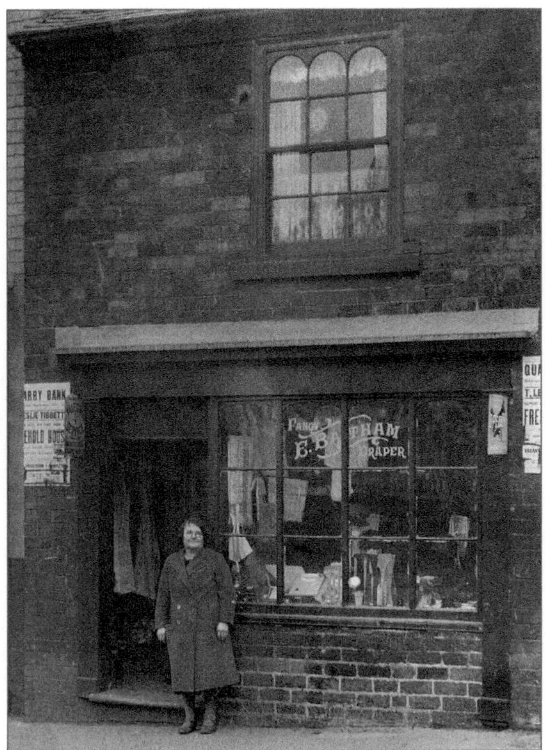

Below: This aerial view features the butcher's shop referred to on the previous page in the top left-hand corner and shows how the High Street winds through the lower part of Quarry Bank. The primary school fills the picture, but it is also possible to make out the Community Centre on the corner of Sheffield Street, the old Sunday school building, and Woodhouse Court under construction. To the right of the school playground is the site of Saltwells No. 33 Colliery, which until about 1912 brought coal working within a few yards of the High Street. (*MPLHG*)

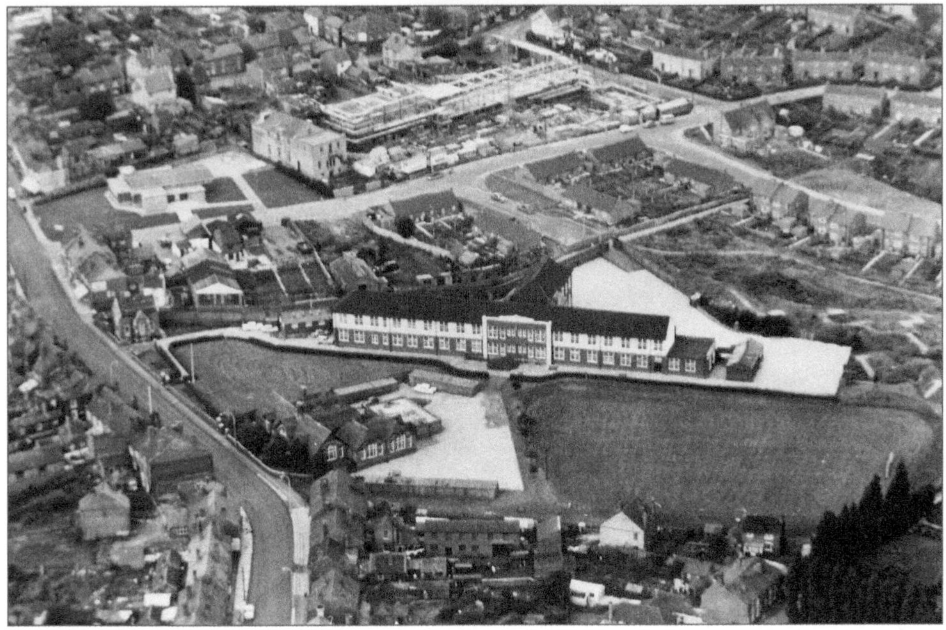

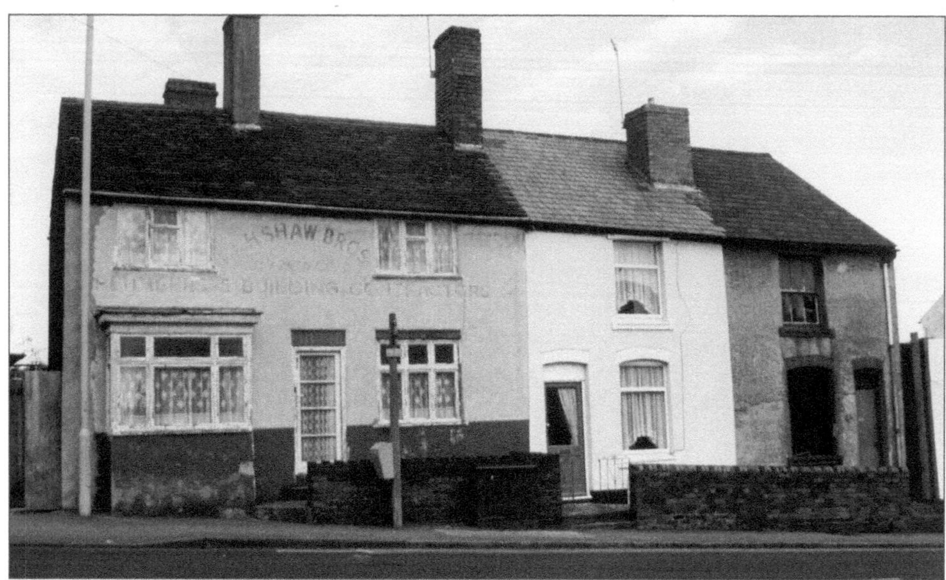

The two pictures on this page illustrate how some things stay the same while others change or disappear in Quarry Bank High Street. The March 1989 photograph, above, shows the cottages next door to The Queens Head, now demolished. The signwriting on the building on the left still proclaims, in faded fashion, that this was the headquarters of F. & H. Shaw Brothers, well-known decorators and building contractors. (*Ned Williams*)

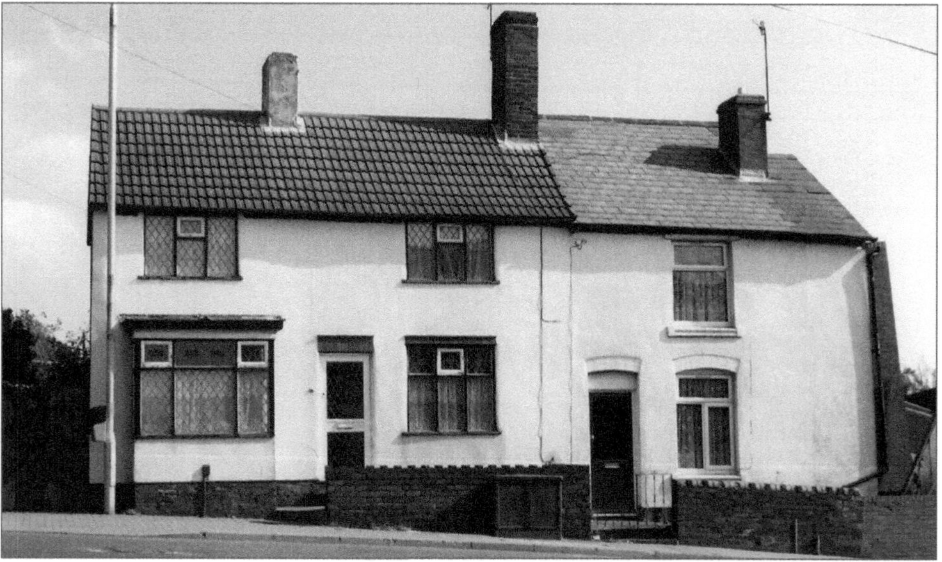

A September 2002 photograph reveals that the Shaw Brothers' premises have been nicely restored but not substantially altered, and the house next door has not changed at all. Meanwhile, the dwelling seen on the right in the upper photograph has disappeared altogether! (Or maybe only half of it?) (*Ned Williams*)

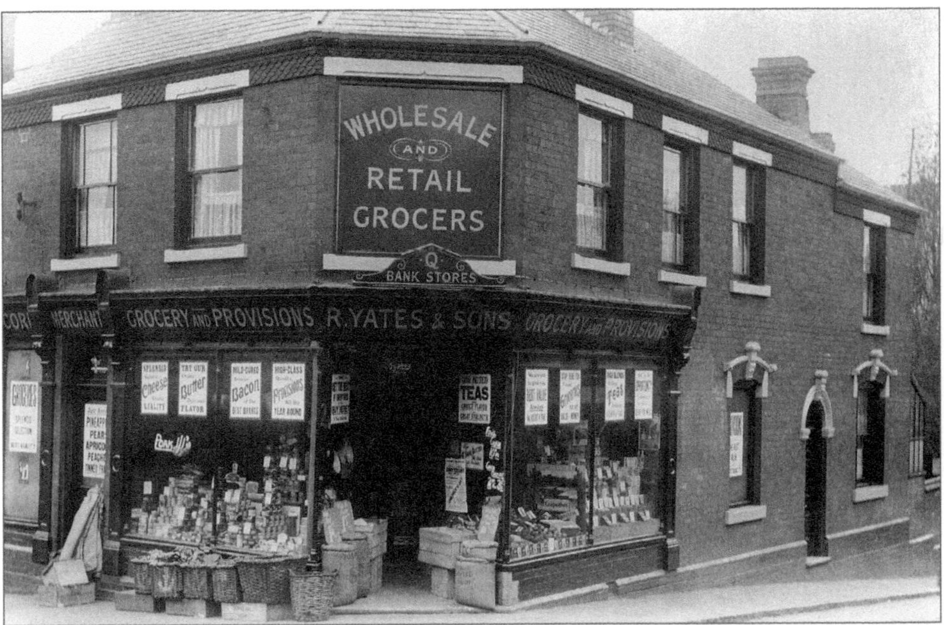

Opposite Shaw Brothers is the entrance to New Street. New Street, lower Maugham Street and Queen Street were probably laid out in the first phase of formal urbanisation of Quarry Bank in the 1880s. Robert Yates's grocery store occupies a prominent corner position – seen here in the 1930s. (*Margaret Yates*)

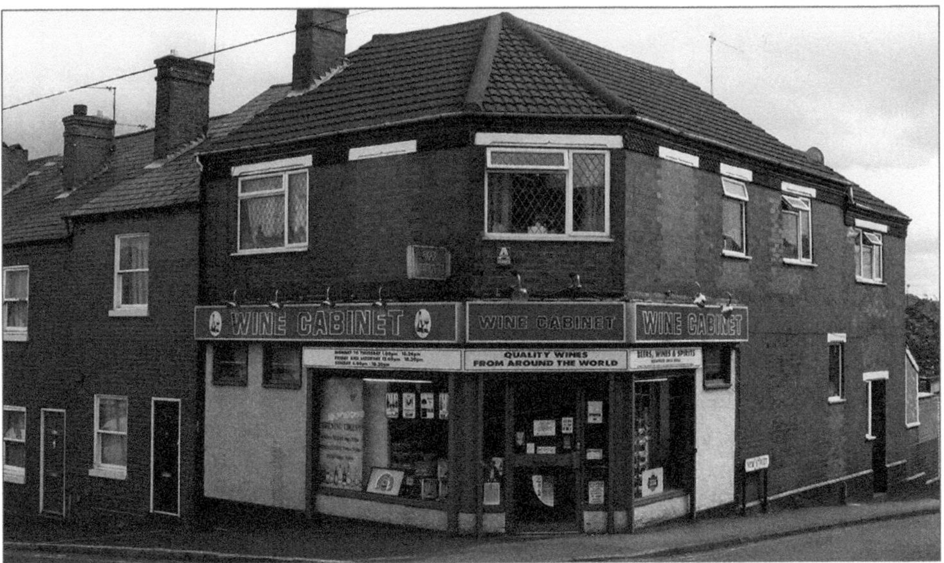

Yates's store has now become an off-licence, the Wine Cabinet, and much of the Victorian quality of the building has been lost by the introduction of modern windows and a new shopfront. (*Ned Williams*)

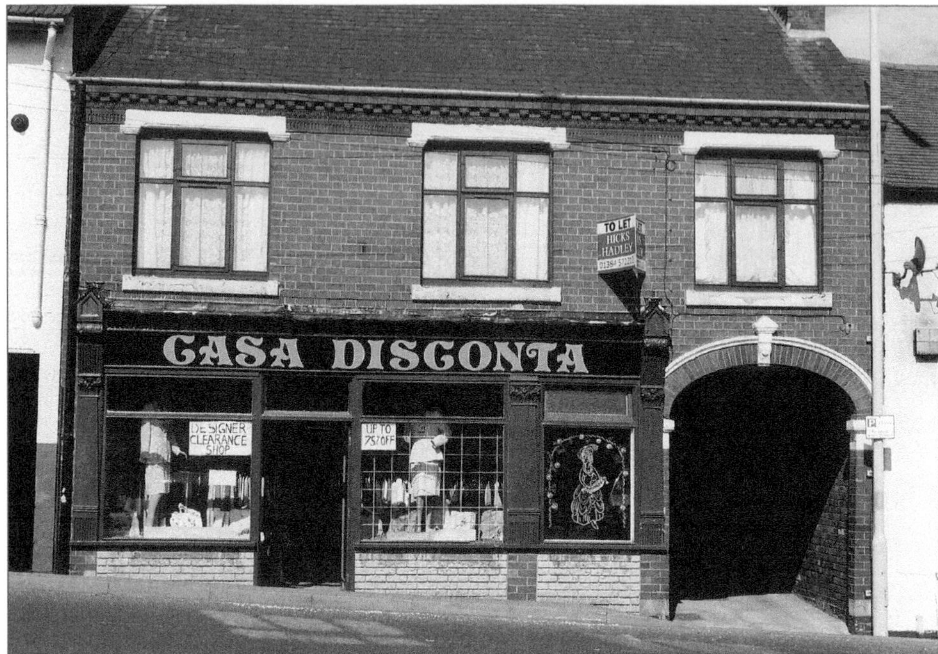

Casa Disconta currently occupies a building that has not altered substantially since it was built in the 1890s. Its distinctive arch, upstairs windows and elegant shopfront can be seen in many photographs of the Lower High Street. Many local people remember the shop as Cox's, the chemist's. (*Ned Williams*)

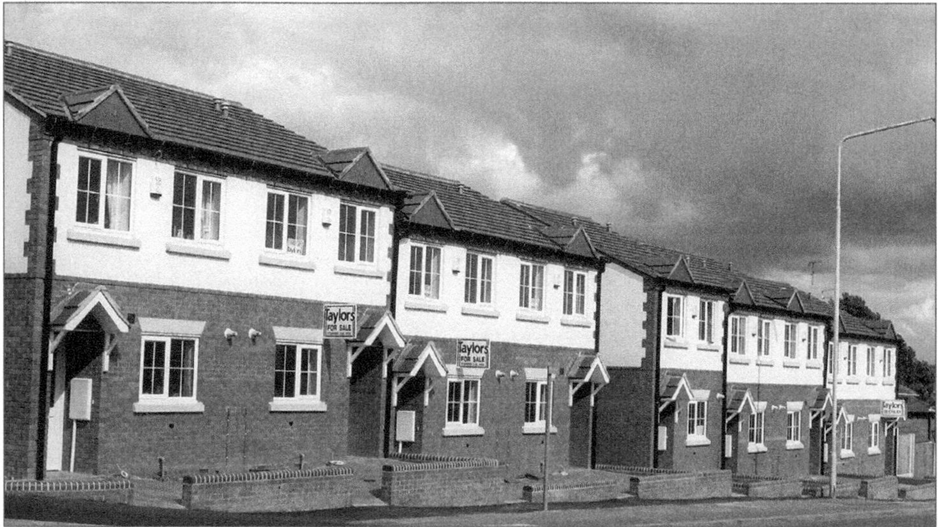

New houses in the Lower High Street now occupy the site of a petrol station that was previously occupied by the Coronet Cinema. The Coronet was a small independent cinema that presented films in Quarry Bank from 1933 until 1960. (*Ned Williams*)

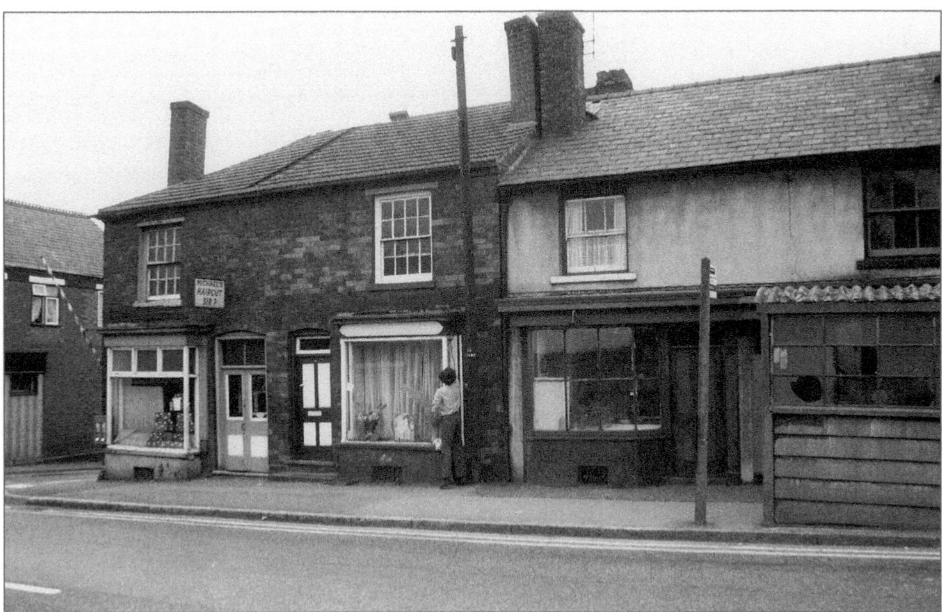

The High Street buildings above the junction with New Street are very old and of 'cottage-like' proportions. The corner shop has long been a gents hairdresser's, for many years known as Duckett's, and the shop just to the left of the bus shelter (no longer there) was Genner's fish and chip shop, now trading as Our Plaice Too. This picture was taken in the early 1970s. (*Dave Whyley*)

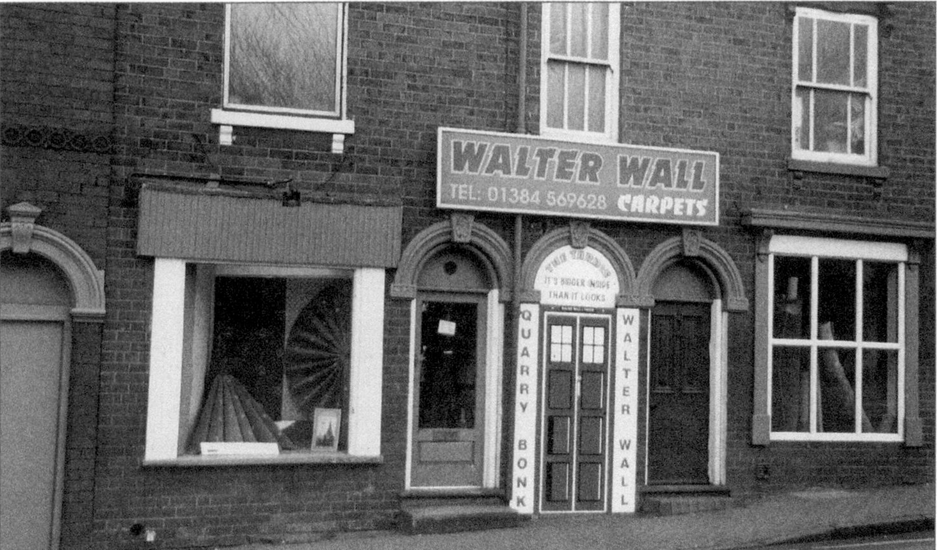

A 1998 picture of the well-established and well-known Quarry Bank business – Walter Wall. Older folk remember the shops run by members of the Thompson family – selling shoes and carrying out shoe repairs. (*Ned Williams*)

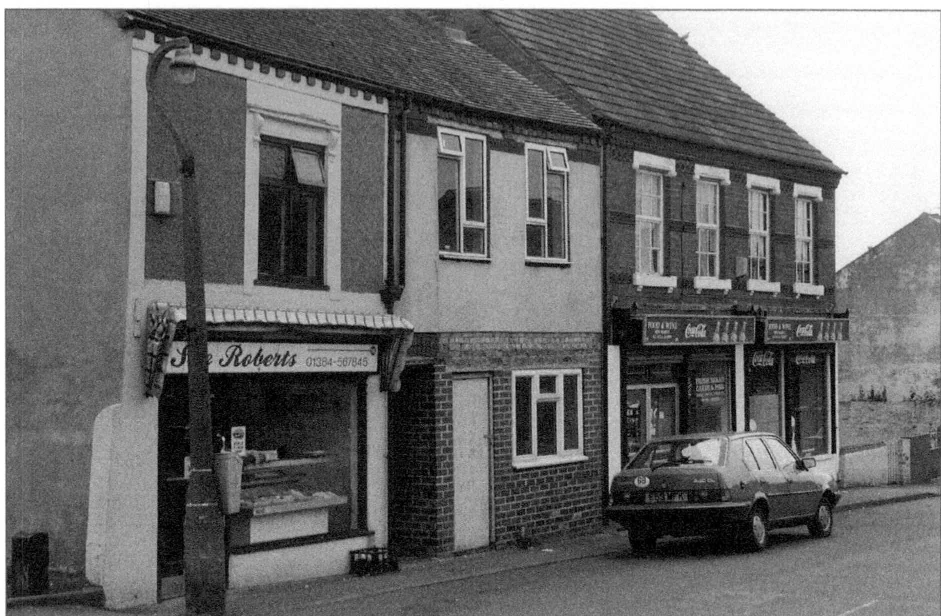

New Street had many shops and seemed to enjoy a commercial independence of its own, separate from the High Street. This 1998 picture shows how shops were disappearing, but they had once included Simmonds's, the grocer's, a fish and chip shop, then Hadley's (once Griffiths's), and Harris's sweet shop. (*Ned Williams*)

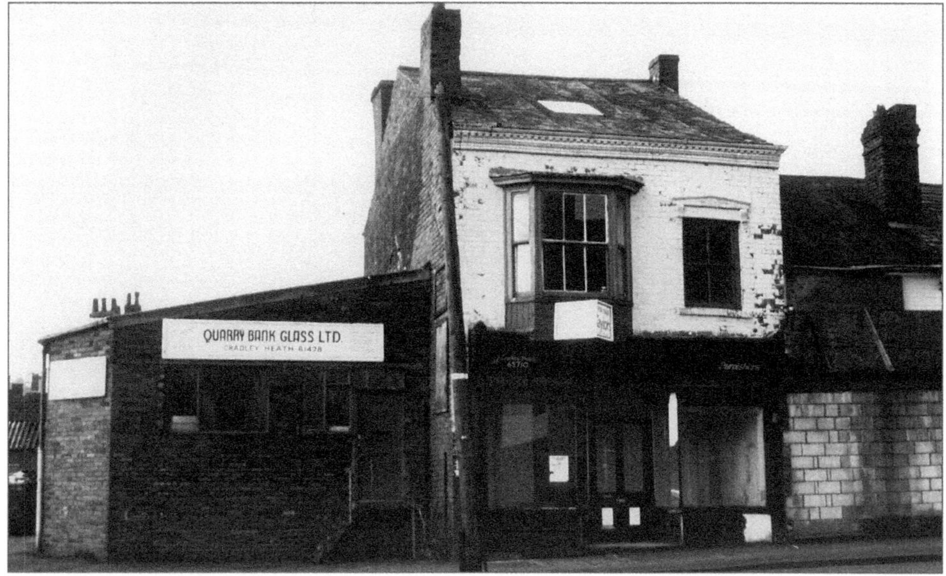

One of the principal shops of New Street had once been Goodwin's (see *Quarry Bank in Old Photographs*, pages 34–5), opened in 1875. It had traded for a century but looks very forlorn in this 1989 photograph. (*Ned Williams*)

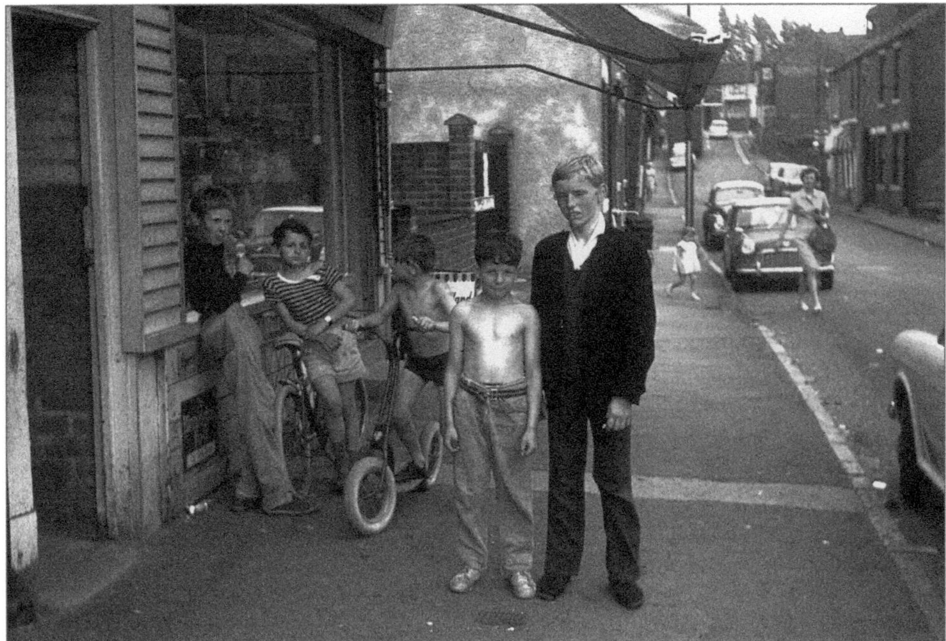

For many years the newsagent shop in New Street was run by George Court. In about 1966 the business was taken over by Ray Lilley, and this picture was taken during his tenure, which lasted until 1970. The Court family continued to wholesale Sunday papers for a while. (*Ray Lilley*)

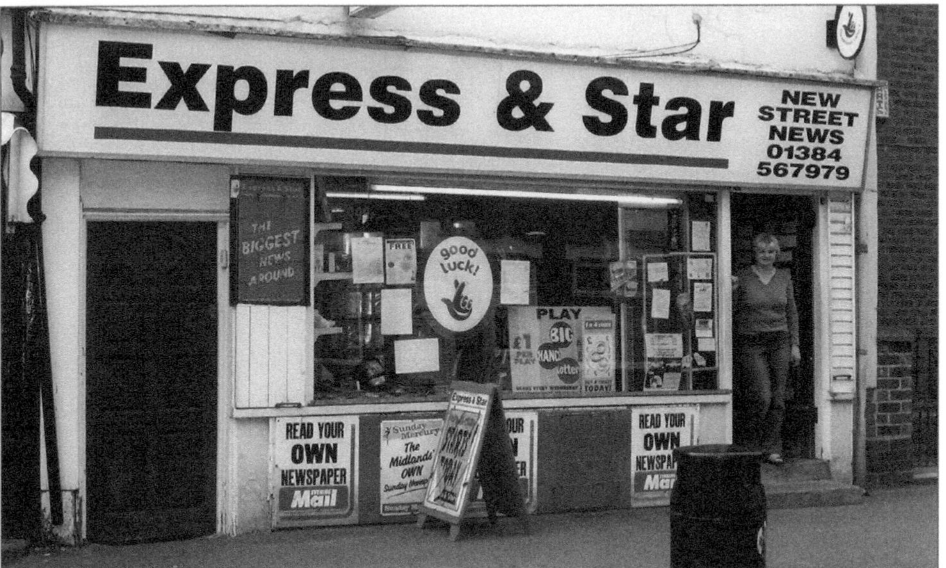

In recent years the newspaper shop in New Street has been run by Mrs Stote and Mrs Walker. Mrs Stote stands in the doorway in July 2003. (*Ned Williams*)

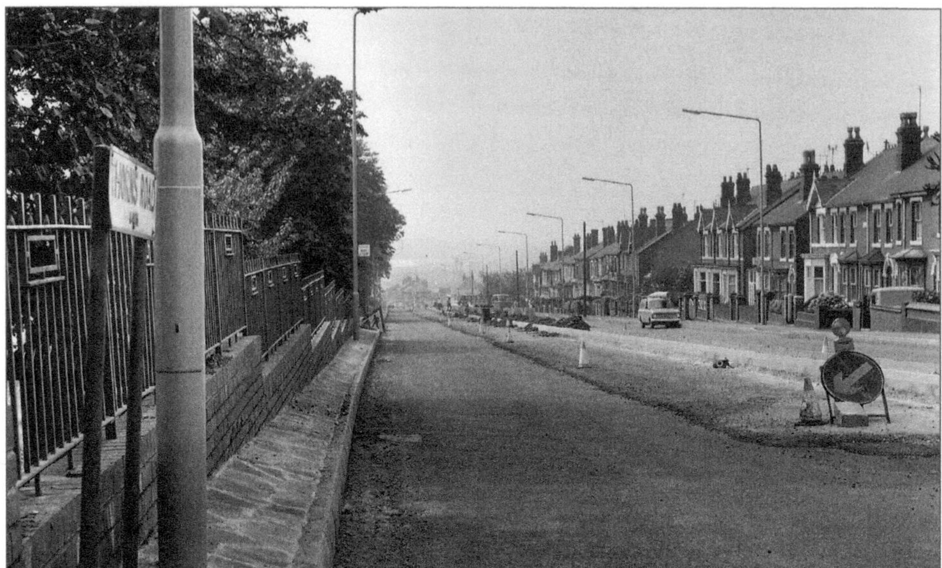

Thorns Road enjoyed a very different kind of development when compared with the High Street. Good-quality Edwardian housing lined the west side of the road – once a main turnpike between Dudley and Kidderminster. Industry exploited the land on the east side of the road, but since the 1920s the impact of this has been lessened by the development of Stevens Park. Here the railings of the park are pushed back to make way for the new dual carriageway. (*John James*)

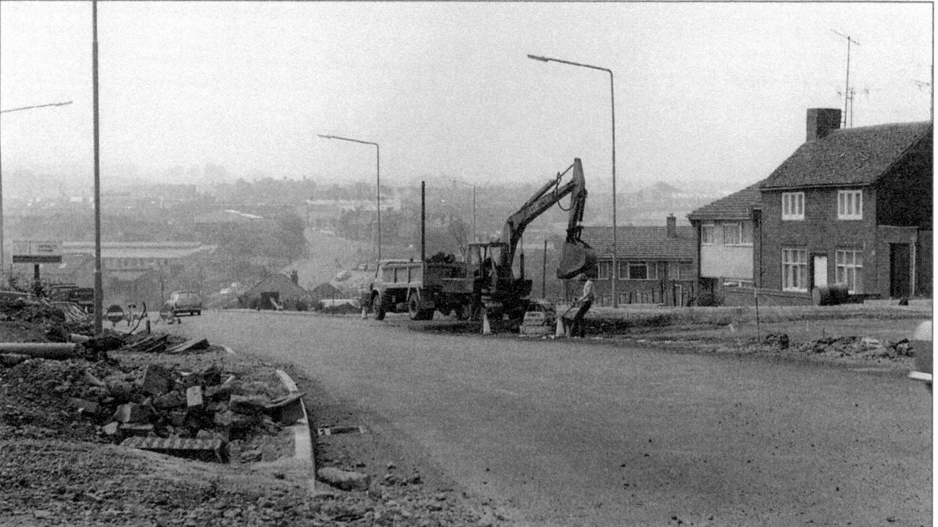

Thorns Road passes through Thorns – one of the subdivisions of Quarry Bank – once with its own post office, pub and local housing, dominated by the Jury Hollow-Ware Works. Here we see Thorns Road heading for the Lye at the time of creating the dual carriageway during the 1970s. (*John James*)

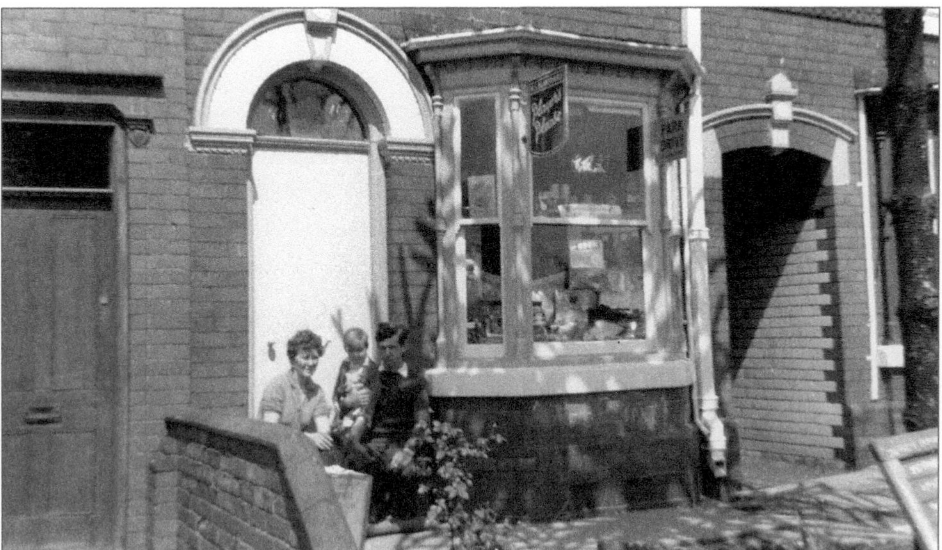

Marjorie Blanshed, née Hackett, ran a shop at 78 Thorns Road from 1959 to 1974. Today the premises have returned to private domestic use, but in this picture the Blanshed family pose for the camera outside their shop. (*Marjorie Blanshed*)

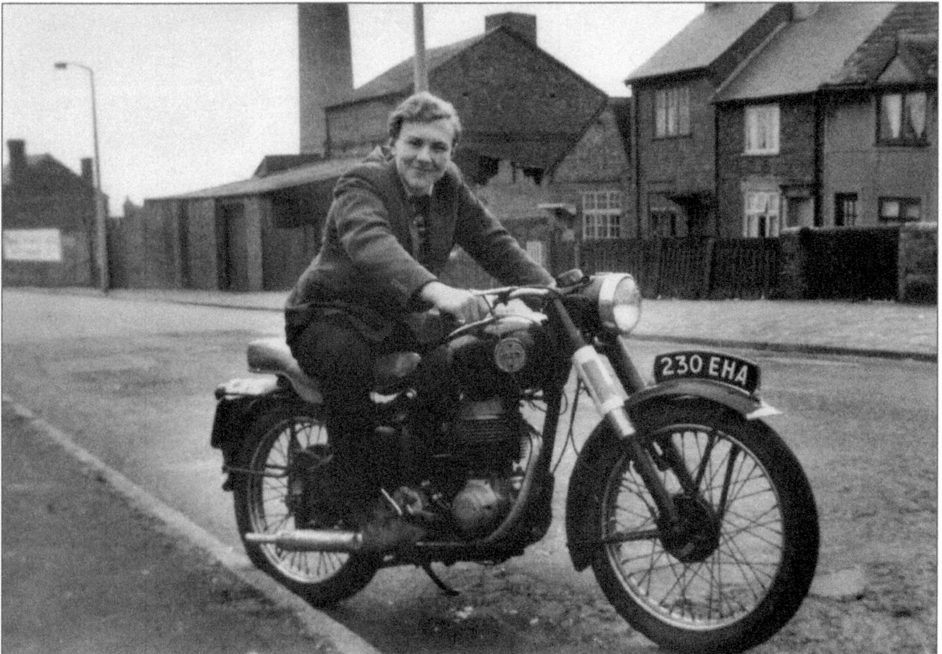

A portrait of Brian Harris and his Ariel Colt motorcycle taken in the early 1960s turns, forty years later, into an interesting visual record of Thorns Road, and the houses and works on the section just above the junction with Caledonia. (*Collected via Marie Billingham*)

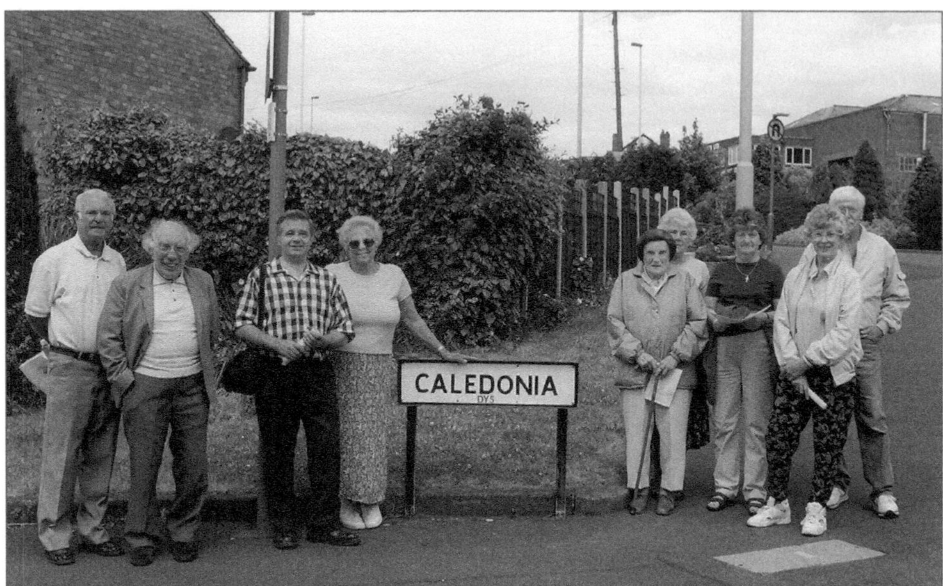

Caledonia was once an isolated hamlet just off Thorns Road built on land that sloped down into the valley of the Stour. Its name comes from the Caledonian clay once mined in the area. The houses that formed the 'old' Caledonia have been swept away with the wholesale development of this area for housing from the 1960s onwards. In 2003 the Local History Group decided to explore Caledonia and its past with the help of Walter Perks (far right), who had grown up in the area. Our journey began here at the junction with Thorns Road. (*Ned Williams*)

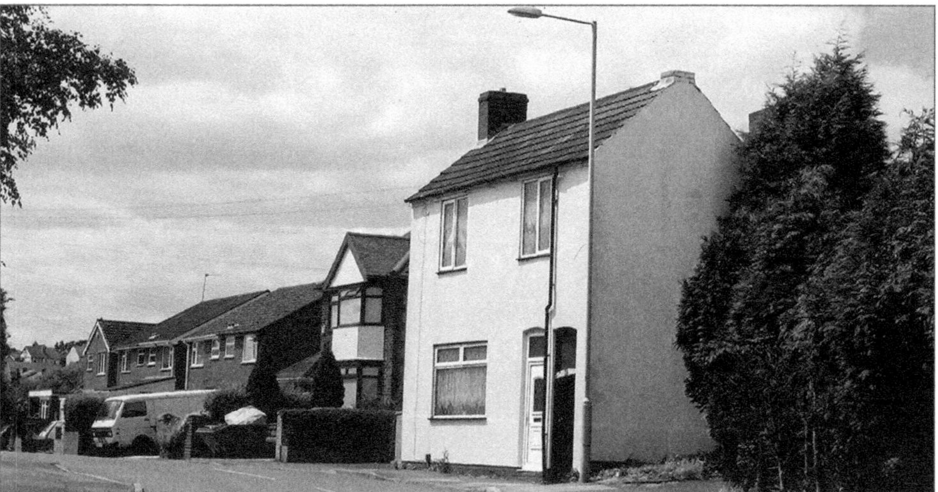

Next to the modern houses stands the only surviving building of the 'old' Caledonia – now a private home, but once a pub called Staffordshire House. (The Stour formed the county boundary and gave the pub's name a special significance.) The modern houses replaced the main row of houses of 'old' Caledonia. (*Ned Williams*)

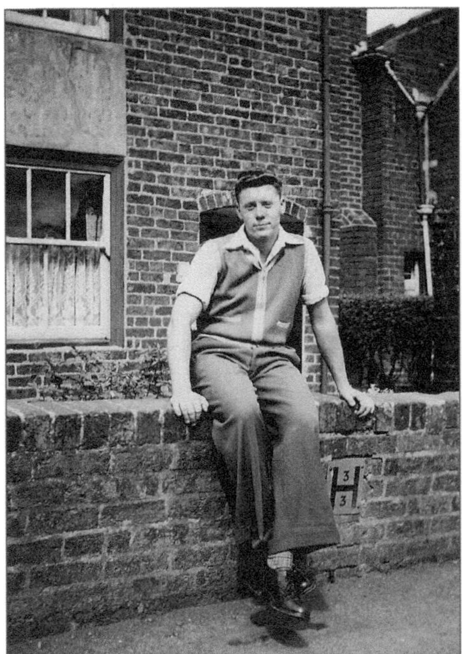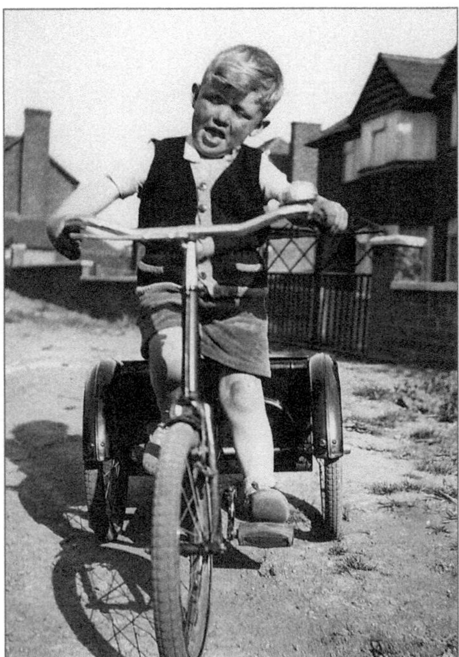

Old and new in Caledonia. *Left*: Walter Perks outside his home at no. 21 in the 'old' Caledonia, *c.* 1953. The house was demolished about ten years later. *Right*: Young Kevin Field on his new trike when new houses (in the background) were beginning to appear in Caledonia, *c.* 1953. (*Walter Perks*)

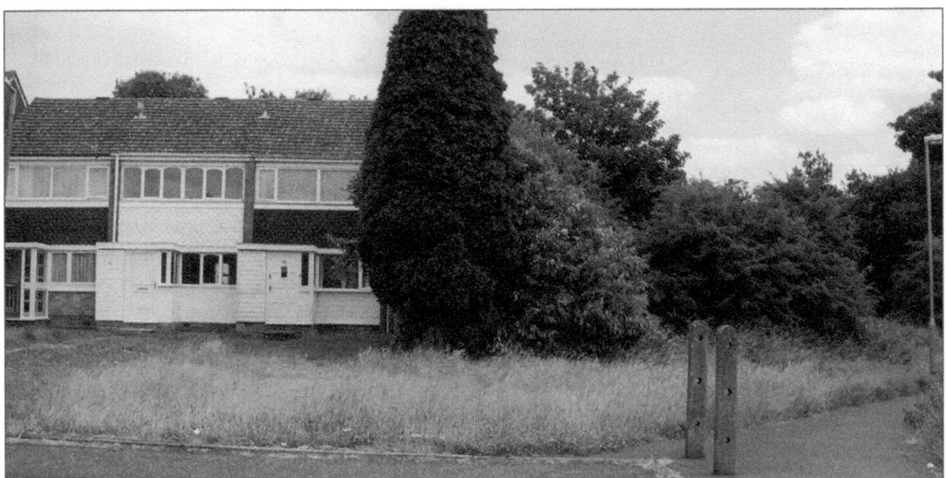

On the right a footpath can be seen that once brought people from Thorns Road into the rough open spaces of Caledonia – overgrown pit banks known locally as The Cricket. After further open-casting and considerable landscaping the area has been covered in houses since the 1960s. Early McClean houses can be seen on the left. The path now stops here at Grosvenor Road. (*Ned Williams*)

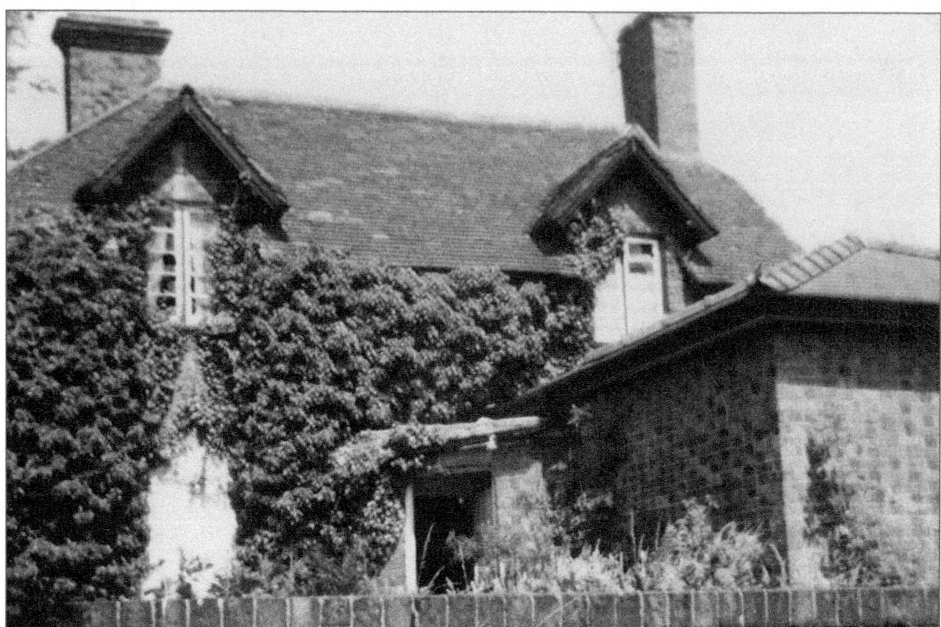

Mousehall Farm was built on land once occupied by the Ranger's lodge when the area was the southernmost part of Pensnett Chase. It was inhabited by the Deeley family in recent times and was compulsorily purchased at the end of the 1960s to prepare a site for the new Thorns Comprehensive School. (*Collected by Margaret Priest*)

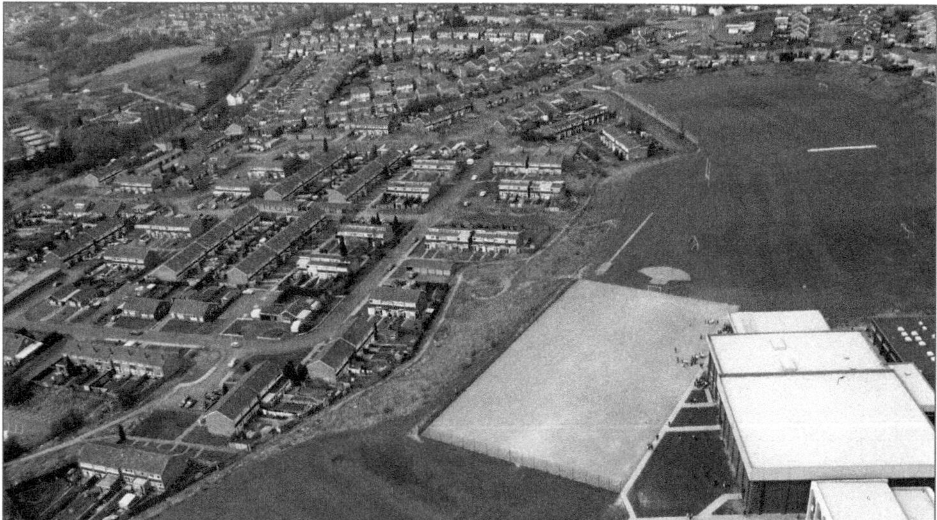

After some frenzied open-cast mining the Mousehall Farm area was levelled and the new school built – the rugby pitch occupies the space where the farmhouse once stood. This aerial view looks from the school, on the right, down towards Caledonia and the Stour Valley, and shows how housing has filled this area since the 1960s. (*MPLHG*)

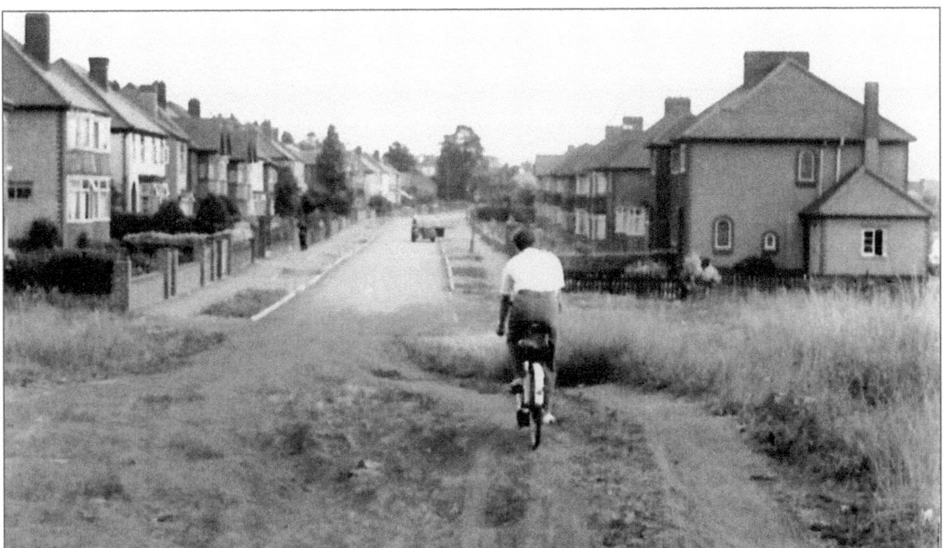

A cyclist, thought to be Michael Claydon, comes off the rough track from Dove Hill into the made-up portion of Acres Road, itself probably only surfaced in the early 1950s. Acres Road at the time, about 1955, stopped at no. 90, the house on the left, at the time occupied by the Stevens family. The last house on the right was occupied by the Robins family. This photograph was taken by Norman Williams, born in 1940 at 72 Acres Road, and forms part of one of the few photographic records of the development of this part of Quarry Bank. (*Norman Williams*)

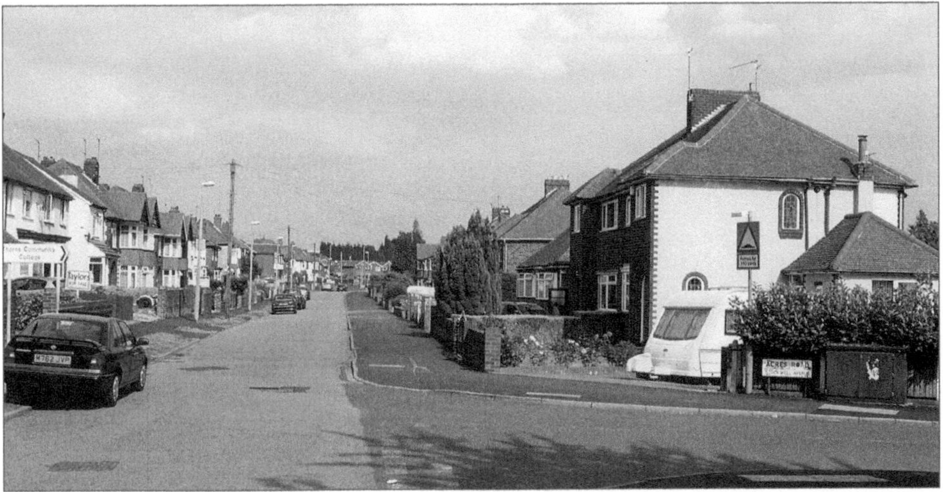

Acres Road today, with hedge and caravan partly obscuring the house seen so clearly above. The sign on the corner reads 'Acres Road, leading to Stockwell Avenue'. Houses were built in this short piece of Acres Road after the war, but Stockwell Road was not created until the 1970s. Acres Road (behind the camera) was completed through to Amblecote Road in the late 1950s. The fields between Thorns Road and Amblecote Road had been known as The Twelve Acres. (*Ned Williams*)

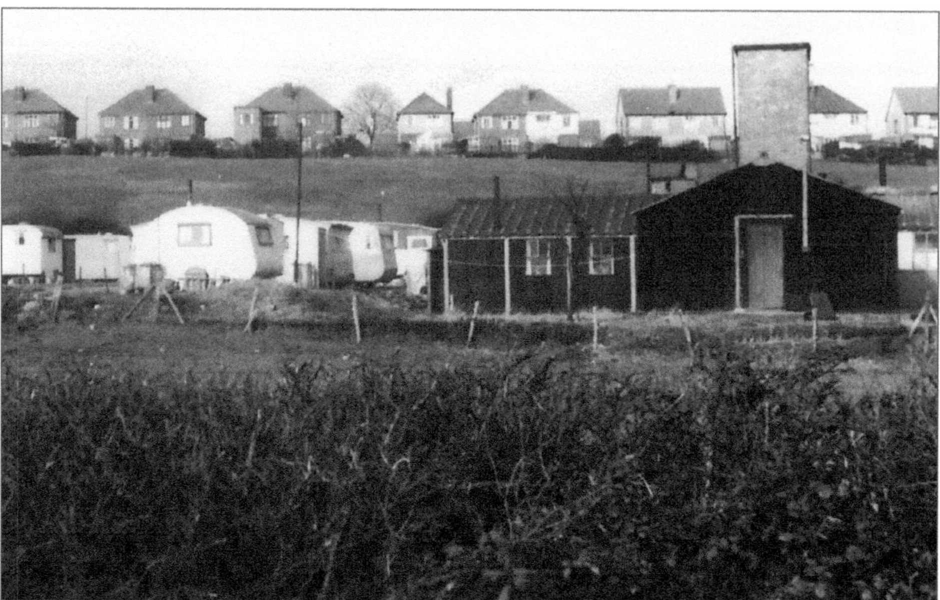

Looking over the hedge in Woods Lane at what is now the top of Calewood Road, this early 1950s view reveals a rare glimpse of the prisoner of war camp built during the Second World War on land requisitioned from Ravensitch Farm. By the time this picture was taken caravans and mobile homes occupied the site. Houses in Amblecote Road provide the backdrop. (*Norman Williams*)

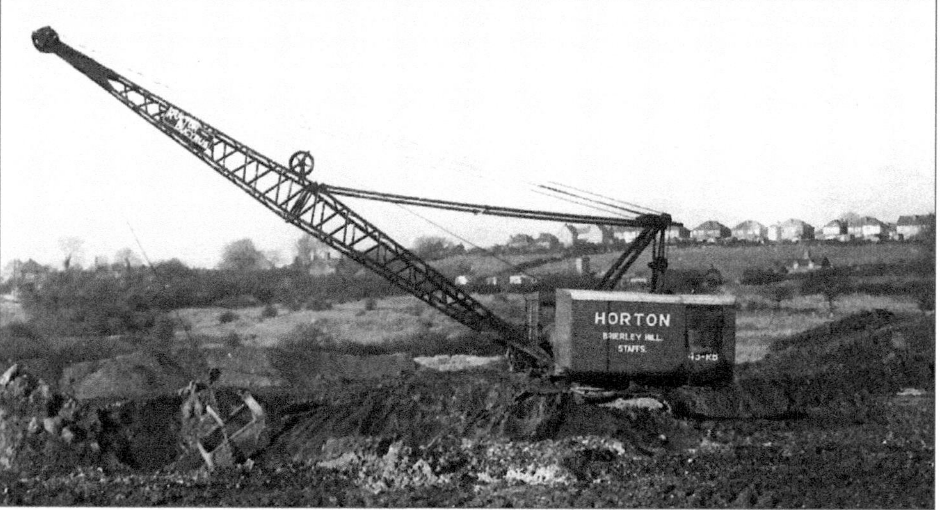

Once again the houses in Amblecote Road form the skyline, and the prisoner of war camp can be seen between the jib of Horton's excavator and the winding mechanism. This 1950s view gives us a glimpse of the amount of open space in Caledonia that has now been filled with the houses of Calewood Road, Walker Avenue, Rodway Close, etc. The trees below the jib conceal Ravensitch Farm – Quarry Bank's last farm. (*Norman Williams*)

CHAPTER TWO

A HOME IN QUARRY BANK

Quarry Bank contains a rich diversity of housing. A few buildings survive from the days when Quarry Bank was an unplanned village made up of rather scattered hamlets. These were small early nineteenth-century cottages, and the survivors have often been extensively rebuilt. The houses that were built in the late nineteenth century and in the first decade of the twentieth century are generally good-quality homes that survive very well, but modern improvements are frequently changing their character. Thorns Road, Mount Pleasant, Victoria Road and parts of the streets built to the south of the High Street provide many examples.

The existence of inter-war housing shows the expansion of Quarry Bank during the 1920s and 1930s. The early council houses in the White City and Woodlands Avenue are precursors of the larger post-war estates. After the Second World War large estates were built, and from the 1960s onwards many rural enclaves and green 'wedges' disappeared under new houses. Hamlets like Caledonia and Dove Hill disappeared in the vast new housing schemes that filled the area between Caledonia and Amblecote Road. Areas like Birch Coppice and Dunns Bank lost their isolation.

Every quarter of Quarry Bank has been created by endless 'infilling', and it is possible to traverse roads containing houses reflecting the fashions of every decade. A walk along Amblecote Road introduces you to every aspect of domestic architecture. A stroll along Birch Coppice, across Caledonia, or out to Dunns Bank will astound you!

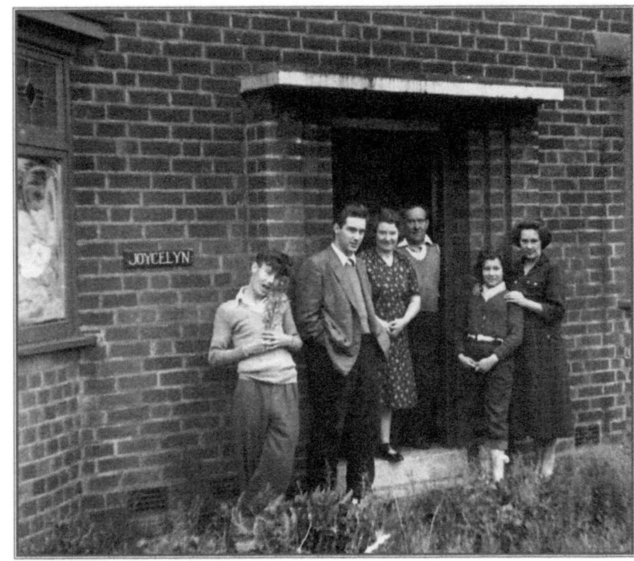

The Amphlett family at their new house at 77 Acres Road in the early 1950s, the first of the new houses to be built just after the war in the 'stub' of Acres Road, which now leads into Stockwell Avenue. Left to right: Michael, Cedric, Mrs and Mr Amphlett, Joyce and Hazel. The house has not changed significantly over the years. (*Norman Williams*)

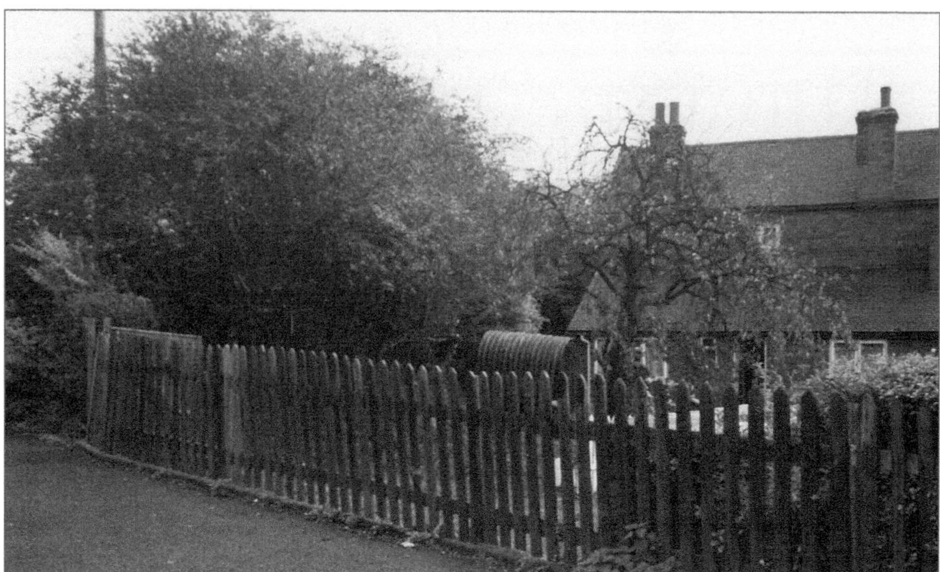

There are many interesting houses in Quarry Bank. New Pool House, seen here in about 1983, was built just below the dam constructed to stem the flow of the Mousesweet Brook and thus create the Cradley Pool. (The water power thus created drove Cradley Forge.) The position and name of this house suggest that it was built in connection with the pool, although it is now reached via Woodland Avenue. *(Clive and Jackie Evers)*

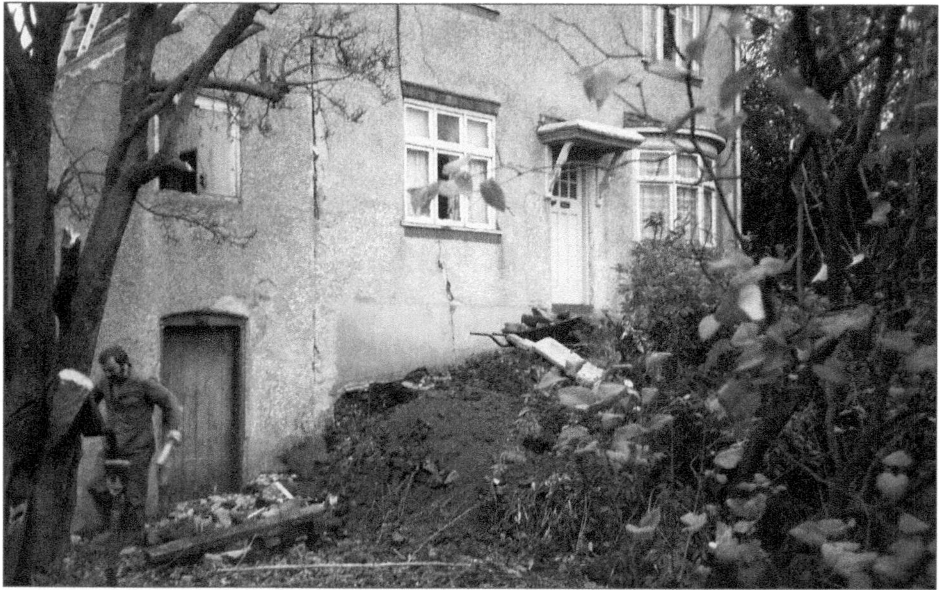

Clive and Jackie Evers bought the house in about 1982 and maintained a photographic record as they set about improving it. The door visible here, at the back of the house, gave access to cellars that appear once to have been a ground floor of the building. *(Clive and Jackie Evers)*

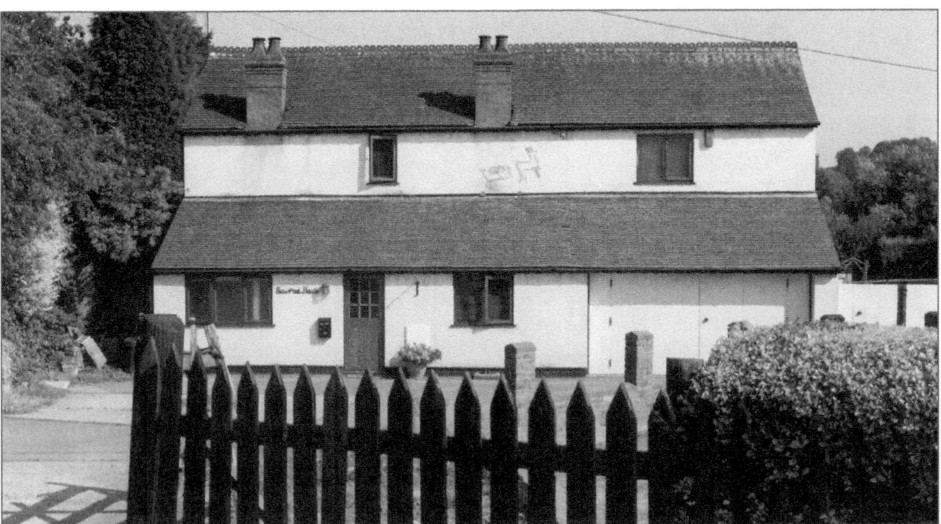

New Pool House in 2003 is wonderfully rebuilt but now conceals its history and the many modifications that have been made to it over the years. The pool itself was drained in the 1880s, but some of the scattered housing and settlements that surrounded the pool have survived. (e.g. Birch Coppice on one side of the pool and Mushroom Green on the other). (*Ned Williams*)

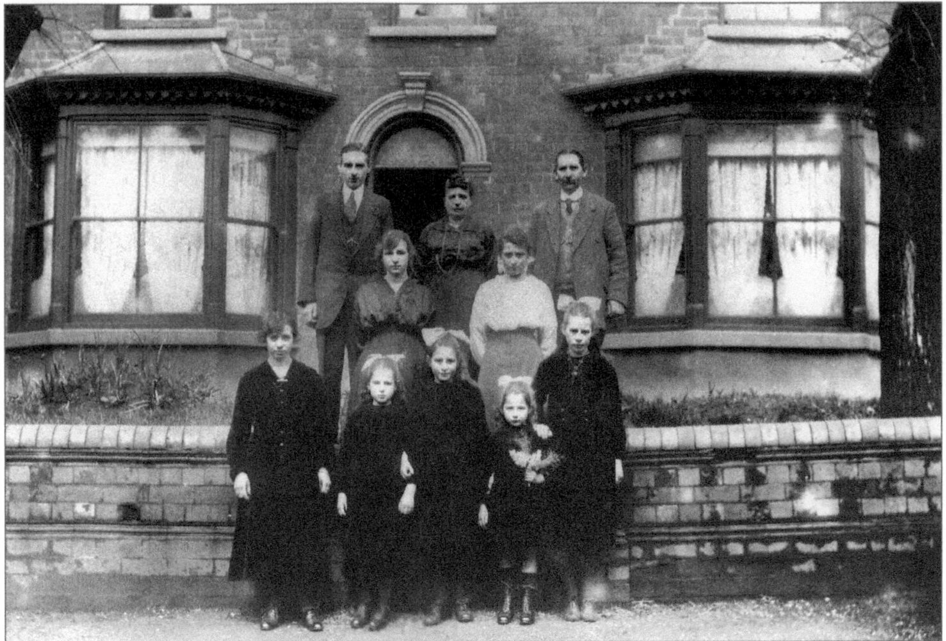

John Henry and Nellie Stringer and family outside their home, Oak Villa, in Oak Street, *c.* 1920. Mr Stringer established his enamel hollow-ware business almost next door and later moved to Verbena, a house in the High Street. (*Olwen Homer*)

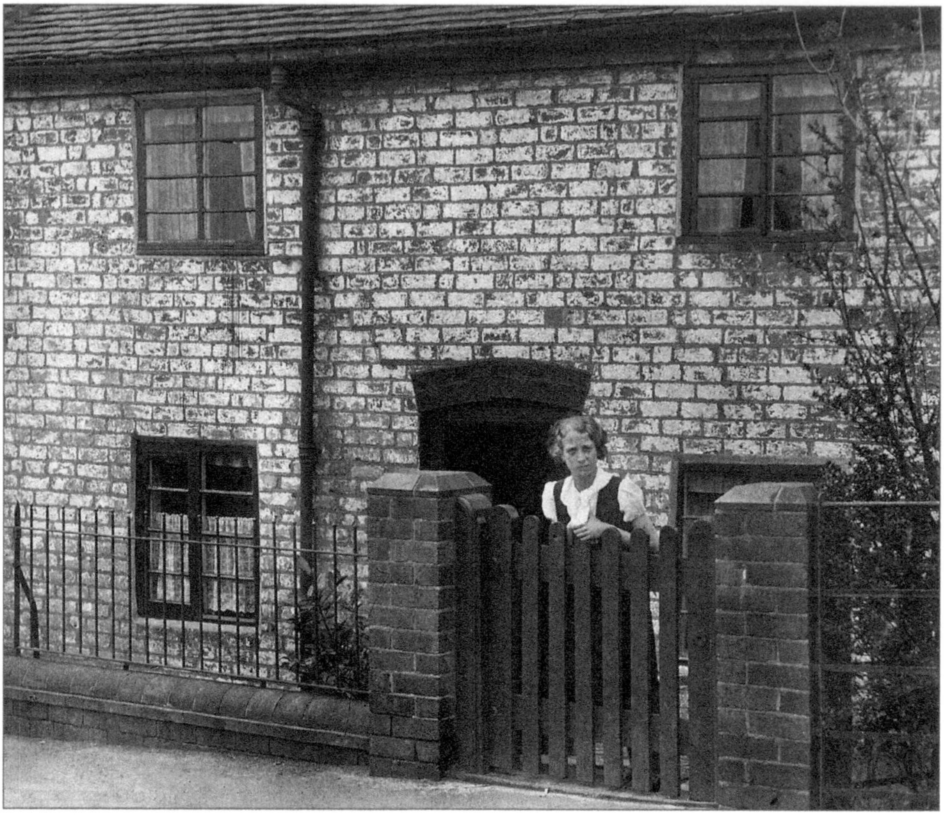

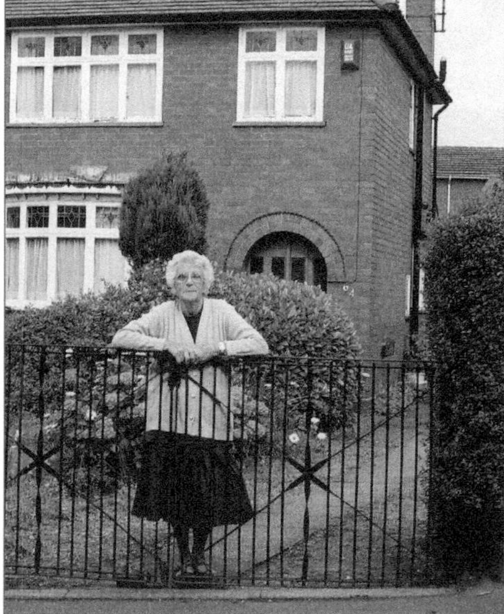

Doris Peat (née Sidaway) stands at the gate of 81 Thorns Road in the mid-1930s. This house was demolished in 1939. *(Doris Peat)*

The house was replaced with a new semi-detached house built on a site behind its predecessor. Doris Peat stands at the gate of the 'new' house in 2002 – on her eightieth birthday. *(John James)*

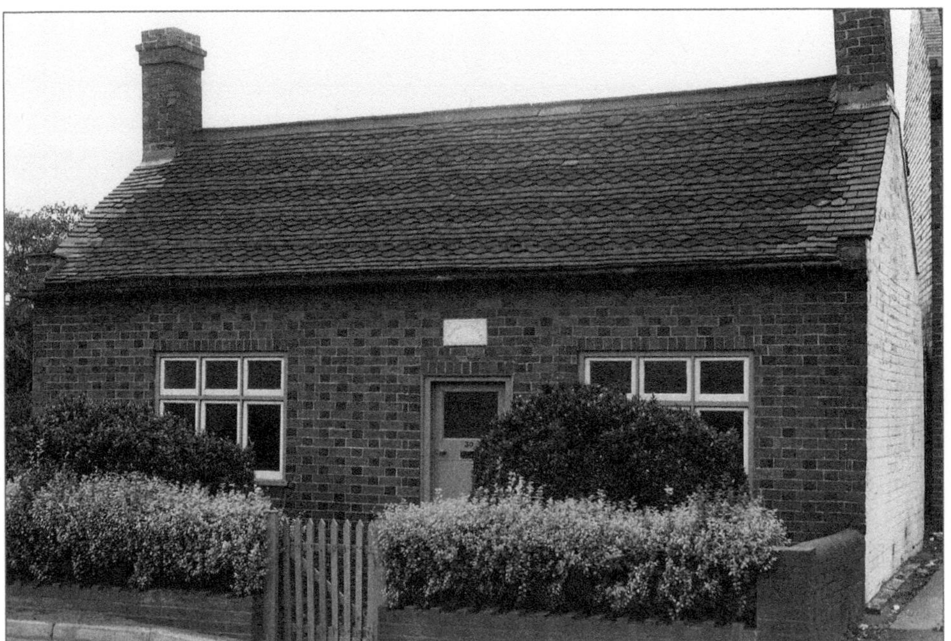

Some cottage-style buildings of early nineteenth-century Quarry Bank still survive but many have been demolished or rebuilt in recent years. Weavers Cottage, seen here in Park Street in the 1970s, has now been demolished. *(Dave Whyley)*

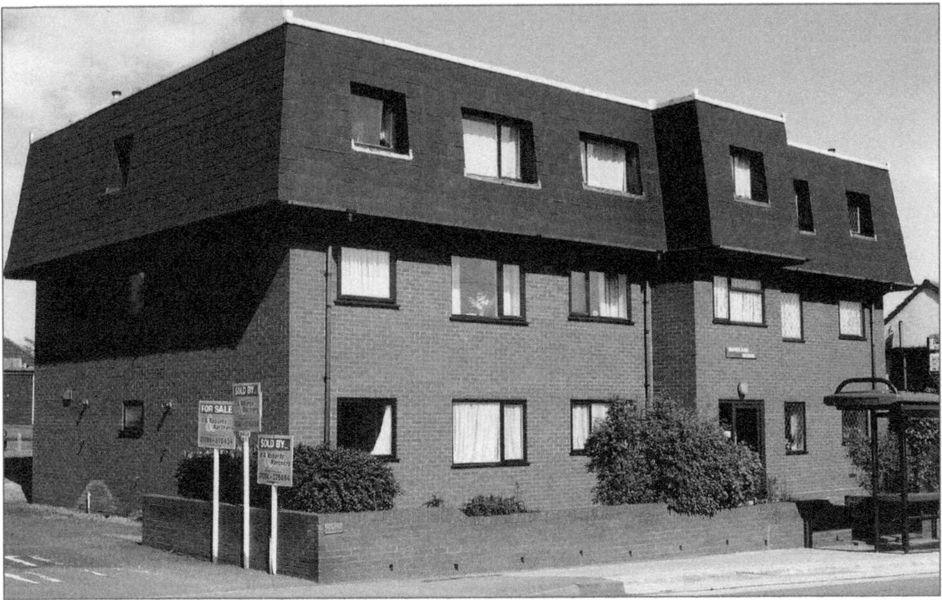

Woodlands Court, in Quarry Bank High Street, is typical of the latest housing being built in the area. (*Ned Williams*)

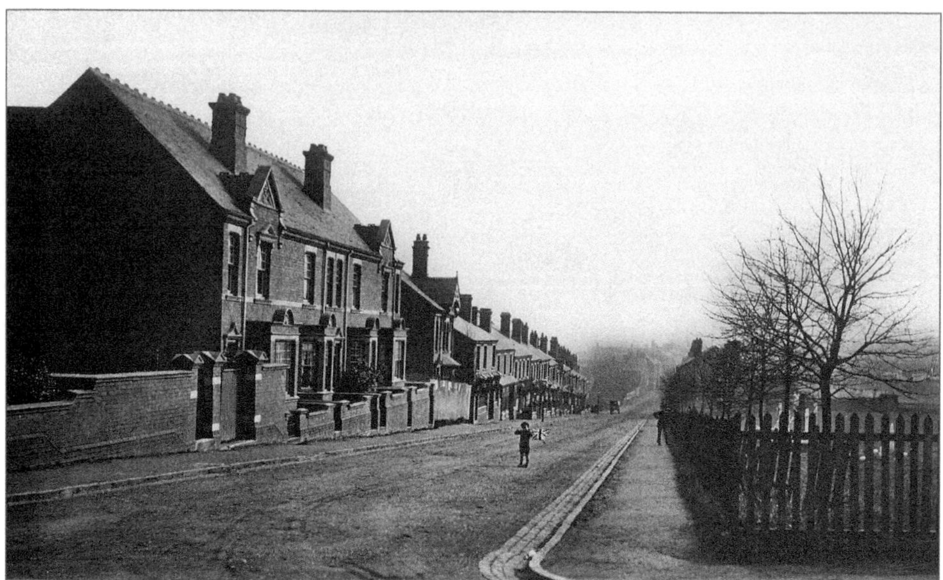

Once the Urban District Council had been formed in 1897, the street pattern of late Victorian Quarry Bank was quickly established and house building proceeded apace. No. 39 Victoria Road, on the corner with Coppice Lane (see *Quarry Bank in Old Photographs*, page 28), and the row of four houses seen here (nos 40–3) were built early on and dominated the skyline until other houses were added. On the right is the 'new' cemetery established by the church in 1900. *(Ken Rock)*

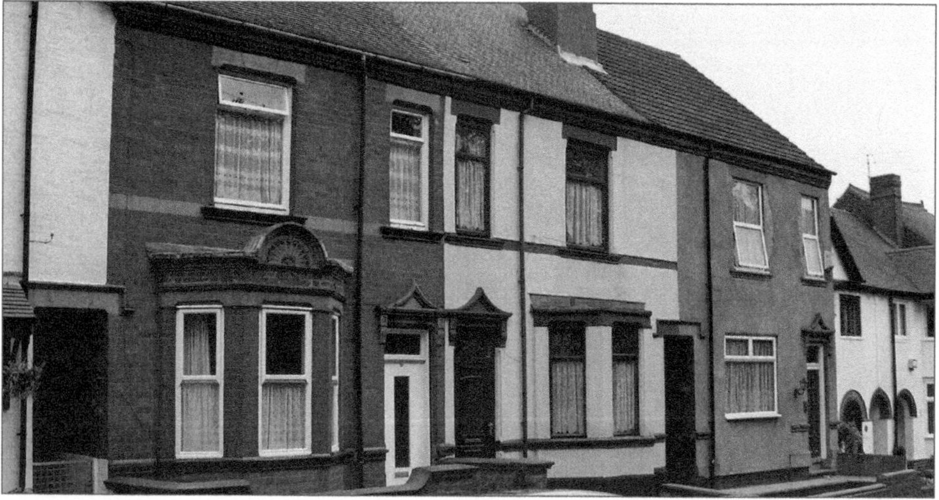

Nos 40–3 Victoria Road today make an interesting comparison with the above picture. No. 41 still has the original front wall, plus the distinctive moulded terracotta brickwork above the bay and door, but rendering and alterations to the windows, plus drastic changes at roof level, have changed the appearance of the row. The space next door was 'infilled' in the 1930s. *(Ned Williams)*

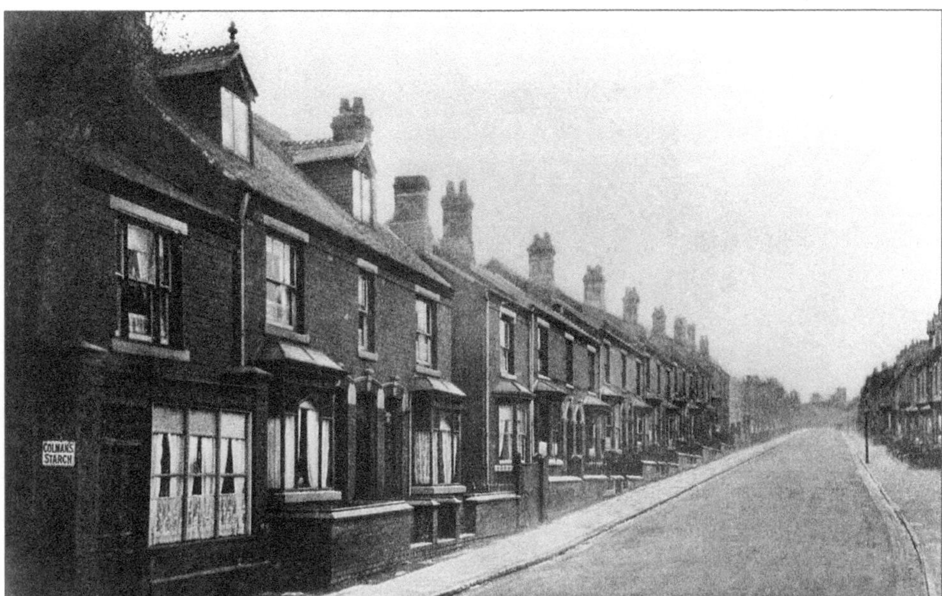

Arthur Webb built many of the houses of late Victorian and Edwardian Quarry Bank, for example these houses at the High Street end of Victoria Road. Many of the 'new' streets off Quarry Bank High Street supported a few local shops, such as the one seen on the left. *(MPLHG)*

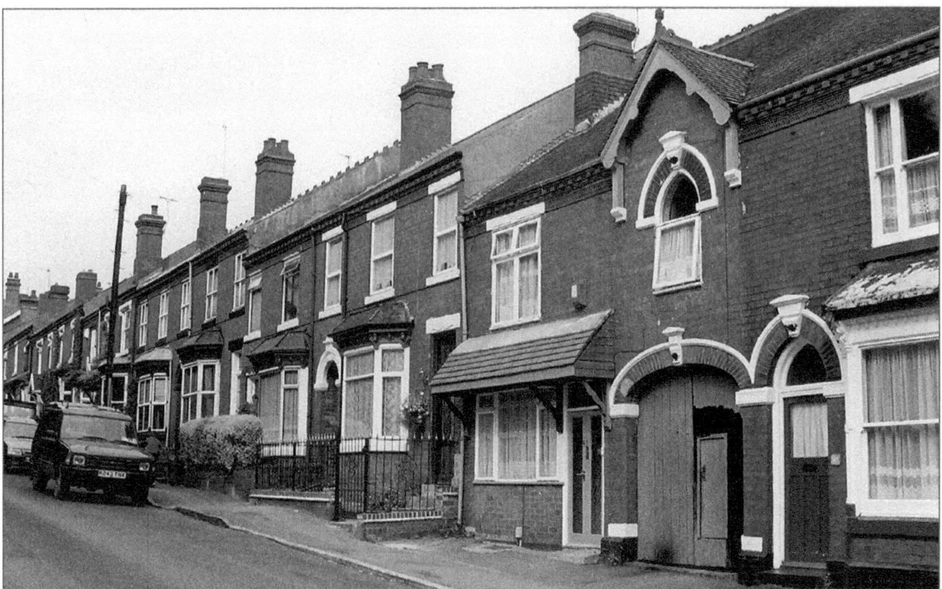

Looking at the opposite side of Victoria Road today, we see that many of the bays of the distinctive Edwardian semis remain intact, plus some interesting gables and arches. *(Ned Williams)*

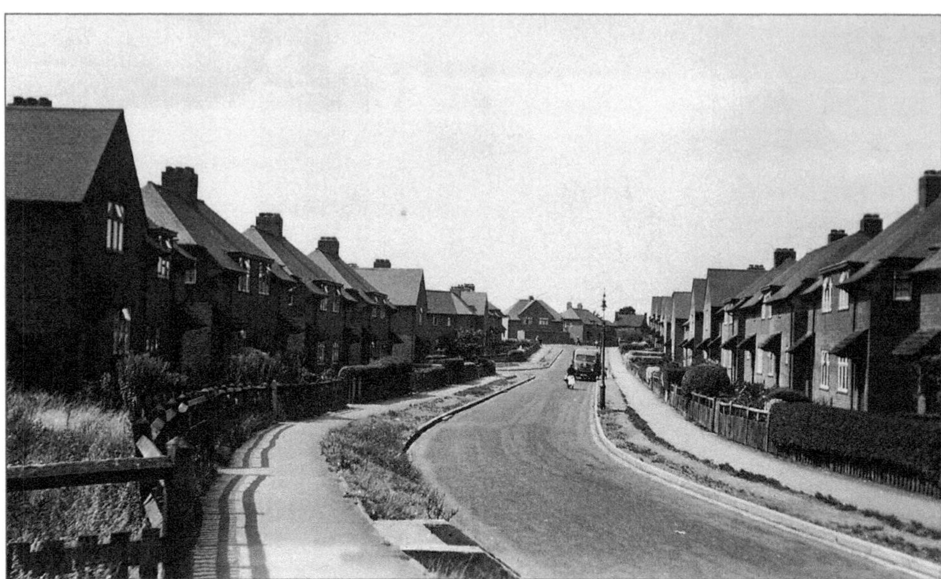

In the 1900s the area to the south of Mount Pleasant and west of Thorns Road was occupied by the open fields of Thorns Farm – reached by a track that left Thorns Road opposite the Blue Ball. In the 1930s work started on planning council estates that would cover this area, and the track became the basis of Thorns Avenue. Farm Road and Thornhill Road were also provided. It was planned to link Thorns Road with Amblecote Road by building Acres Road, but for many years the road stopped short at what became Stockwell Avenue. *(MPLHG)*

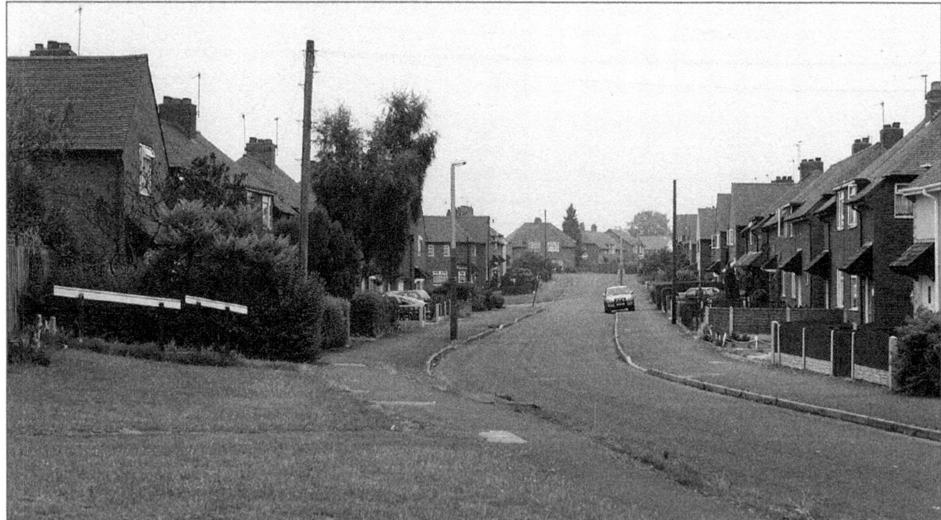

These two pictures of Thorns Avenue, one taken in about 1950 and the other in 2003, show how little such estates have changed – all that has happened is that trees have grown larger and the lamp-post seems to have crossed the road! Webbs built these houses in about 1935. *(John James)*

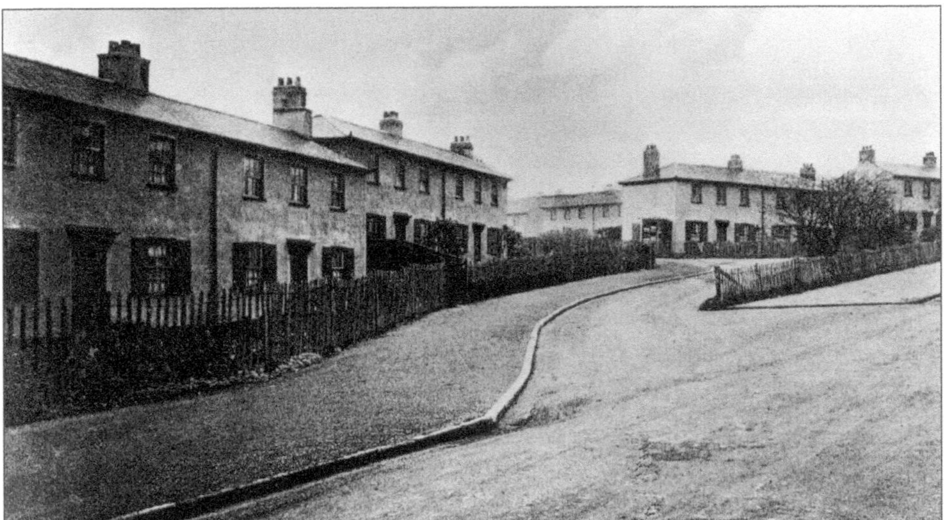

The White City when new – completed in the first wave of council-house building that followed the First World War, along with the first section of Woodland Avenue. The picture is taken from Coppice Lane and shows the houses in their original white rendering – hence the name of the estate. The name of the road through the estate has been changed back and forth over the years, but it is now called White City Road once again! (*MPLHG*)

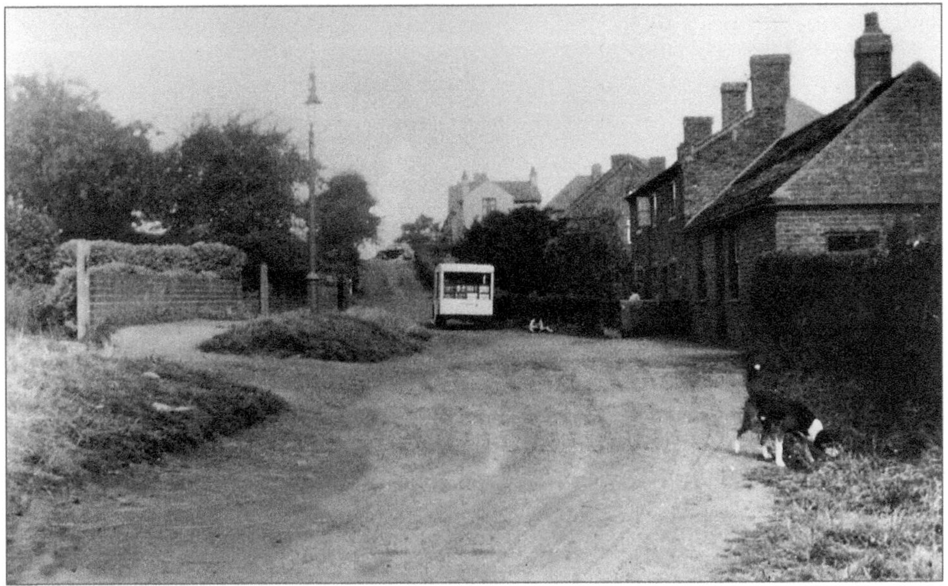

A picture of Belle Vale in 1948 from an interesting collection of snaps taken in this area just after the war. Sandwiched between the White City and Birch Coppice, Belle Vale was an isolated cul-de-sac entered from Coppice Lane. (This view is looking towards Coppice Lane.) The picture captures the feel of the scattered settlements that once made up Quarry Bank. (*Dawn Shaw*)

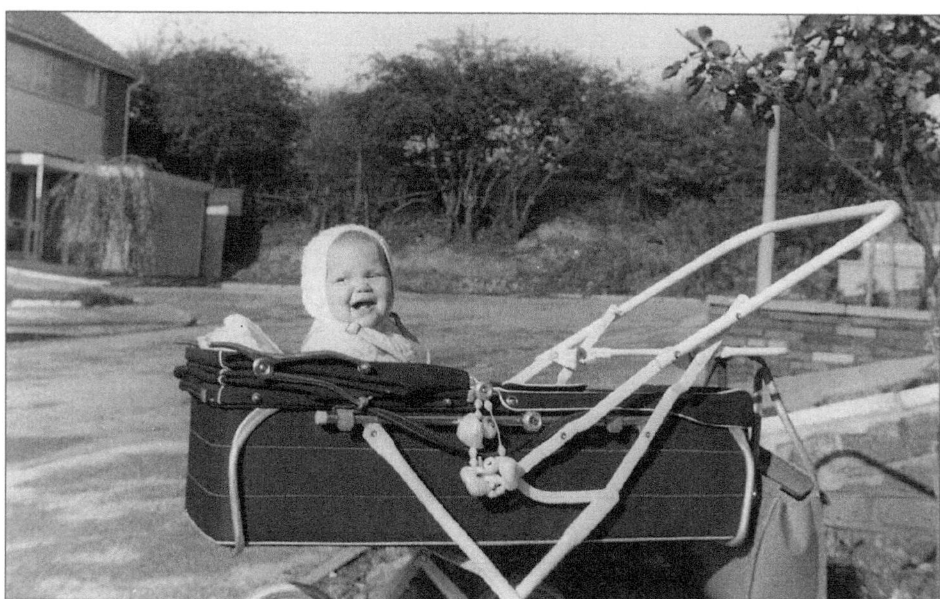

Young Stephen Priest seen enjoying life in his pram in 1963 – in Astons Close, a quiet cul-de- sac in the new streets provided in Caledonia as housing changed the face of the whole area. Wright's Farm (Ravensitch) was beyond the hedgerow in the background. *(Margaret Priest)*

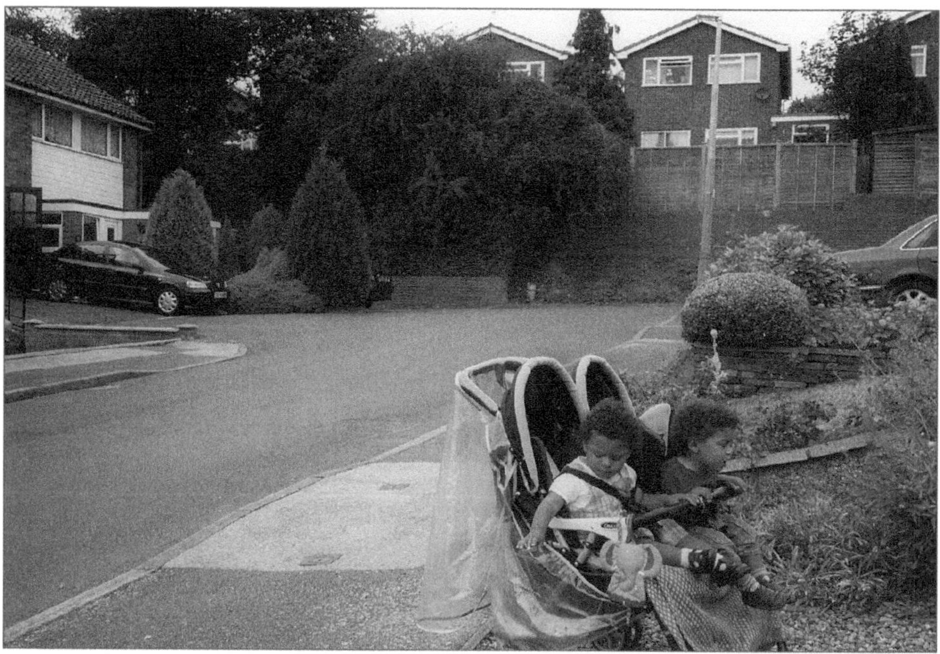

New houses now form the backdrop, as Ebologu and Olise Priest occupy the same position in Astons Close in 2003. *(Margaret Priest)*

CHAPTER THREE

THE CHURCHES

For as long as most people can remember there have been five or six churches in Quarry Bank: the parish church of Christ Church, the Congregationalists in the High Street, the Wesleyan Methodists at Cradley Forge, the Wesleyan Methodists at Mount Pleasant, the Primitive Methodists at Birch Coppice, and until 1981 in New Street. Earlier chapels are now forgotten.

The history of these churches was outlined in *Quarry Bank in Old Photographs*, and it can be noted that each church has played a considerable part in the history of Quarry Bank. Congregations grew and found the funds to replace buildings; Sunday schools and choirs, youth groups, women's groups and men's groups all flourished and contributed to the fabric of life in Quarry Bank. The churches also played a part in the development of education in Quarry Bank.

Early photographs portray the processions and festivities that made the churches such a visible part of the community. Today these events no longer take place. The churches still celebrate their anniversaries, but their Sunday schools and choirs are smaller, or non-existent.

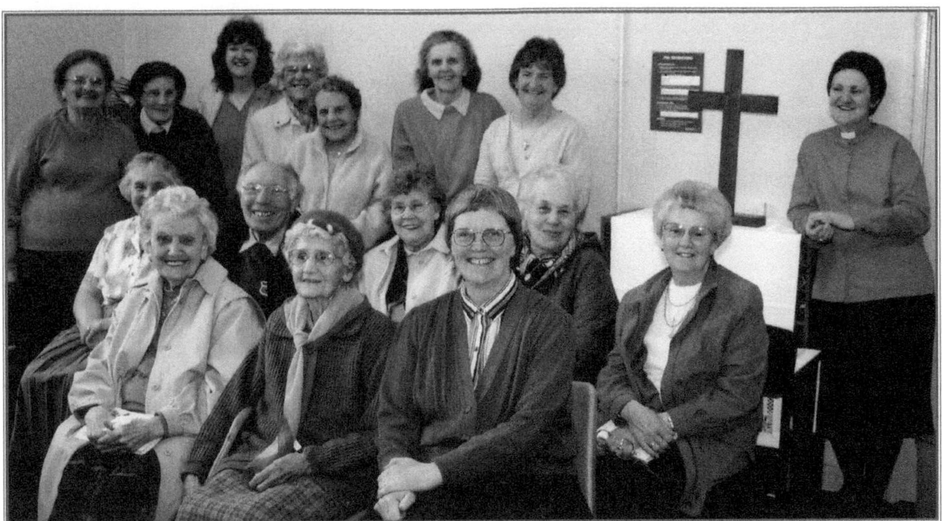

Since 2002 the Vicar of Christ Church, the Revd Caroline Windley, has organised a regular Monday morning meeting of Christian worship and fellowship, followed by a simple meal. This is held in the Community Centre and is open to all members of the community, to all church-goers and to non-church-goers. There is also a combined choir in Quarry Bank, reflecting the degree of cooperation that exists between local churches today. *(Ned Williams)*

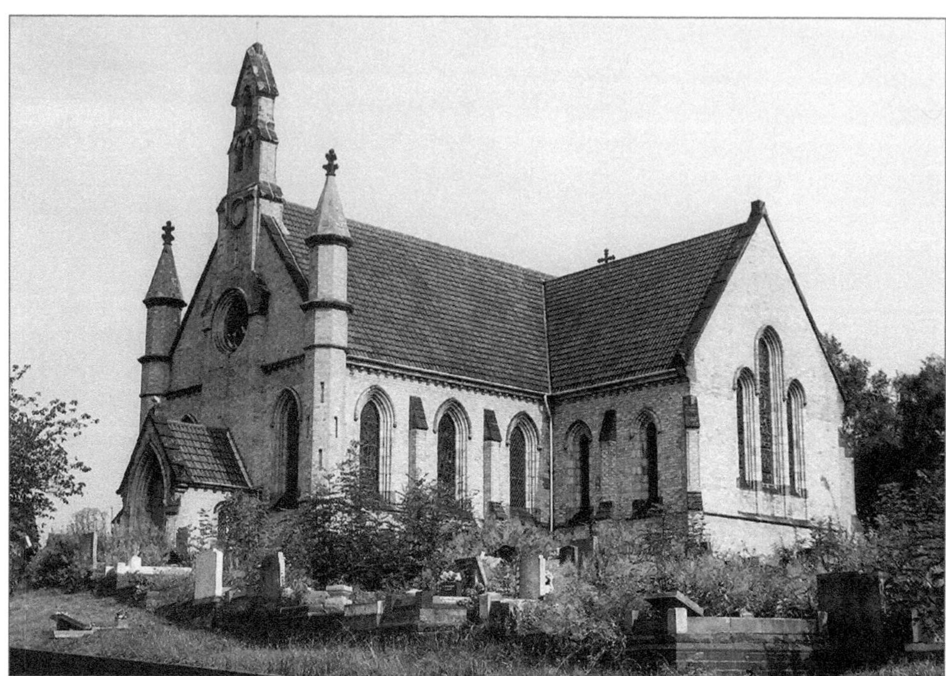

Christ Church, Quarry Bank, was consecrated in 1847, reflecting the population growth and urbanisation in the area. Built in cream refractory brick, it occupies a fine position in the centre of its parish. *(Ned Williams)*

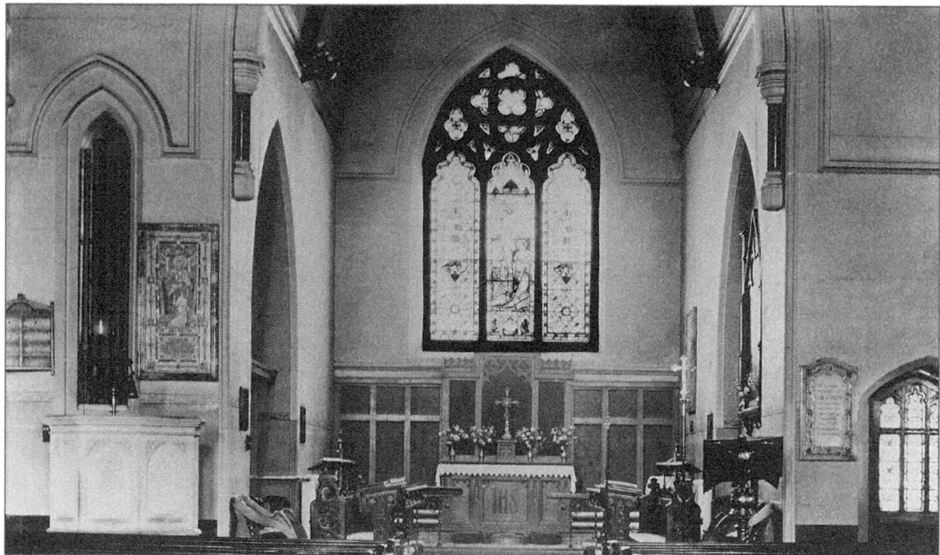

An Edwardian postcard view of the interior of Christ Church produced by Walter Wootton, photographer and picture-framer of 1 Merry Hill, Quarry Bank. The firm had been photographing local scenes and events since 1894. *(MPLHG)*

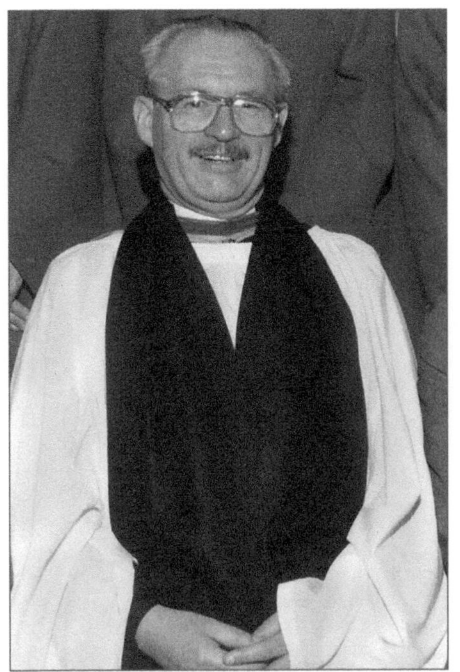

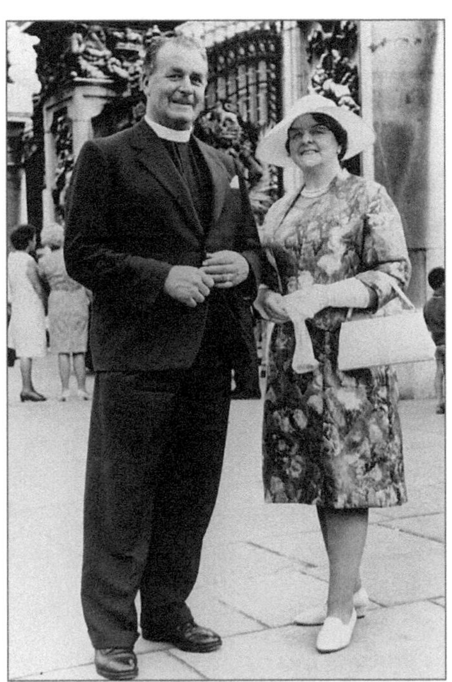

Above left: The Revd Tom Chapman (1981–99).
Above right: The Revd George Larkin (1946–72)
and his wife, Marie.
Below right: Judy McArthur-Edwards – new
curate at Christ Church, 2003.
Below: The Revd Caroline Windley, Vicar
since 2001. (*NPLHG Collection*)

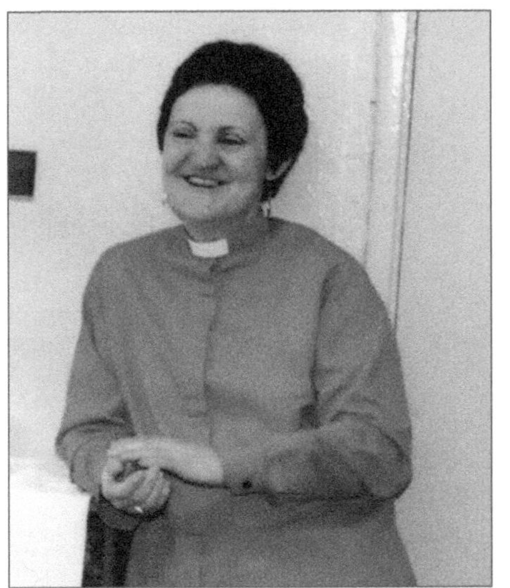

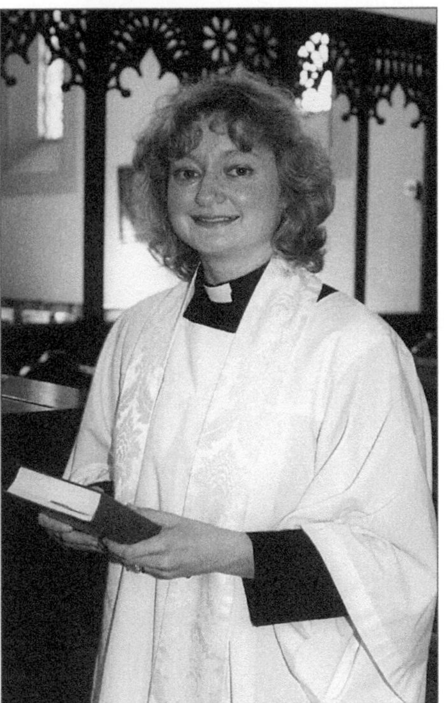

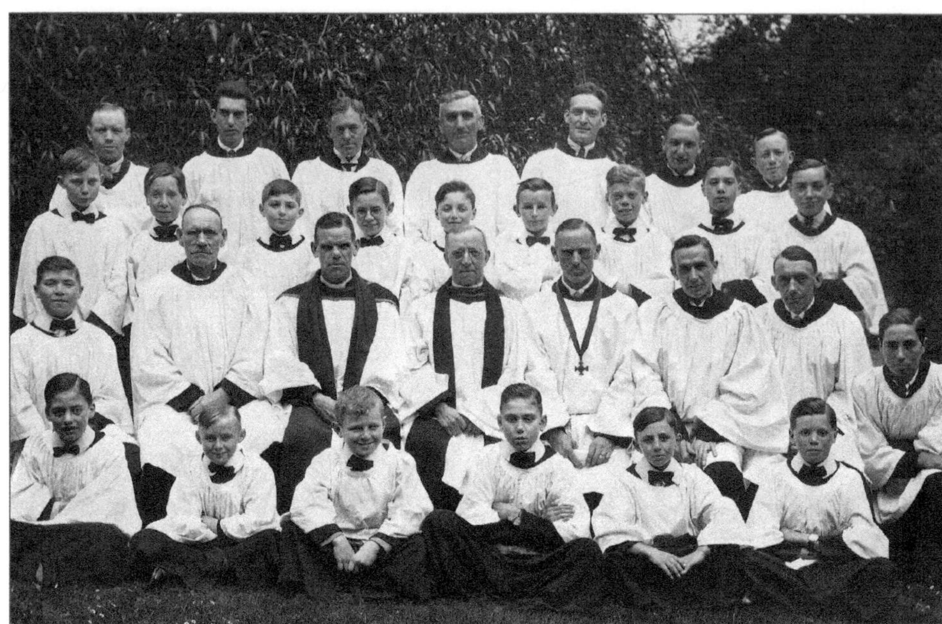

Christ Church choir, mid-1930s. In the centre is the Revd Mr McCarthy, flanked by the Revd Mr Lawton (left) and Herbert Dunn. *(Ursula Griffiths, whose father, Mr Griffiths, is sitting next to Herbert Dunn.)*

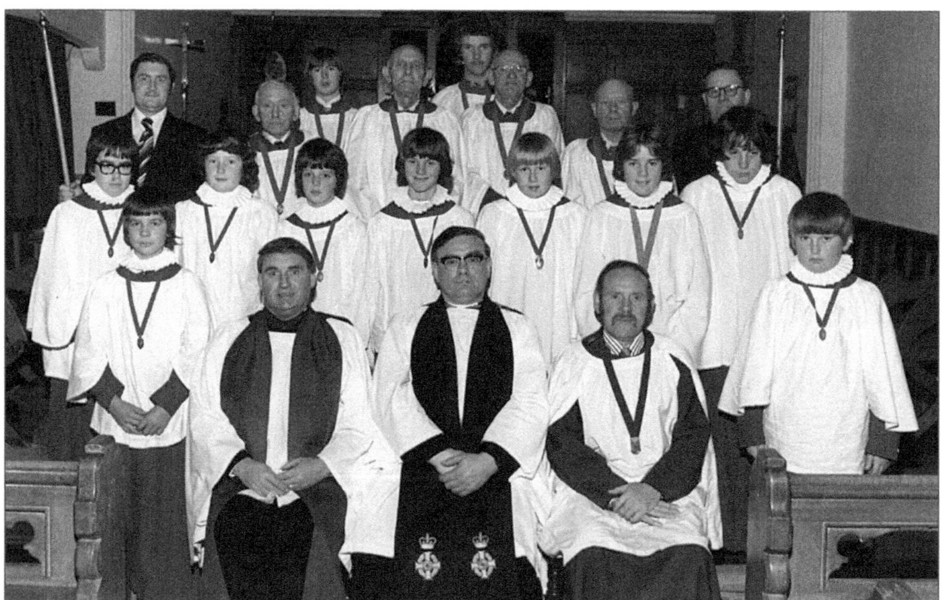

Christ Church choir photographed on Choir Festival Day, 31 October 1976. Back row left and right are the churchwardens, Ray Grove and Albert Peat. Front row: John Symonds (Reader), Vicar Irwin and Aubrey Burrows (organist). *(Margaret Priest)*

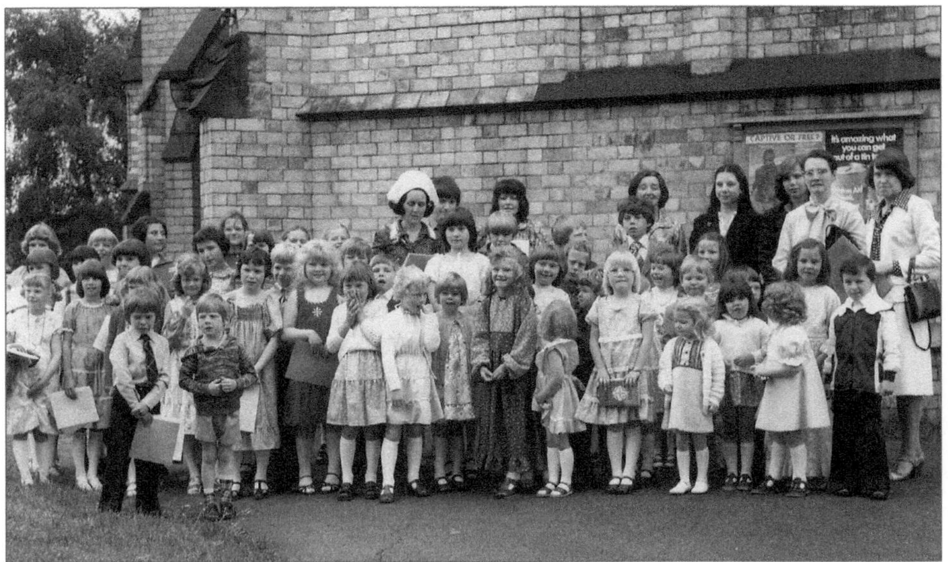

Vera Hegedus (right) and June Grove (centre) and children from the Christ Church Sunday School in 1979. The parish church no longer runs a Sunday school and Quarry Bank's other churches have much diminished Sunday schools. *(Margaret Priest)*

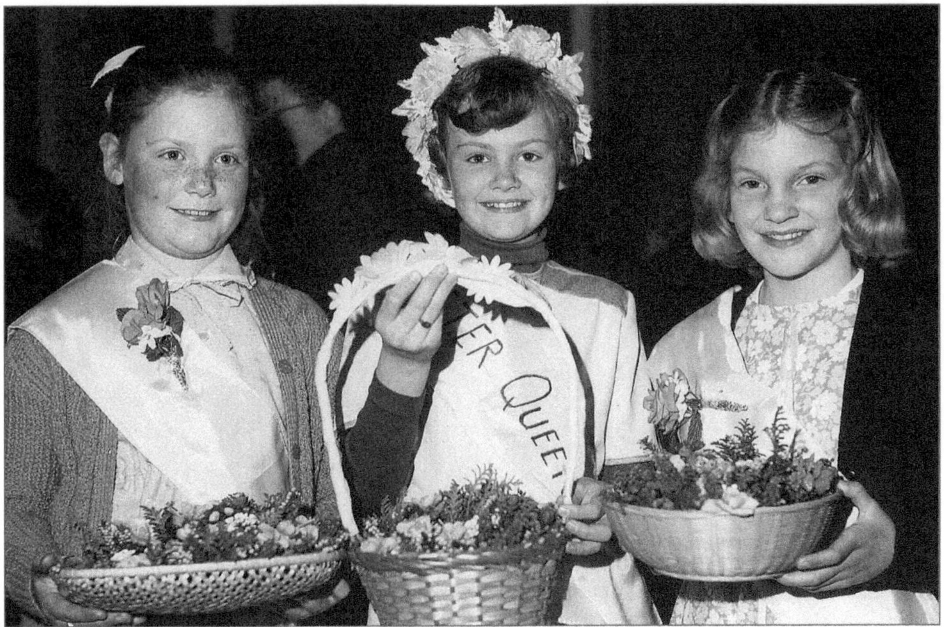

In 1979 it was still the custom to have a May Queen in the Christ Church Sunday School at Easter. Left to right: Anne Marie Simpson, Lisa Thompson and Caroline Priest. *(Margaret Priest)*

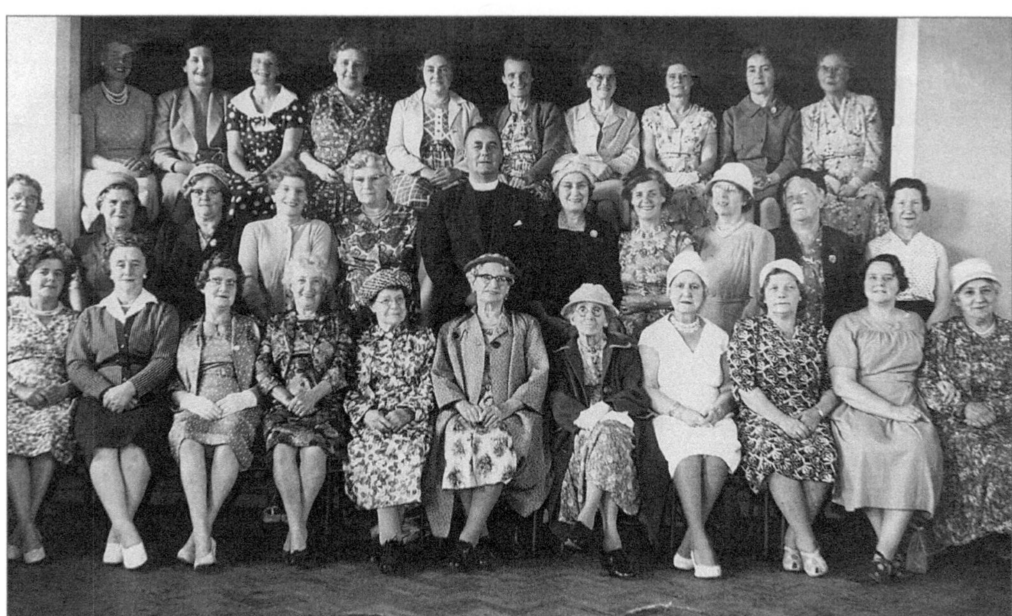

The Revd George Larkin and members of the Mothers' Union at Christ Church in the 1950s, photographed by the stage in the Church Hall in Victoria Street. *(Collected by Bessie Cranton)*

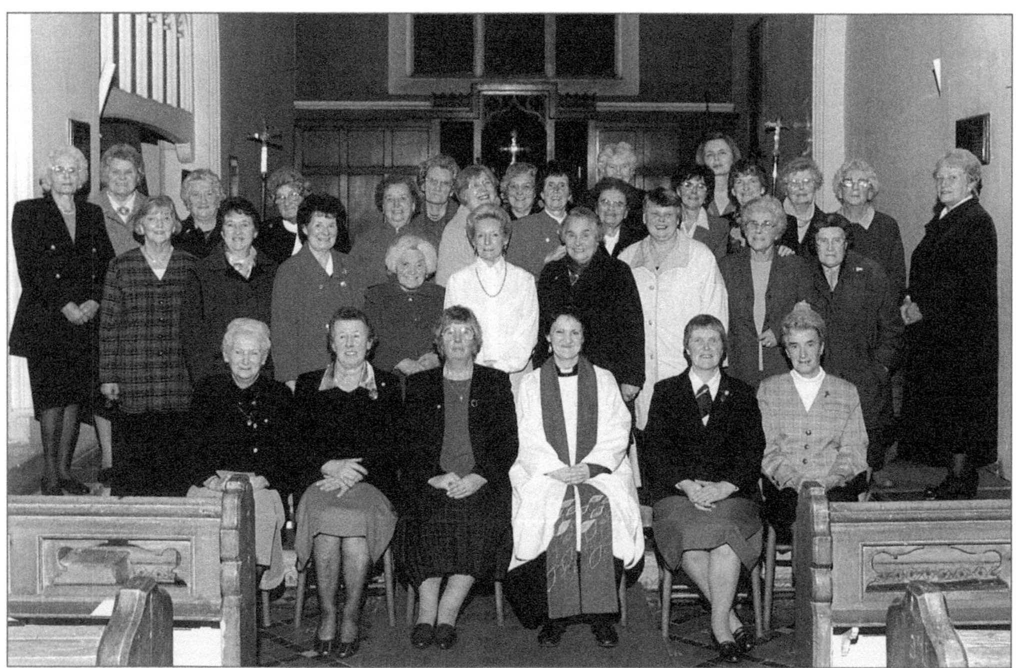

The Revd Caroline Windley, Vicar of Christ Church, and members of the Mothers' Union in 2002, photographed in the church. *(Roger Pirie)*

Right: The Mothers' Union banner at Christ Church still exists and is still in use. It is held here by Vera Hegedus and was photographed in 2002. (*Ned Williams*)

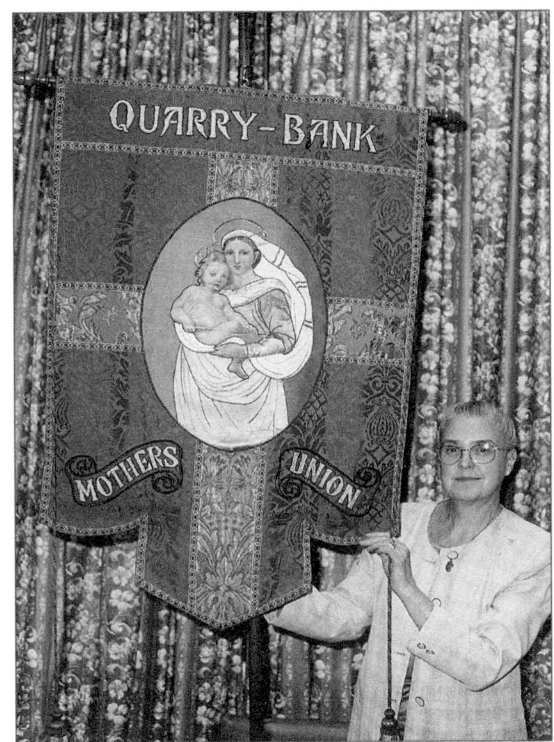

Below: Members of the Girls' Friendly Society pose with their banner at the back of Herbert Dunn's home at 126 Thorns Road. Herbert Dunn played a major part in the life of Christ Church and it is thought that the GFS was formed at the church between the wars. Left: Jessie Shaw (later Pargetter), right: Beatrice Johnson (later Siviter). A number of Sunday school and Friendly Society banners once existed in Quarry Bank, but where are they now? (*Derek Siviter*)

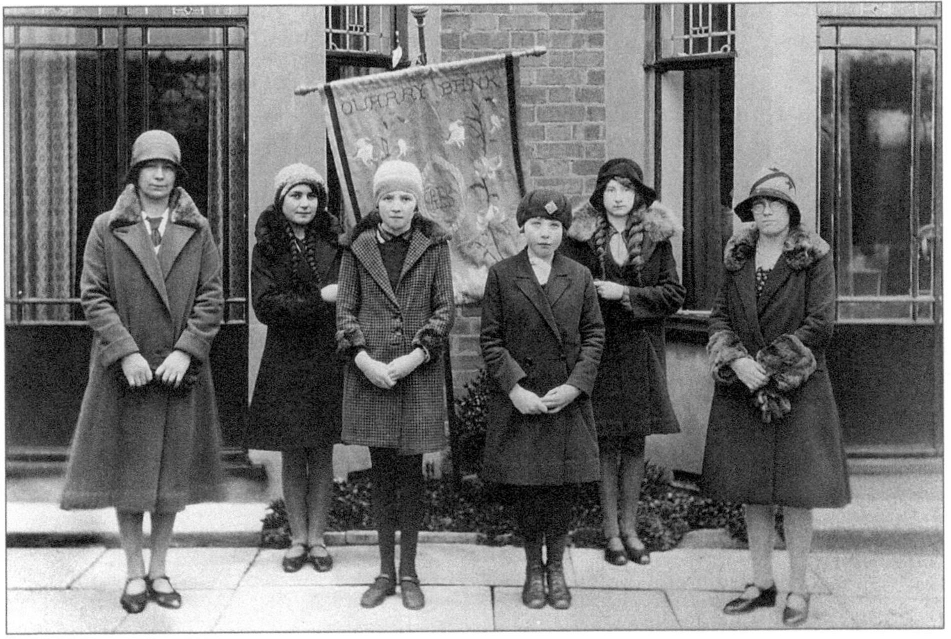

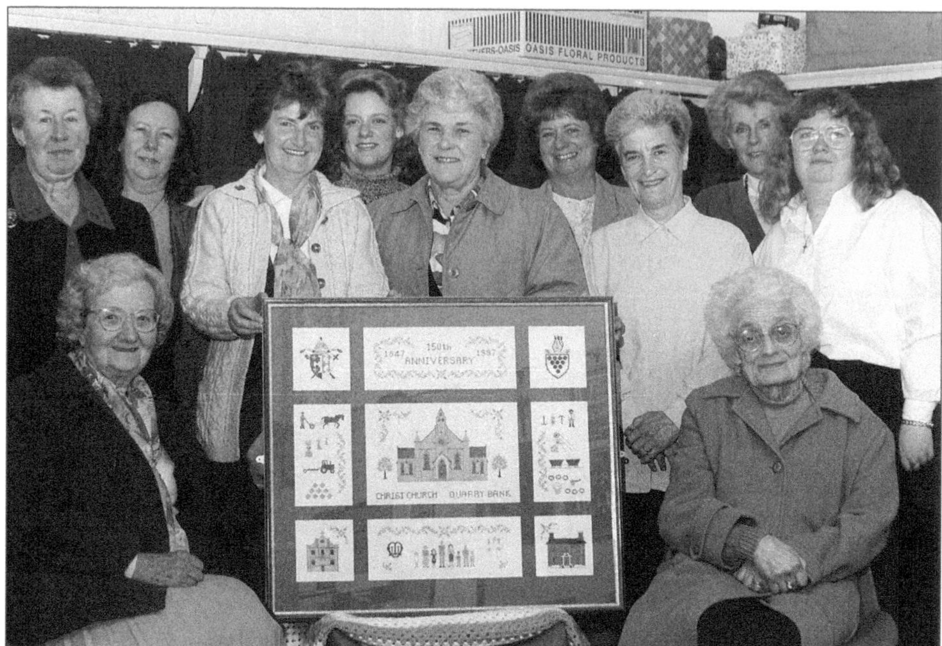

The ladies of Christ Church celebrate the church's 150th Anniversary in 1997. Back row, left to right: Briony Symonds, Sheila Hadlington, Audrey Davies, Judith Simpson, Joan Pearson, Anne Marie Simpson, Margaret Priest, Pauline Astley, Sylvia Chapman. Seated: Anne Willetts and Ivy Astley. *(John James)*

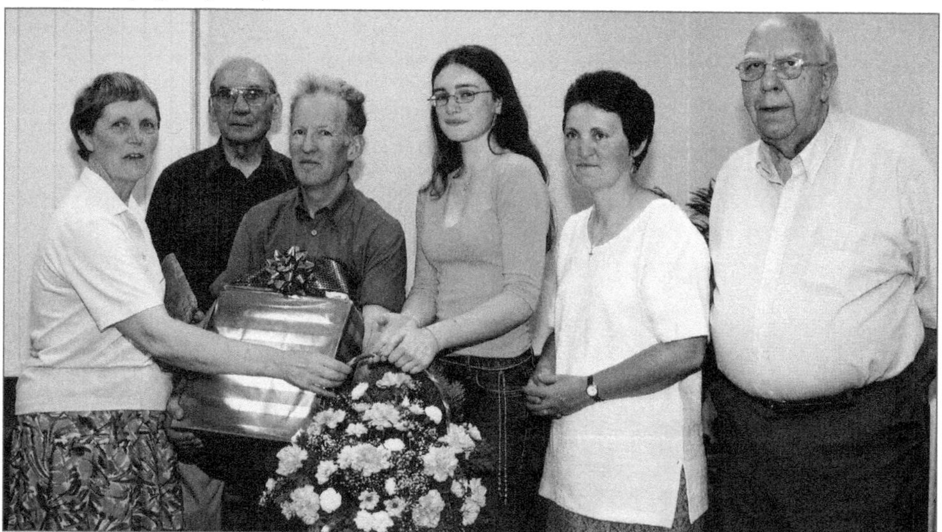

Sister Janice Mills retired from her work at Christ Church Quarry Bank and received a special farewell presentation on 19 July 2002. The Revd Caroline Windley and church wardens Jack Hill and Geoffrey Harper were on hand to make the presentations to Janice and her husband at the Sheffield Street Community Centre. *(Ned Williams)*

The Primitive Methodist church in New Street was completed in 1902 to replace an earlier chapel built in 1860. Both buildings were the victim of subsidence, and this one eventually closed and was demolished in 1981. It was a large building constructed in red brick and moulded stonework, like many Nonconformist chapels built at the time. (*Colin Southall*)

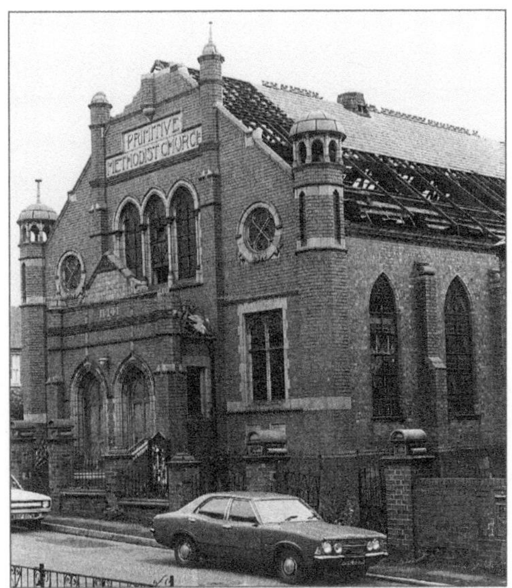

Below: A silver trowel used at the stone-laying ceremony for this church and presented to Mrs W. Weaver in 1902. (*Ned Williams*)

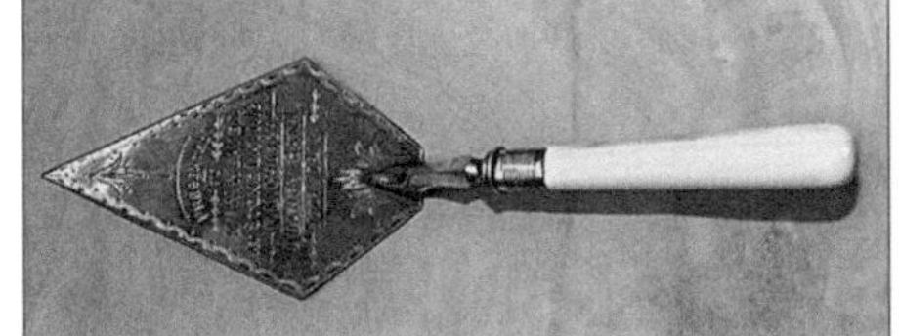

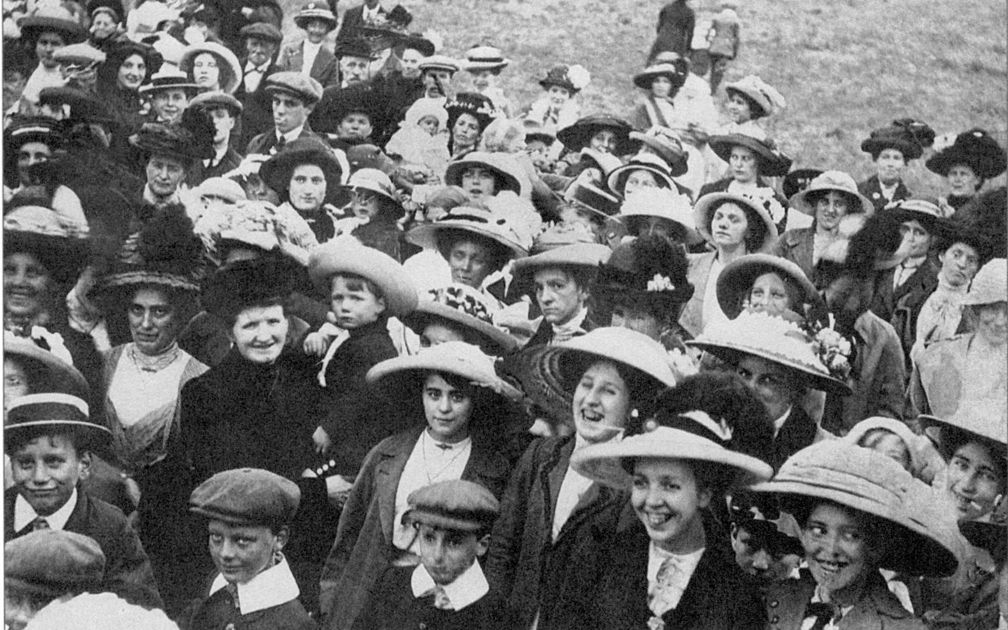

Both the parish church and the Nonconformist churches took pride in organising parades and picnics in Quarry Bank during the years before the First World War. These were often photographed and show Quarry Bankers all dressed up for an important day out. This picture was taken at the Primitive Methodists' Sunday School Festival in 1908; everyone has a hat for the event. Although there were obviously exceptions, it was thought that lower Quarry Bank, centred around New Street, was Nonconformist and Liberal, while upper Quarry Bank was Anglican and Conservative! (*Julie Bird*)

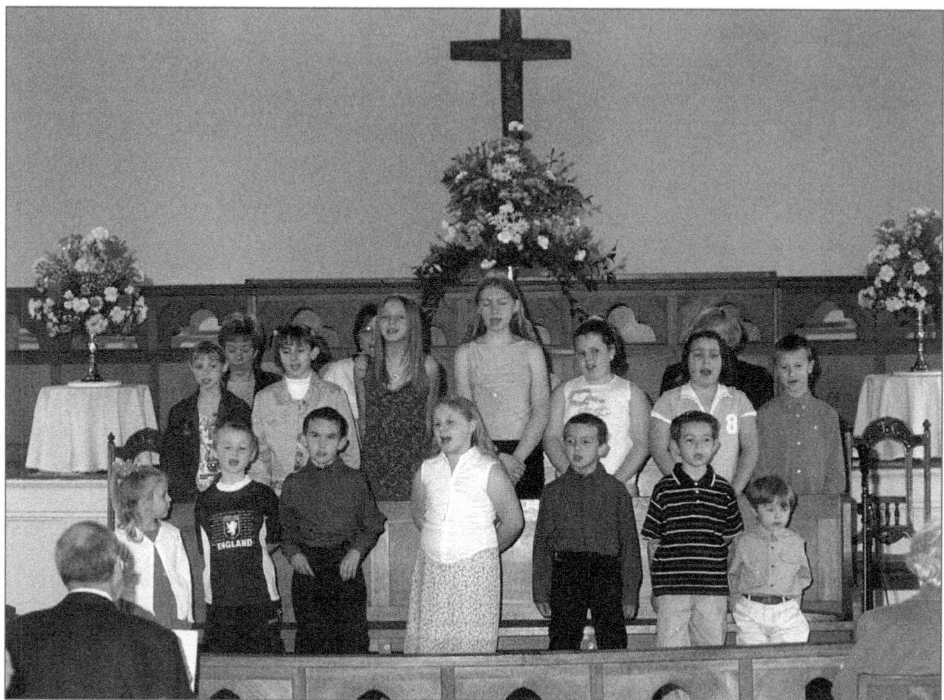

Sunday school anniversaries have always played an important part in the local calendar of events, although much diminished in size in recent years. Here we see Cradley Forge Methodist Sunday School celebrating its anniversary in April 2002. *(David Bills/Sybil Genner)*

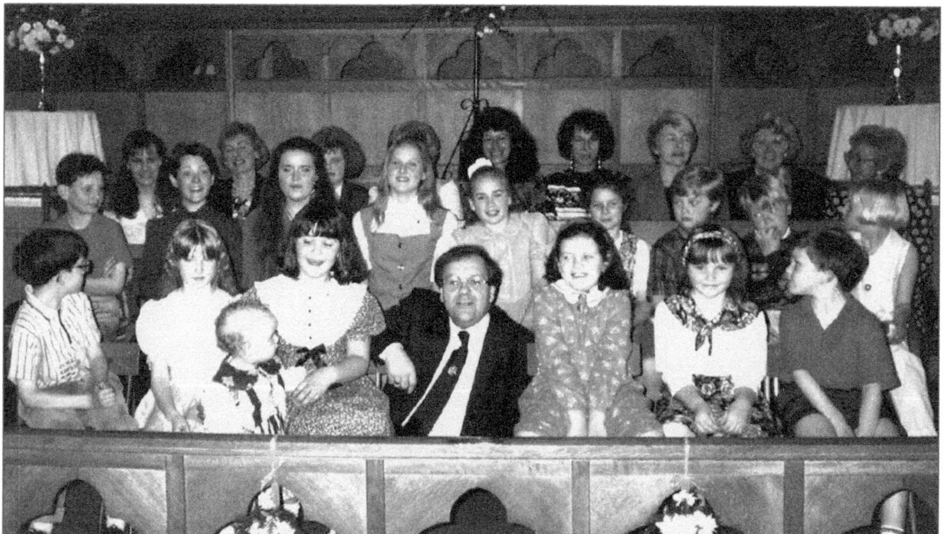

Even a decade earlier there seemed to be slightly more people at the Sunday school anniversary. This picture was taken at Cradley Forge Church in 1993. *(Joyce Webb)*

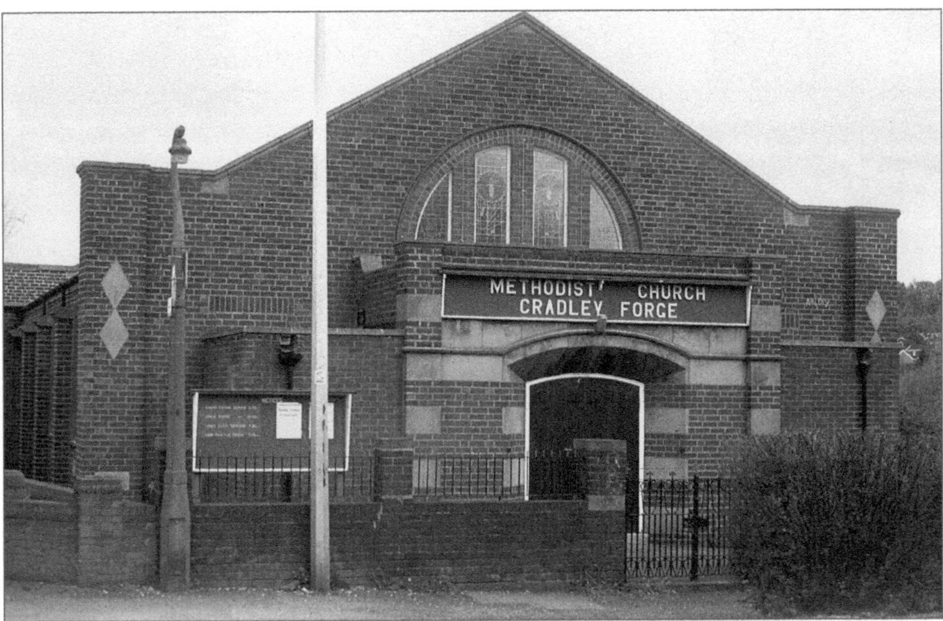

The Methodists at Cradley Forge have a long history – first coming to Quarry Bank in 1796 from Cradley. In 1850 they built a chapel at the foot of Hammer Bank, but that was demolished in 1938 when the road was widened. By then the congregation had built a Sunday school building on the top of Hammer Bank, which then became the church itself. For a time it was home to an amateur operatic and dramatic company, whose shows helped pay for the building. Here is the building in 2002. *(Ned Williams)*

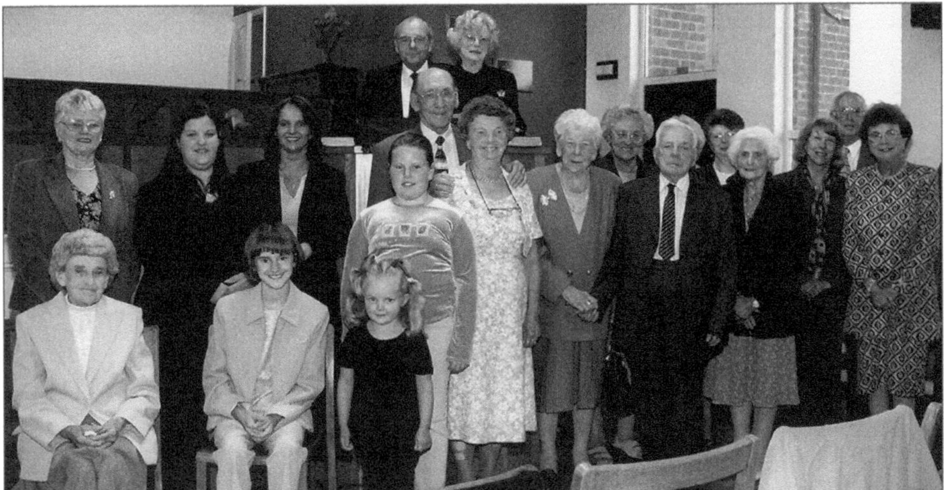

Musicians, choir and some members of the congregation of Cradley Forge church assemble on 8 September 2002 for a musical evening. Sybil Genner, who had presided over the event, is in the pulpit, alongside Brian Clarke, chief steward of the church and Sunday school superintendent. *(Ned Williams)*

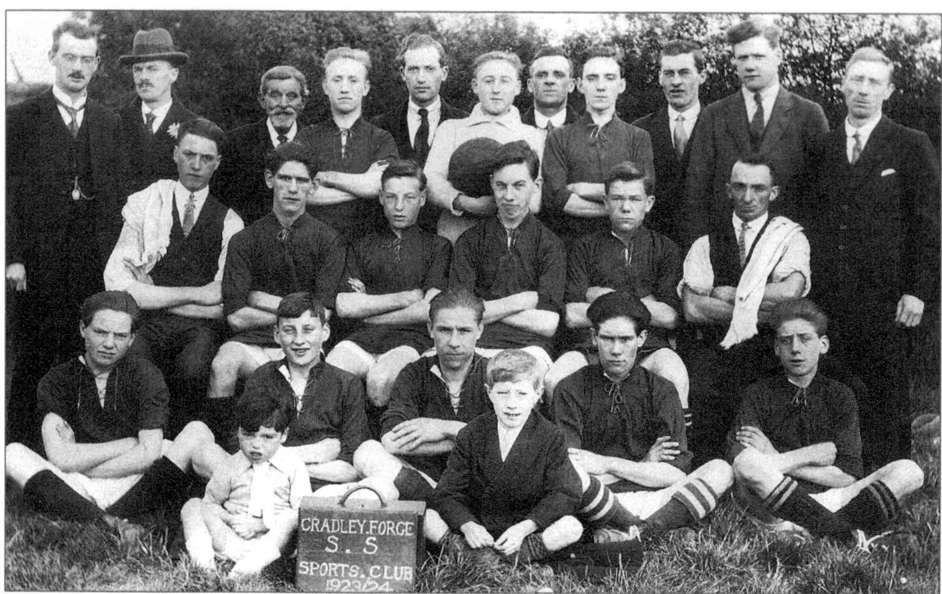

Like other churches, Cradley Forge Sunday School once produced its own football team – seen here as the Sports Club of 1923/4. *(Church Archives)*

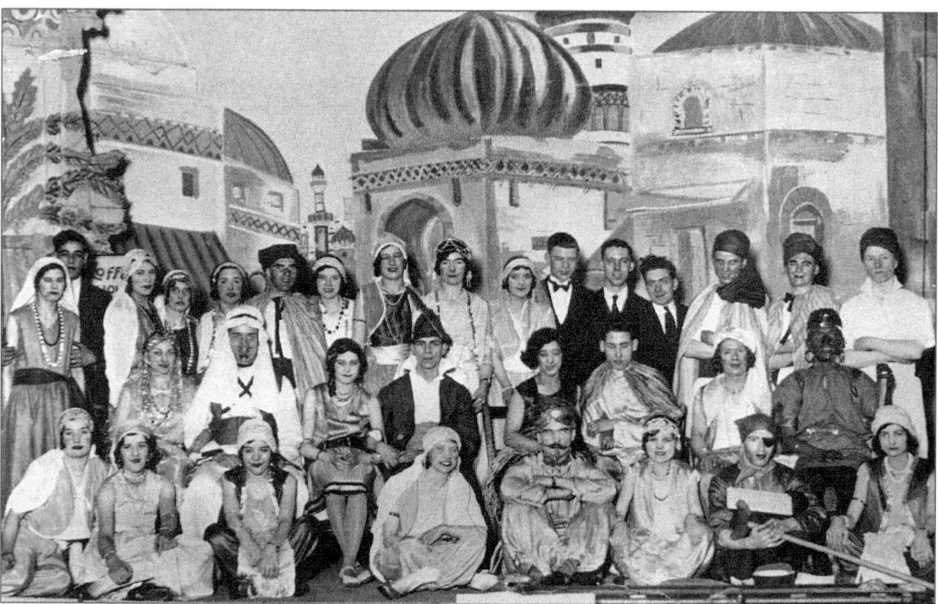

The new Sunday school building, built at Cradley Forge in 1928, was home to a musical society, which became the Amateur Operatic and Dramatic Society. Middle row, fourth from left, is Ernie Webb, who became a star of the company. From 1938 onwards the building became the church itself, and eventually the society separated entirely from the church. *(Margaret Yates)*

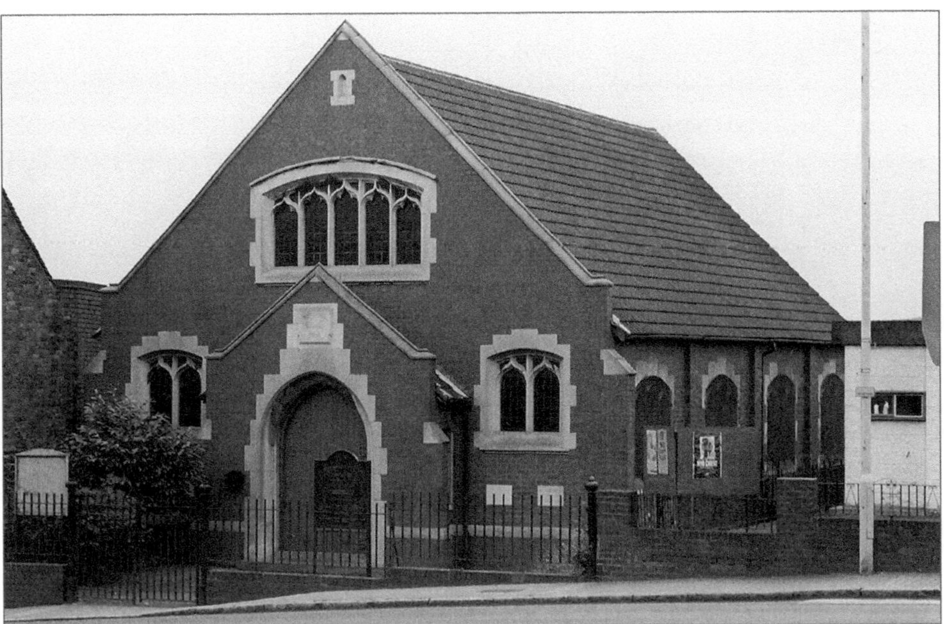

The Congregational church, Quarry Bank High Street, was built in 1935, and the Sunday school building and Church Hall next door was opened in 1967. The congregation itself dates back to the 1880s and came to this part of Quarry Bank in 1897 when they opened a chapel in Z Street – now called Chapel Street. When the United Reformed Church was created, this congregation opted to remain within the Evangelical Fellowship of Congregational Churches. *(Ned Williams)*

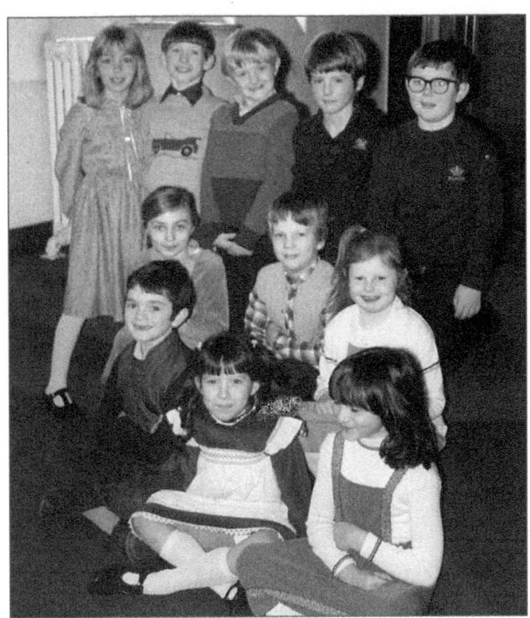

Right: The Congregationalists prided themselves on their choir and the Quarry Bank Silver Band probably grew out of the temperance band that had once been part of this church.
They also provided a Sunday school, and in this picture we see the class of 1983. *(Rose Williams)*

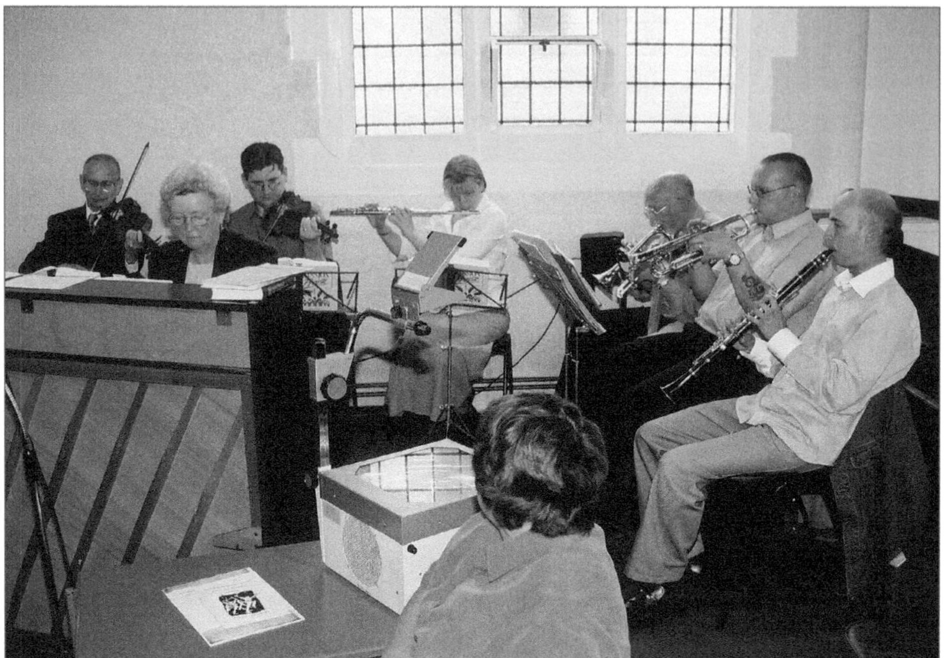

The musical traditions of the Congregationalists seemed alive and well at their Sunday school anniversary on 19 May 2002, when a seven-piece orchestra was assembled for the occasion. *(Ned Williams)*

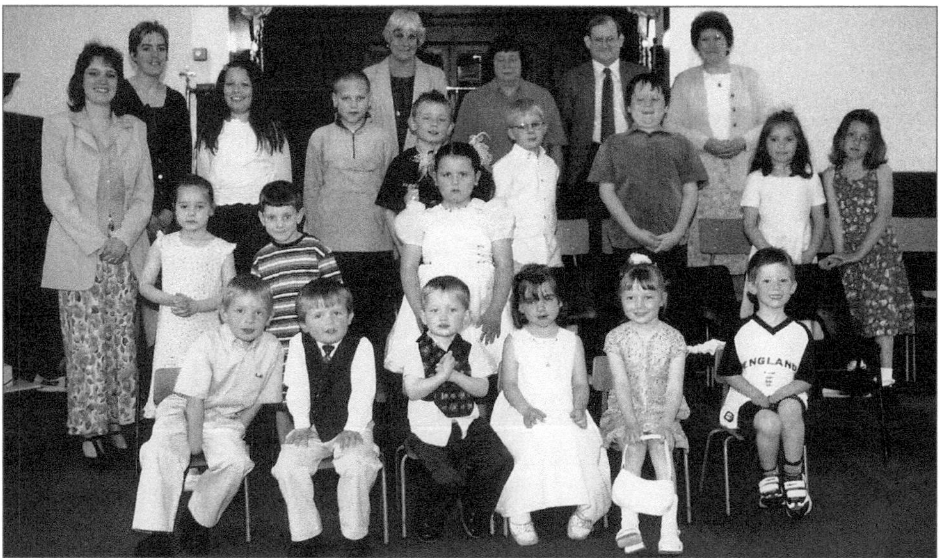

The Congregationalists' Sunday school anniversary, 19 May 2002: Sunday school teachers Ruth Stuart, Hannah Warwick and Angela Hodgetts plus Superintendent Vera Wright and Church Secretary Ian Wright. *(Ned Williams)*

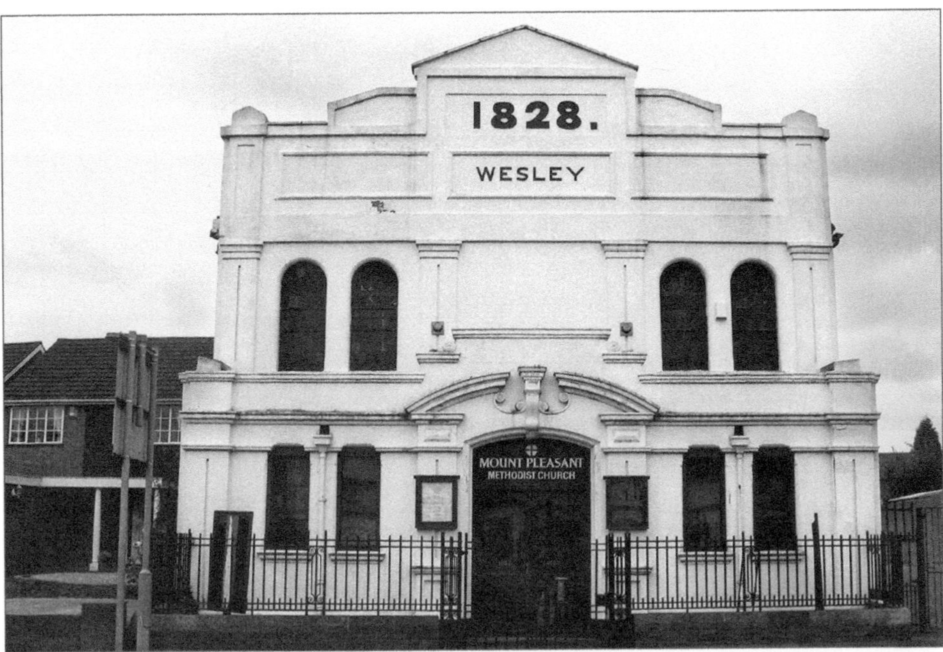

The Wesleyan Methodist church in Mount Pleasant proudly carries the date 1828 – the year when the congregation purchased the land and laid the foundation stone of this building. In 1927 an extension was built on the front of this church, creating its present appearance. This was funded by Ernest Stevens, whose wife Mary had been a member of the congregation. *(Ned Williams)*

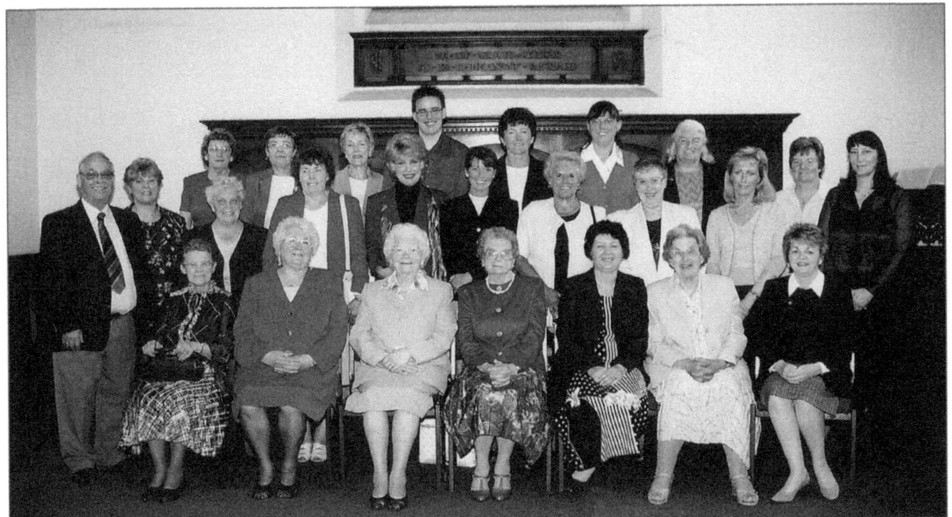

Rather than hold a Sunday school anniversary, the Wesleyans have, in recent years, opted to hold a Sunday school reunion, which has become a successful event. The picture was taken at the reunion held on 12 May 2002. *(Ned Williams)*

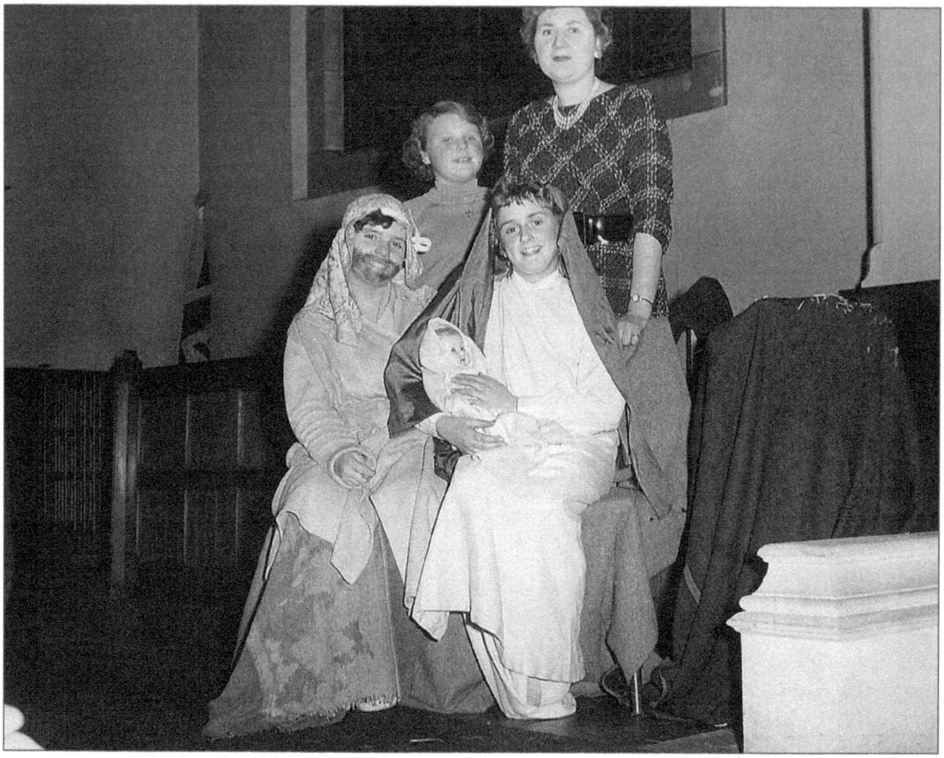

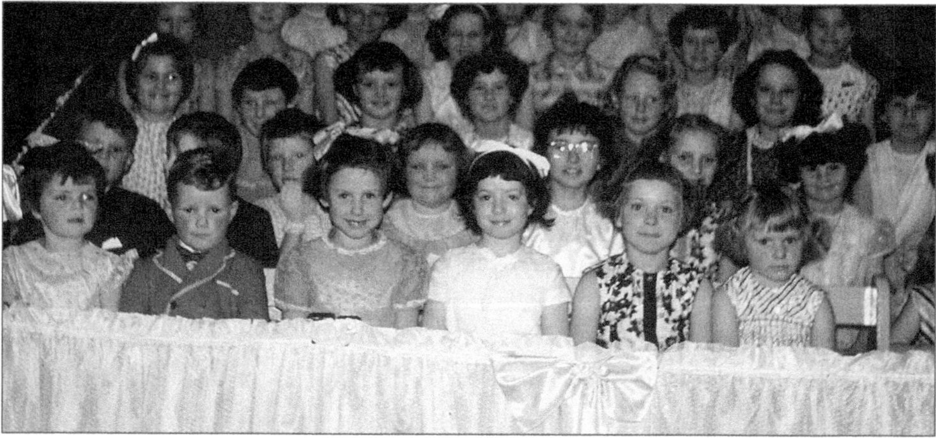

Sunday school children at Mount Pleasant Wesleyan Church putting on a nativity play during the 1960s. The church once had thriving Sunday schools, youth clubs, etc., and the hall behind the church had also been used by a dame school and the first Mount Pleasant Board School in the 1880s. *(June Price)*

Girls outnumber boys at the 1962 Sunday school anniversary at the Mount Pleasant Wesleyan church. How many of them now reappear at the church's Sunday school reunions? *(Olive Allchurch)*

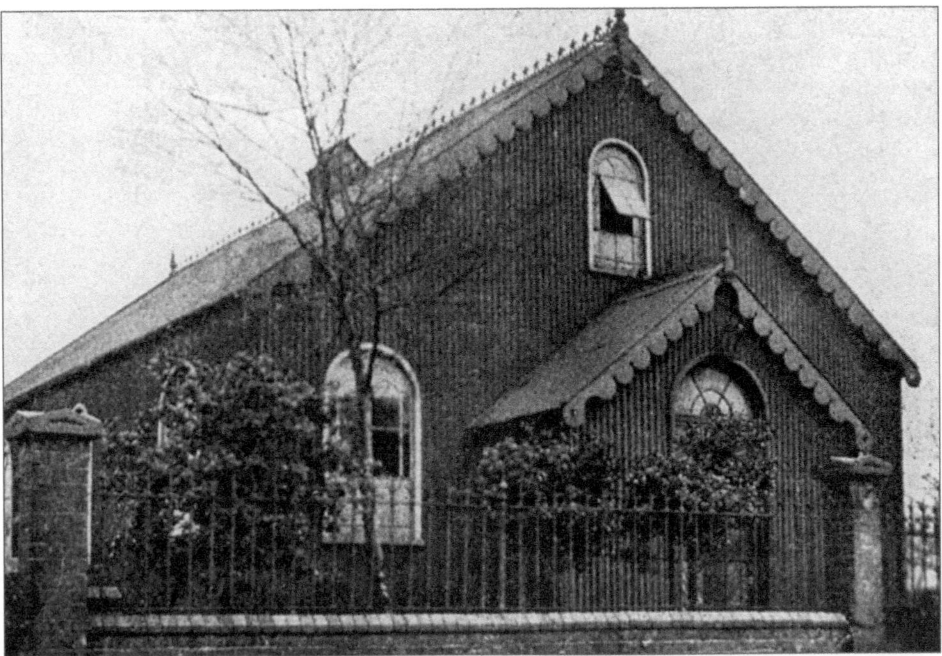

The Primitive Methodists in New Street established a wooden 'mission church' in Birch Coppice in 1884. Four years later the congregation was able to provide a 'tin tabernacle', which was a great success. It was a wooden-framed building clad in corrugated iron, and lined on the inside with wood. *(Mary Rousell)*

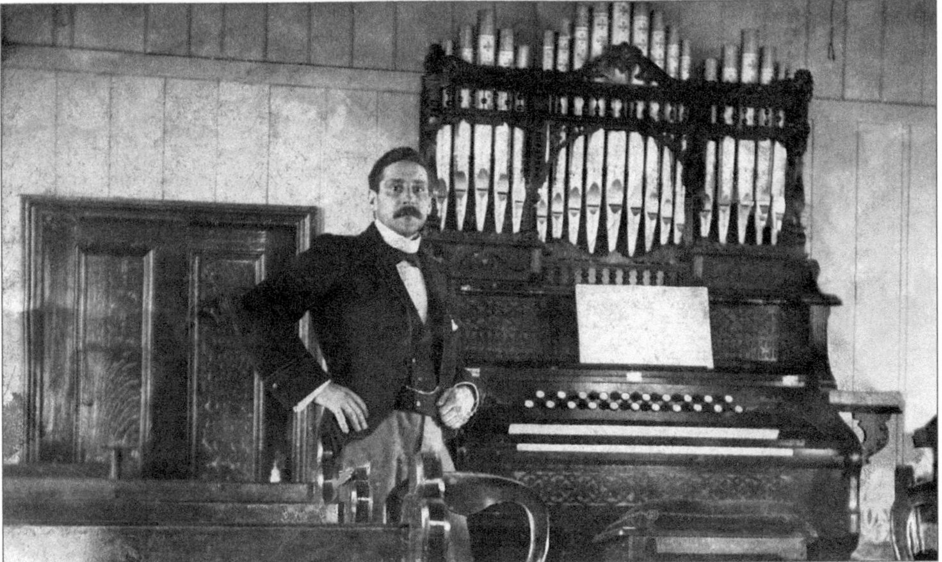

The interior of the tin chapel at Birch Coppice is seen here in this picture of the organist, Mr Brown. *(Margaret Price)*

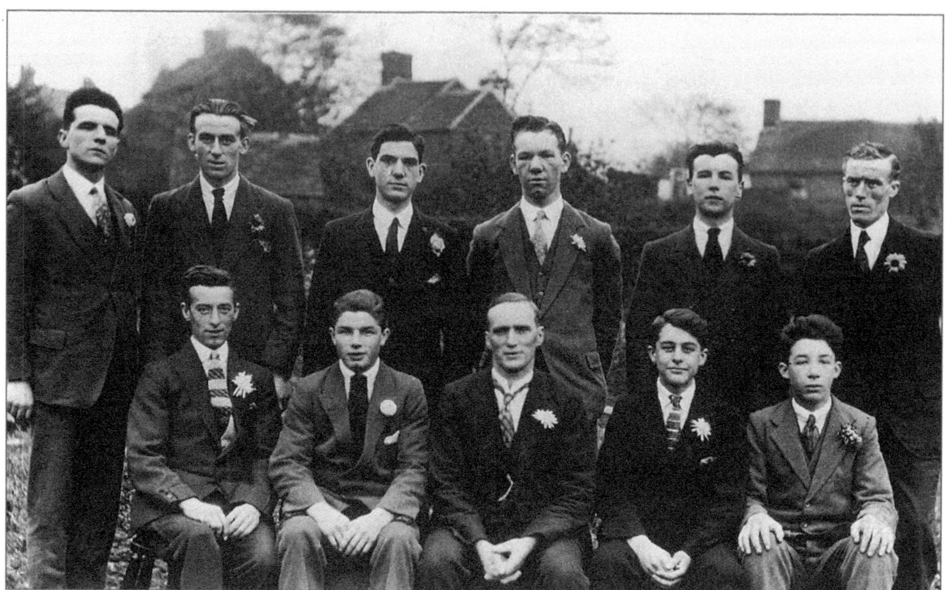

The Birch Coppice Church Young Men's Class of 1927. Back row, left to right: B. Smith, R. Cooper, H. Marsh, O. Jones, J. Fieldhouse, E. Raybould. Front row: J. Clee, H. Thombs, J. Billingham, J. Genner, J. Greenway. *(Jabe Edwards)*

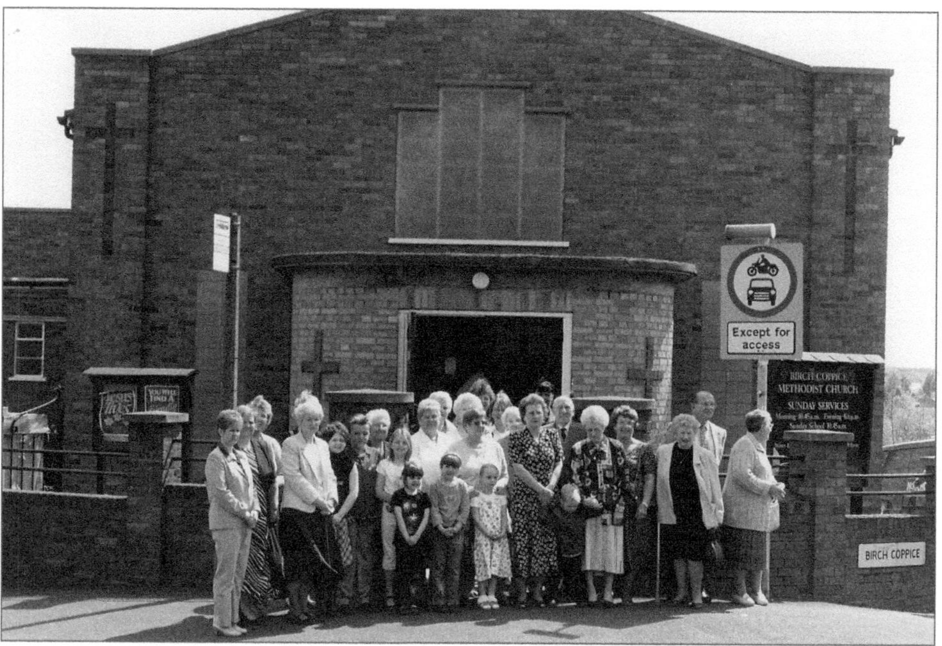

The congregation at Birch Coppice assemble outside the present-day church after their Sunday school anniversary of 5 May 2002. This brick-built replacement for the tin chapel was opened in August 1958. *(Ned Williams)*

In 1988 this tin chapel cake was made as part of the centenary celebrations at Birch Coppice Church. It was also fifty years since the brick building had been completed and was the 250th Anniversary of John Wesley! The cake, made by Mrs Joy Woodhouse, was unveiled at the Flower Festival. Among the flowers are Mrs Clee, Mrs Flohr, Mrs Newey, Mrs Cartwright and Mrs Penn – all of whom had connections with the tin chapel. (*Margaret Price*)

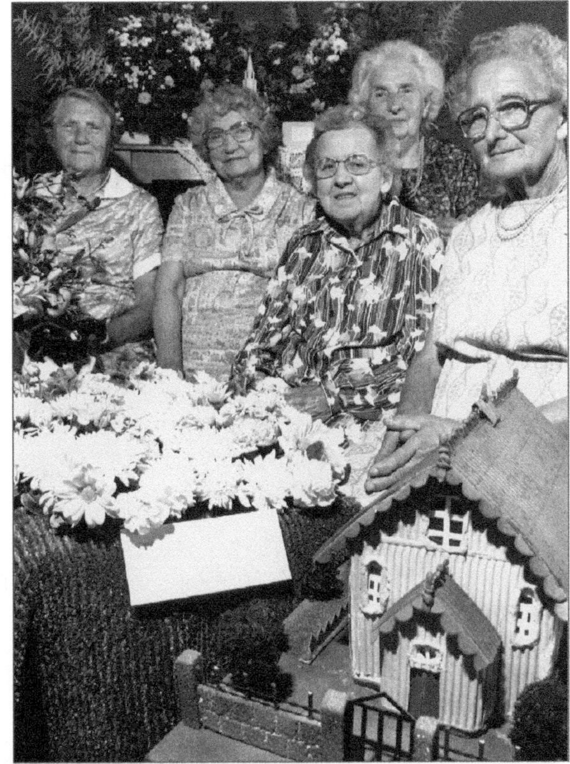

Below: The cast of a Birch Coppice Sunday school nativity play are seen here in a mid-1980s photograph. (*Margaret Price*)

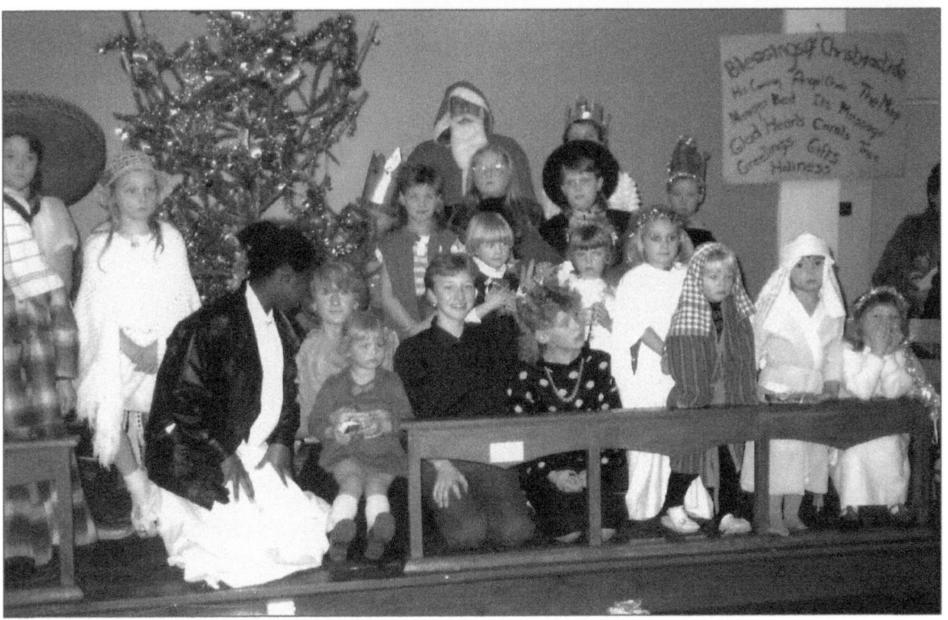

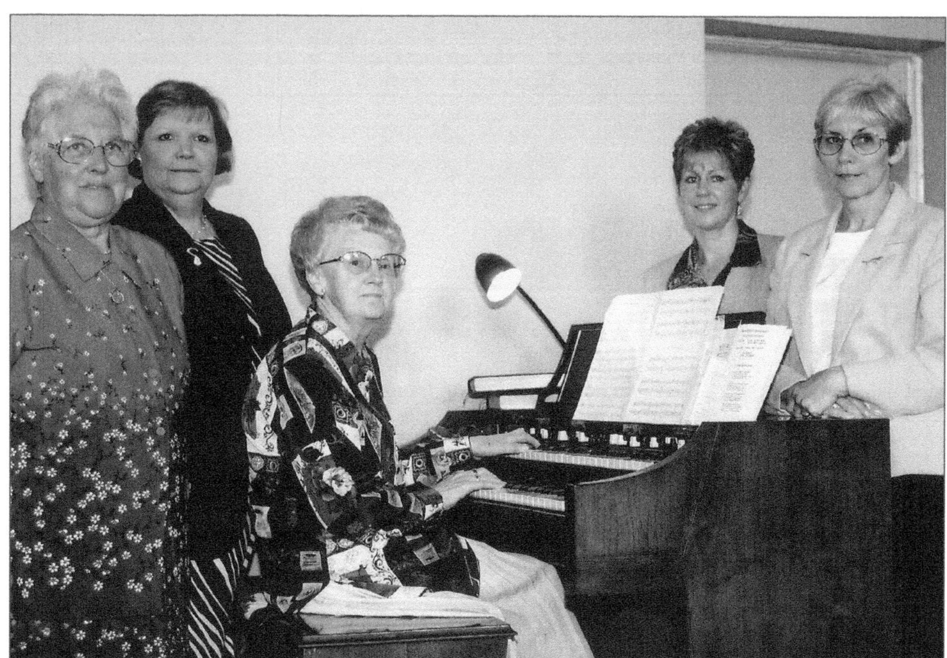

The Birch Coppice Methodist Church annual Sunday school anniversary, 5 May 2002. *Left to right*: Mary Rousell (church secretary), Janet Kirkham (conductor), Margaret Price (organist), Janet Price (Sunday school teacher) and Sue Parkes (Sunday school superintendent). (*Ned Williams*)

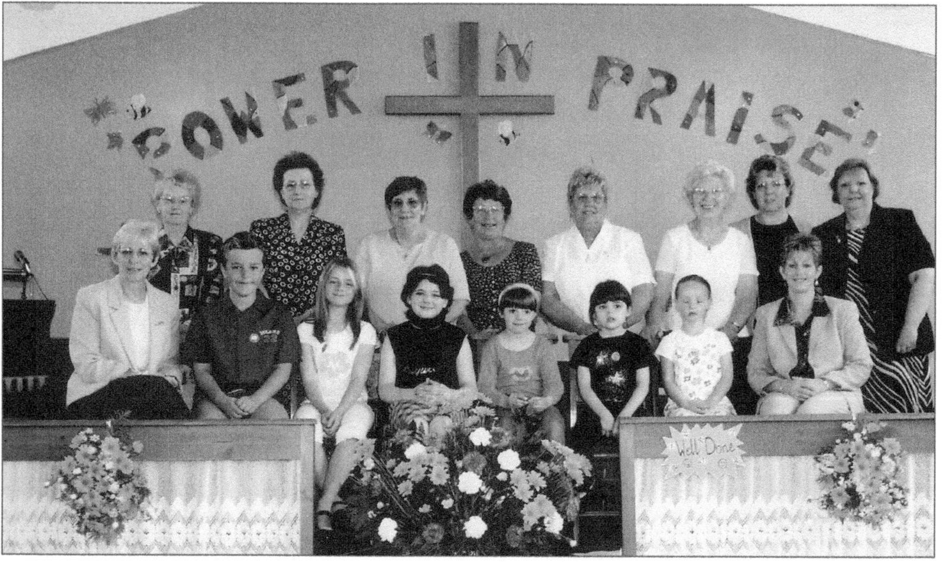

Sunday school children and adults at the same occasion. The anniversary took a 'Power in Praise' theme, hence the decoration. (*Ned Williams*)

FOR BETTER, FOR WORSE

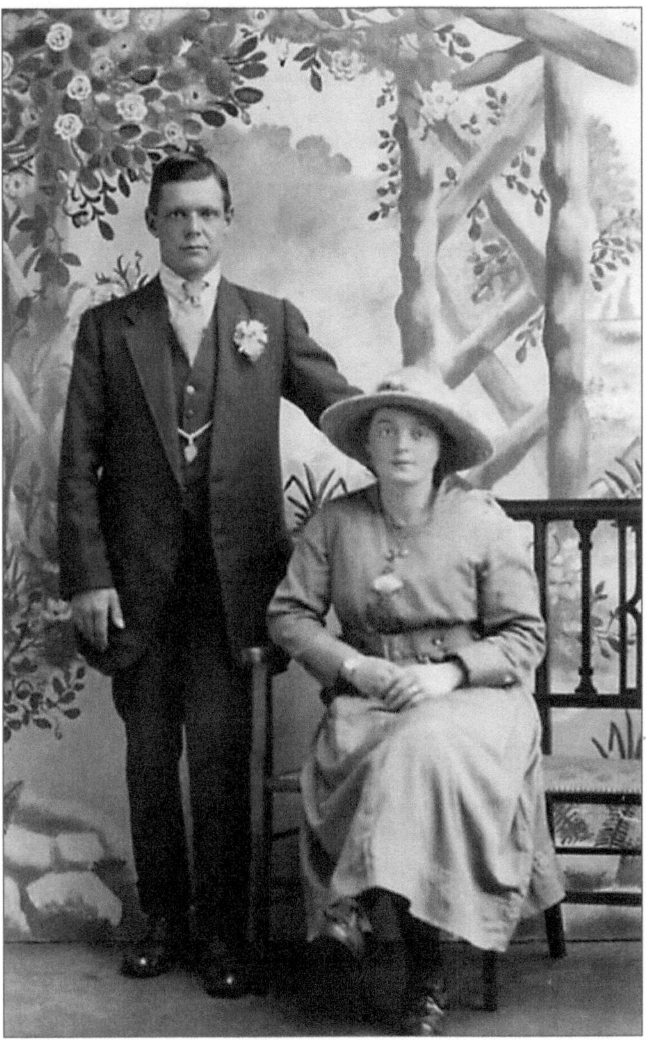

A selection of local wedding photographs reflects the changing fashions of the twentieth century. The selection begins in William Pardoe's studio in the Lye in 1918. The Quarry Bankers getting married are Owen Stevens and Ethel Pewton. Owen had survived the Battle of the Somme during the First World War, but was gassed at Ypres. While still recovering he was married on 7 September 1918, and the couple lived in Quarry Bank for the rest of their lives. Owen travelled by train every day to work at Fort Dunlop in Birmingham. (*Joyce Parkes*)

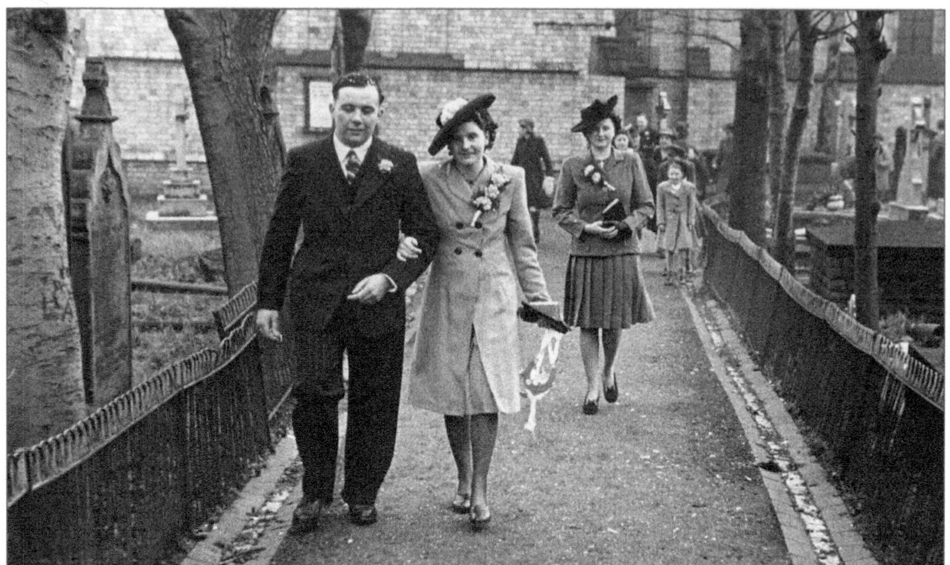

Arthur King married Bessie Tibbetts at Christ Church in January 1947. The couple are photographed leaving the church and are just passing the grave of Thomas Attwood (1815–78), who was Bessie's great-great-grandfather. Behind Bessie are her sisters, Doris and Hazel Tibbetts. (*Sylvia Shaw*)

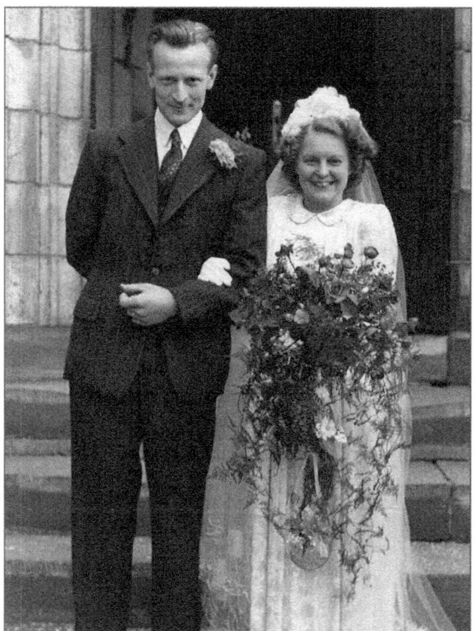

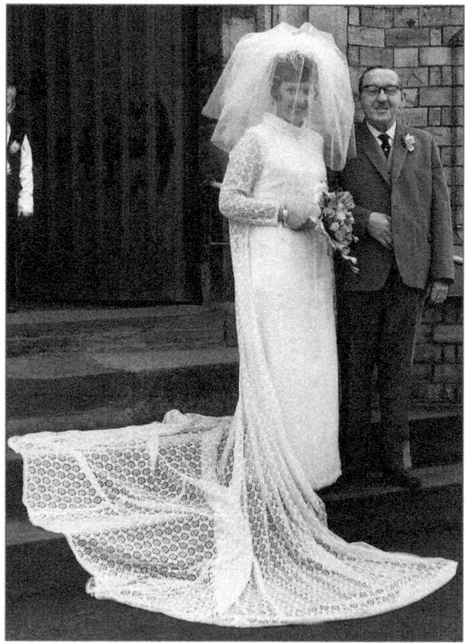

Left: John Parkes marries Joyce Stevens at Christ Church on 24 July 1948. *Right*: Jack Brookes gives away his daughter Susanne at her marriage to Terry Parkes at Christ Church on 26 December 1961. (*Family collections*)

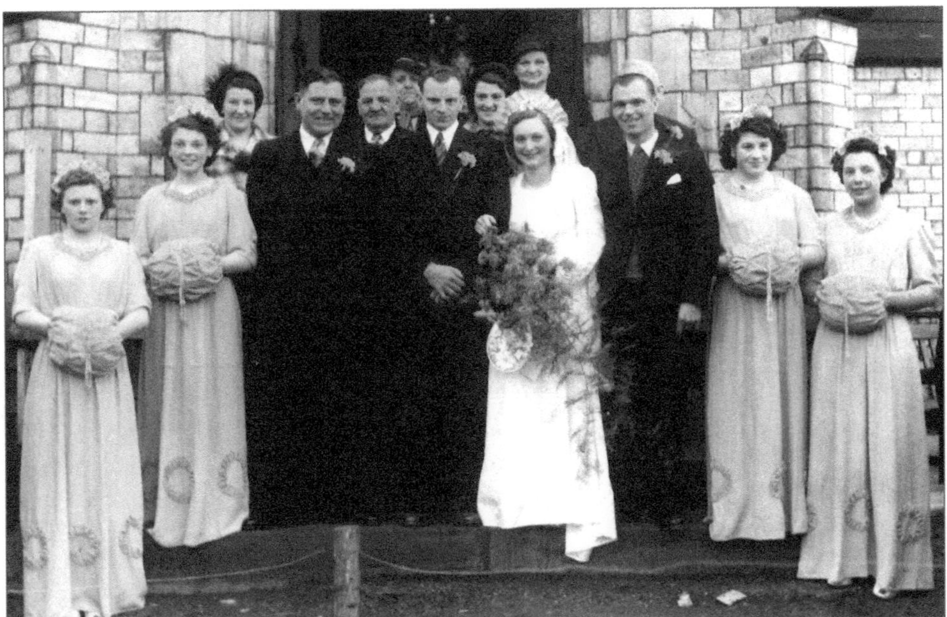

On 3 February 1951 Phyllis Brettle married Les Willetts at Christ Church, Quarry Bank. Les was the nephew of Bert Willetts, who ran the corner shop in Birch Road. (*Jannine Willetts*)

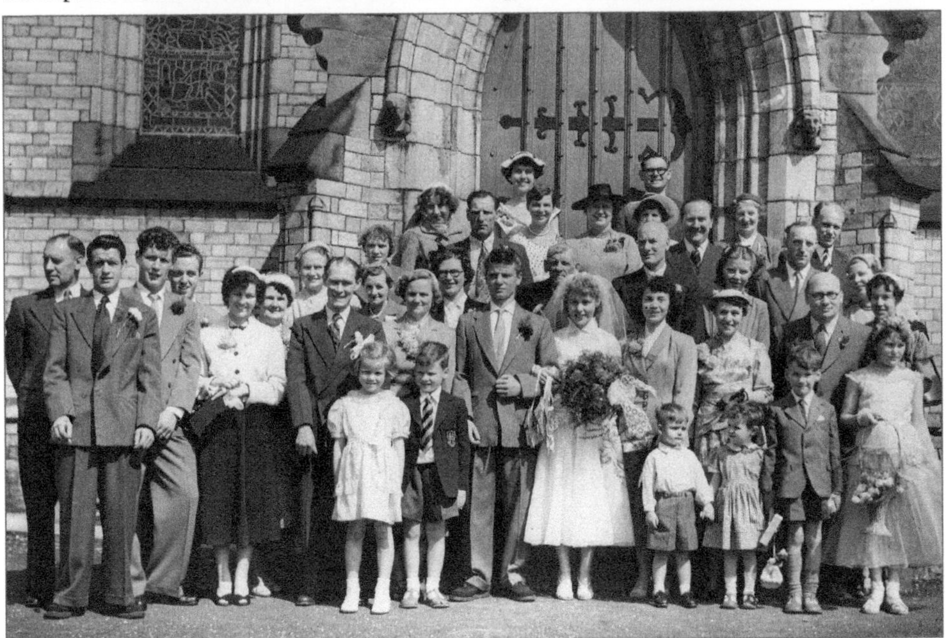

On 9 July 1955 Pat Goodwin of Quarry Bank married Edward Mattocks of Dudley at Christ Church. Eddy and his best man, Trevor Woodcock, were very fashion-conscious young men! (*Pat and Eddy Mattocks*)

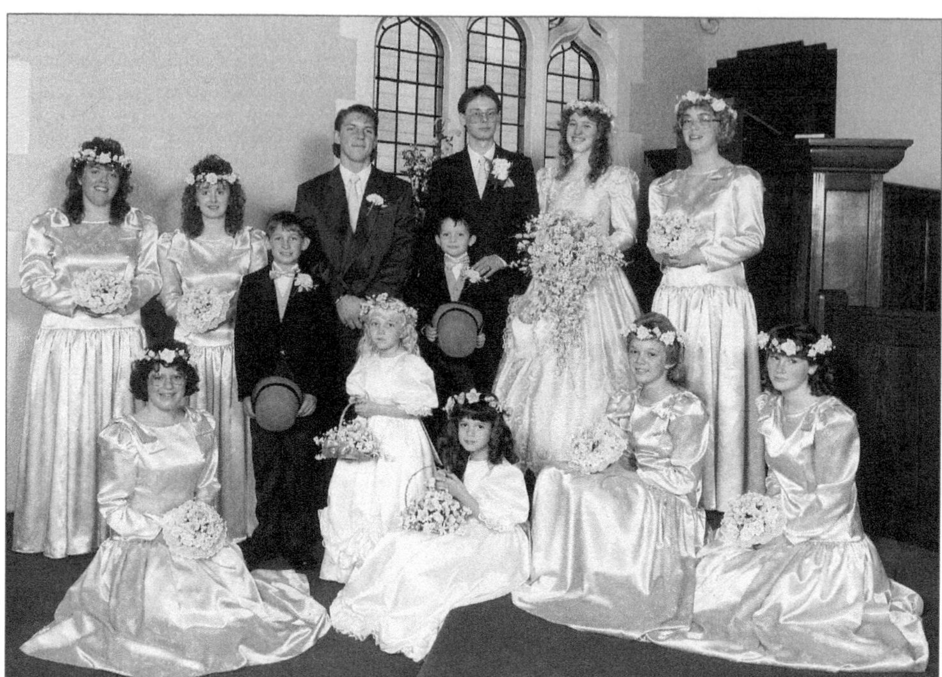

The wedding of Ruth Williams and Brian Shuard took place in the Congregational Church, Quarry Bank, on 21 October 1989 and was photographed by Roger Pirie, the Quarry Bank photographer. Ruth has been a Sunday school teacher at the Congregational Church, and she and Brian still attend this church. (*Ruth and Brian Shuard*)

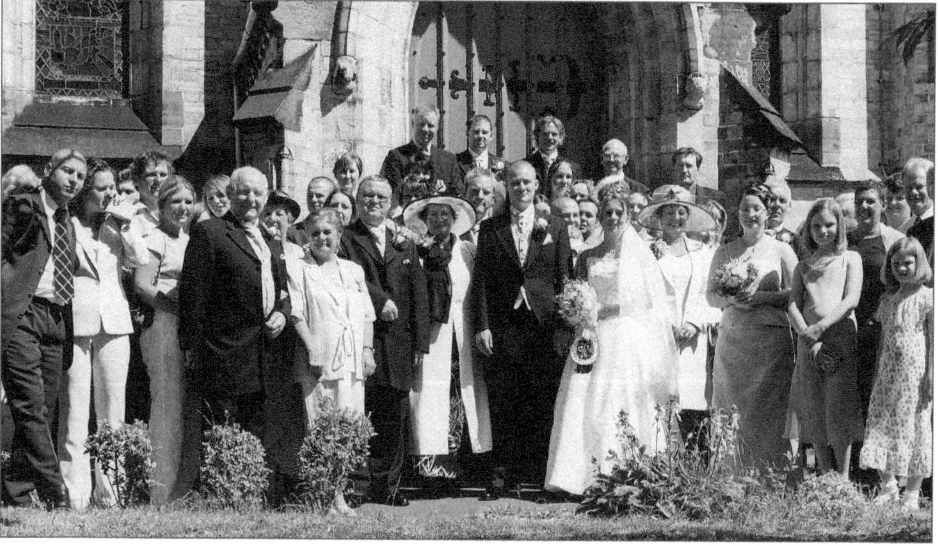

And into the twenty-first century: Rachel Cooper marries Christian Bastable, both of Quarry Bank, on 12 July 2003 at Christ Church. (*John James*)

CHAPTER FIVE

SCHOOLS

The Education Act of 1870 established local School Boards to organise universal education. Before that time some education had been provided by the churches – particularly by the parish church, which had established a 'national school', and some private education. The Kingswinford School Board made reasonable progress in building and opening new schools in the township. The first of these opened in 1872 in the Lower High Street, and the second opened in 1882 in temporary premises in Mount Pleasant.

Demolition of the 1872 buildings in the Lower High Street will mean that parts of the Mount Pleasant site, dating back to 1888, will become the sole surviving legacy of the old School Board. Mount Pleasant School still carries a 'KSB' emblem on the front wall to remind us of the Board's work – later taken over by local government. Quarry Bank's third primary school did not open until 1969 – at the Thorns.

Secondary education in Quarry Bank took a step forward with the building of two secondary schools in Coppice Lane – one for boys and one for girls. Nothing of these two schools now remains. Secondary education is now provided at the Thorns School and Community College in a part of Quarry Bank that was developed in the second half of the twentieth century.

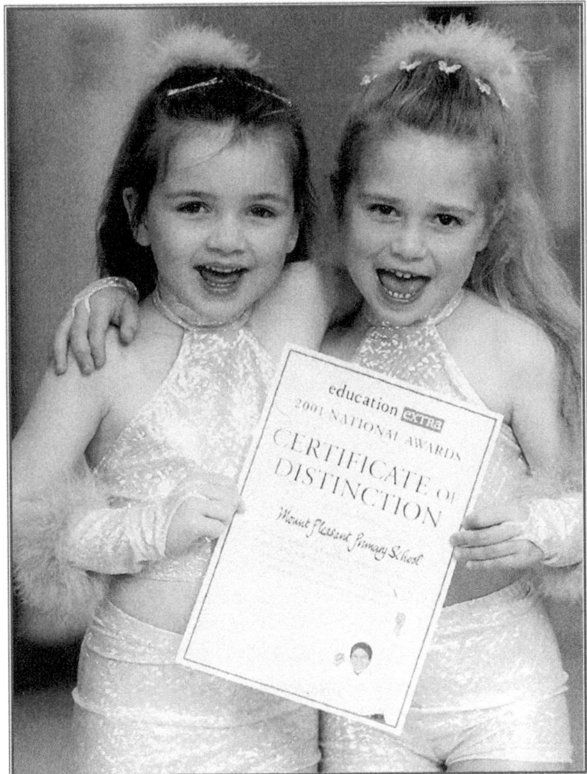

Mount Pleasant pupils Gemma Raybould and Olivia Fullwood display a Certificate of Distinction granted to the school in 2001 for its outstanding scheme of 'out-of-school-hours' learning activities. (*School Archive*)

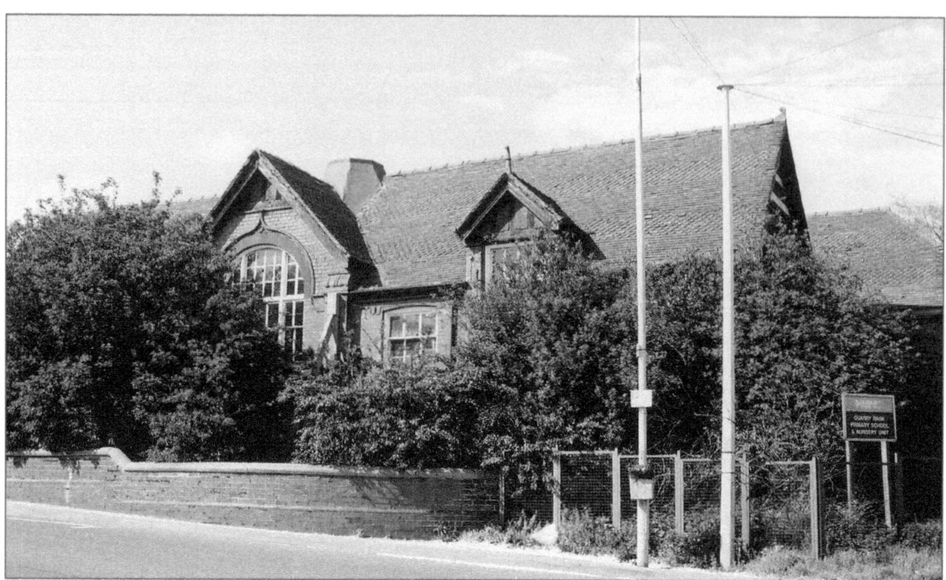

The local School Board opened the first 'state' school in Quarry Bank on 15 July 1872, presumably in this building. In 1877 the school was much enlarged and this building then became for 'mixed-infant' use only. The 1877 building was replaced with the current primary school building in the mid-1930s. By 2002 the infants school building was much the worse for wear and had lost the bell tower that had been a prominent local landmark. (*Ned Williams*)

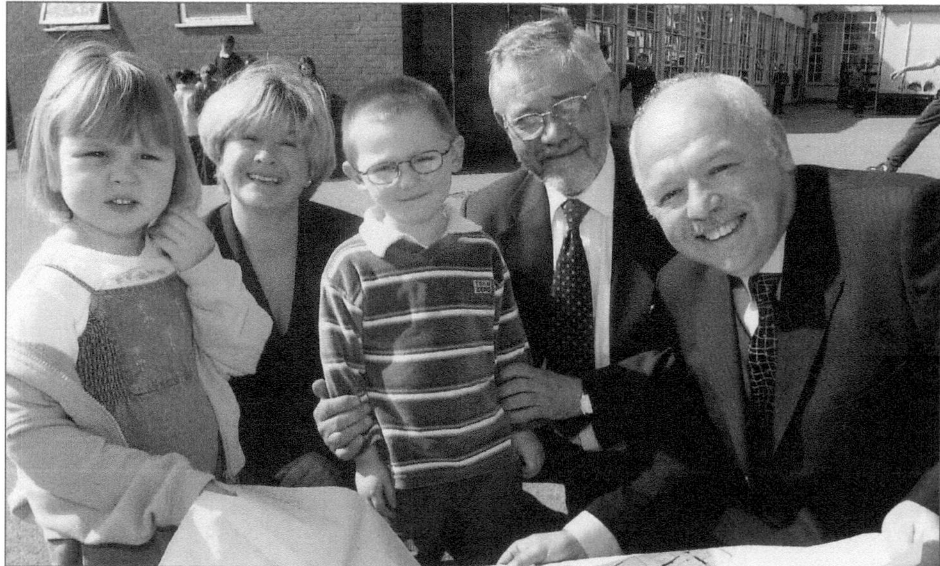

In May 2002 two three-year-old pupils at the Nursery, Grace Donelly and Kieran Kelly, are invited to join Councillors Brian Cotterell and David Sparks and Deputy Head Elaine Perrins to inspect plans for the new building that will replace the old school building of 1872. (*Express & Star*)

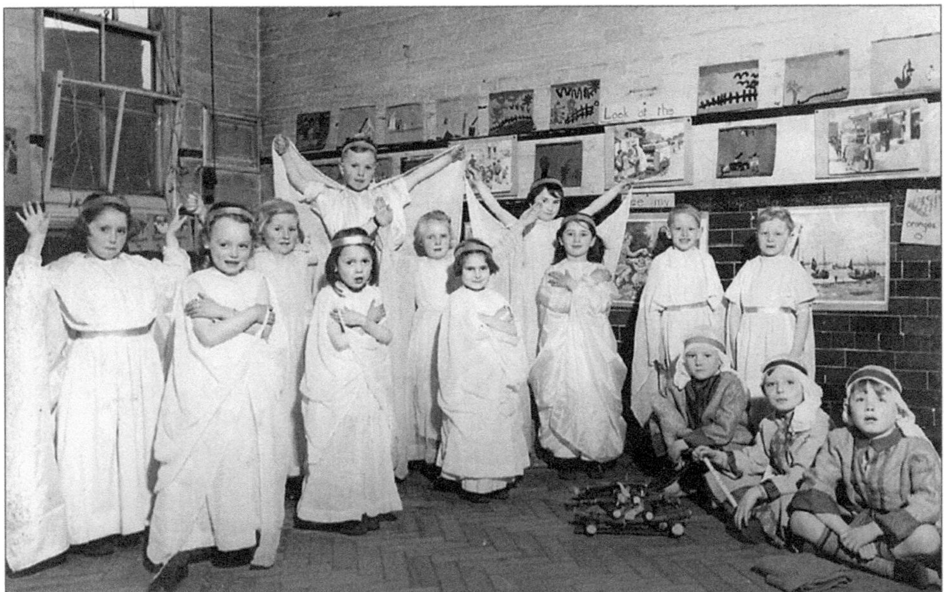

A Christmas play at Quarry Bank Primary School in about 1956 seems to feature three young shepherds overcome by a 'host' of angels. Note the school environment – bare wooden floors, tiled and painted brick walls. (*Joyce Parkes*)

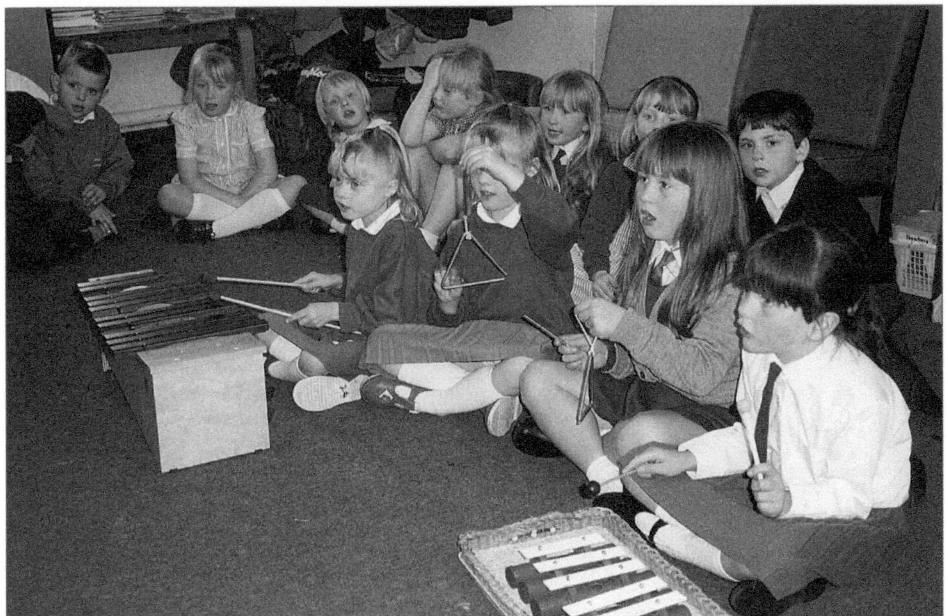

Quarry Bank Primary School in more recent times shows participation in a music lesson in a rather different environment – carpets and school uniforms prevail. (*Quarry Bank Primary School Archive*)

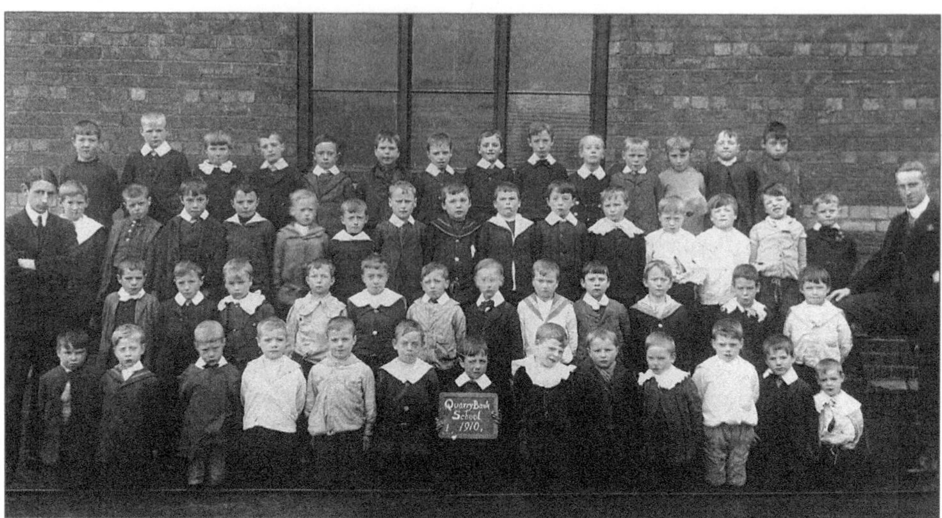

At the Quarry Bank School girls and boys were segregated between the ages of seven and fourteen – a practice that was perpetuated from the mid-1930s onwards with new secondary schools being built in Coppice Lane and the new junior school putting boys on the ground floor and the girls upstairs. This class photo at the junior school of 1910 vintage shows master, pupil teacher and the boys. (*Mary Stevens*)

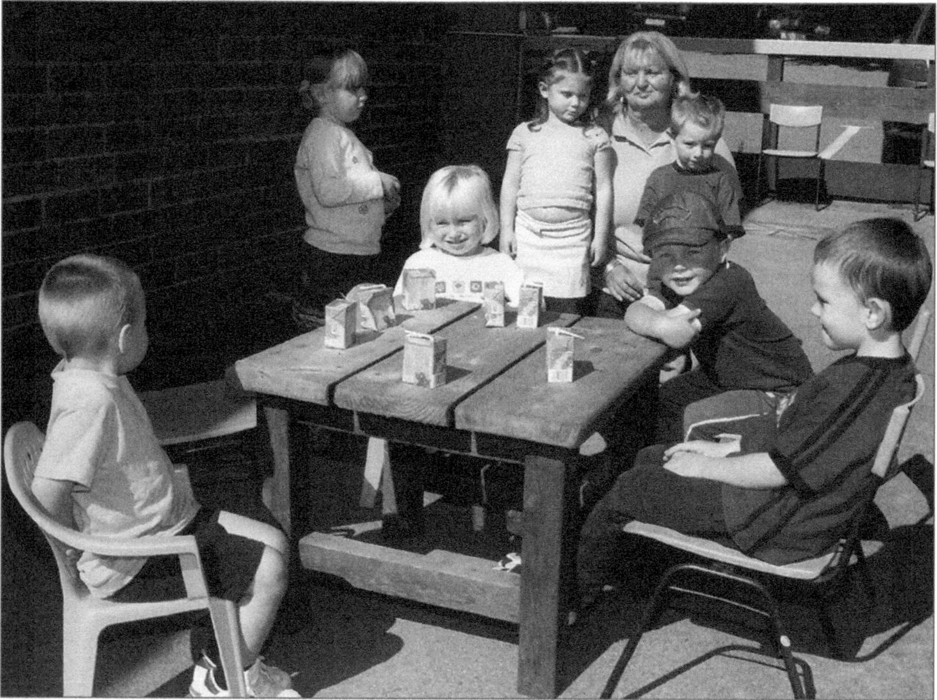

Pupils in the nursery class at Quarry Bank Primary School in 2002. (*Ned Williams*)

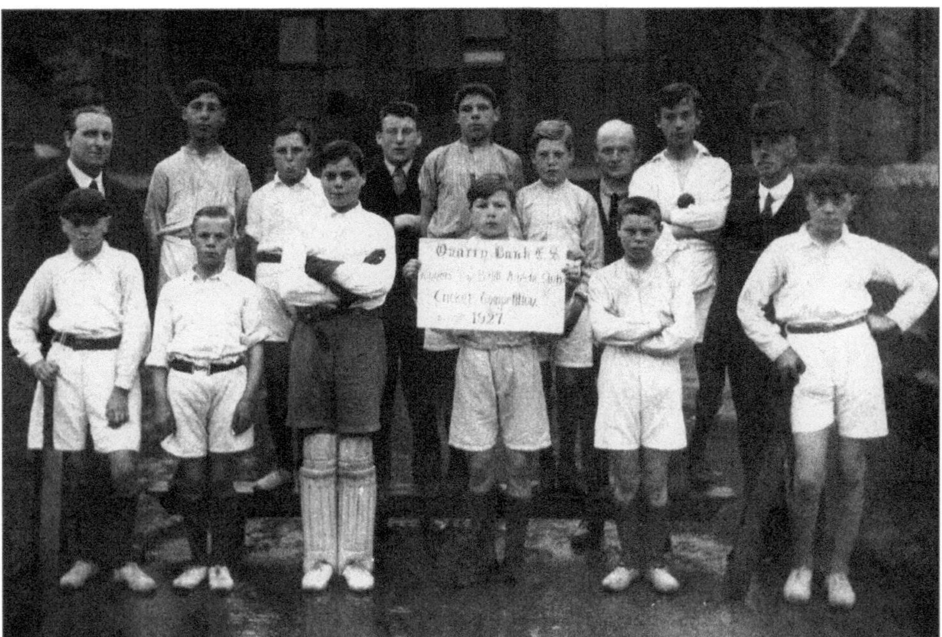

Boys of Quarry Bank Junior School of 1927 pose with headmaster Isaac Badger on the right and well-known sports master Harry Scriven on the left. Albert Tipper is in the centre of the back row. (*MPLHG*)

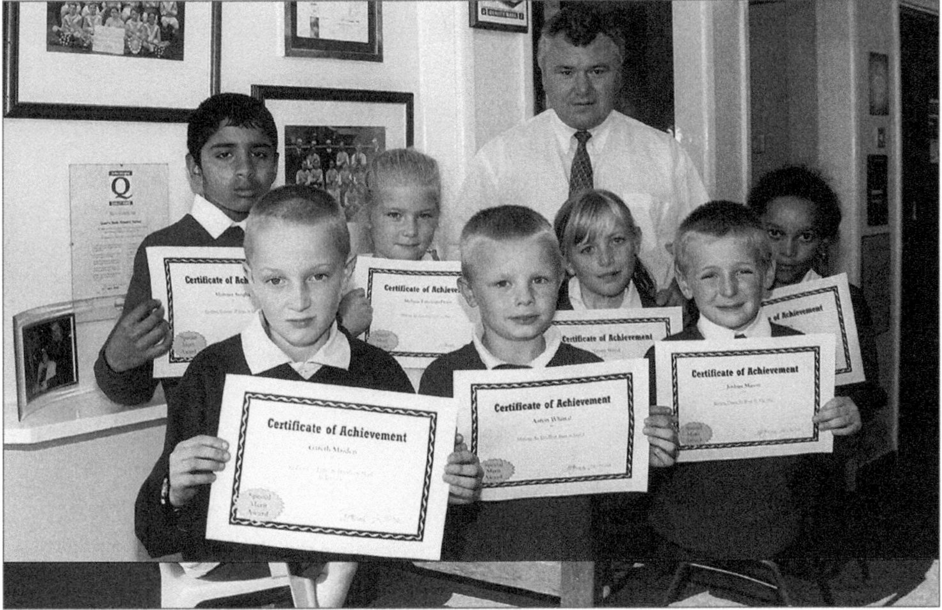

Head teacher Dave Evans and some of the pupils of Quarry Bank Primary School displaying their end-of-week achievement certificates in June 2002. (*Ned Williams*)

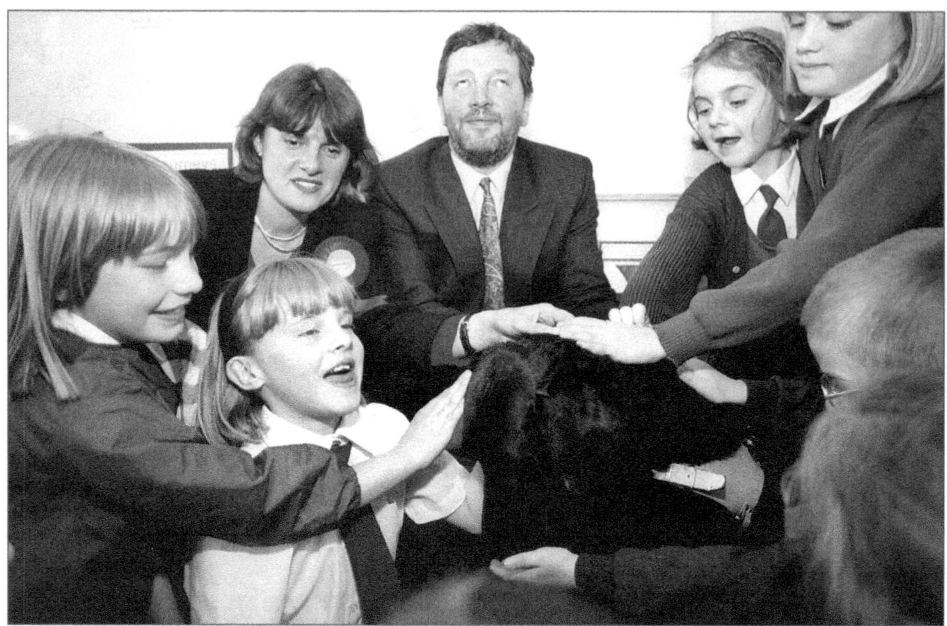

David Blunkett, Secretary of State for Education and Employment, visited Quarry Bank Primary School with local MP Debra Shipley in May 1997. (*Express & Star*)

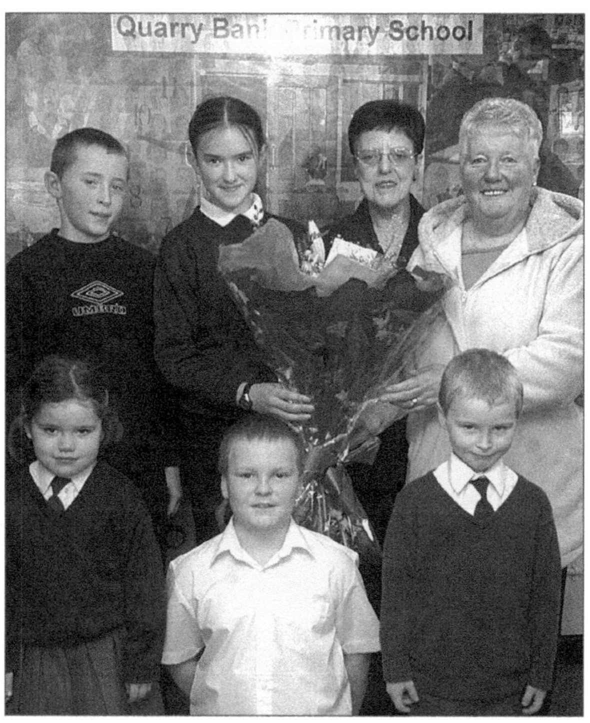

Mrs Jill Southall, a lunchtime supervisor, is presented with a bouquet to mark twenty-five years' of service at Quarry Bank Primary School. Back row, left to right: Duncan Crofts, Rebekah Boddy, supervisor Margaret Sutcliffe and Jill Southall. Front row: Chelsea Massey, Joseph Bridgewater and Jamie Field. In a local school 'archive' a lunchtime supervisor with twenty-five years service, or the schools crossing patrol staff, share equality with head teachers and secretaries of state. (*Quarry Bank Primary School*)

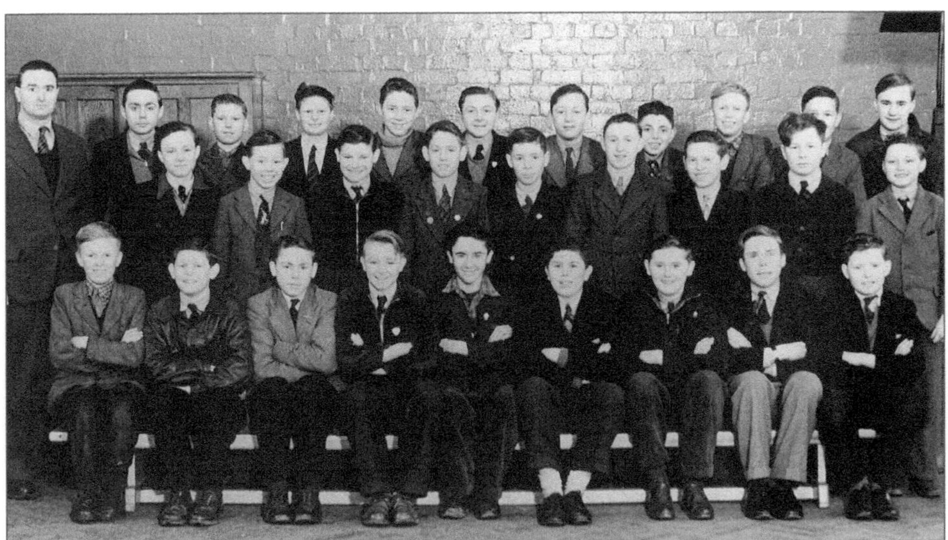

Form 3A at Quarry Bank Boys' Secondary School, 3 March 1953. Back row, left to right: Tom Cooper, C. Homer, J. Little, J. Mountford, R. Homer, G. Dimmock, W. Stafford, P. Dobson, G. Westwood, S. Haynes. Middle row: Mr Evans, N. Raybould, J. Davies, T. Ashman, B. Stevens, D. Round, L. Head, F. Deeley, T. Hill, A. Harris. Front row: B. Dobson, R. Brookes, B. Tyler, F. Hart, R. Haynes, B. Jones, I. Hart, J. Beddard, D. Priest. (*Mary Stevens*)

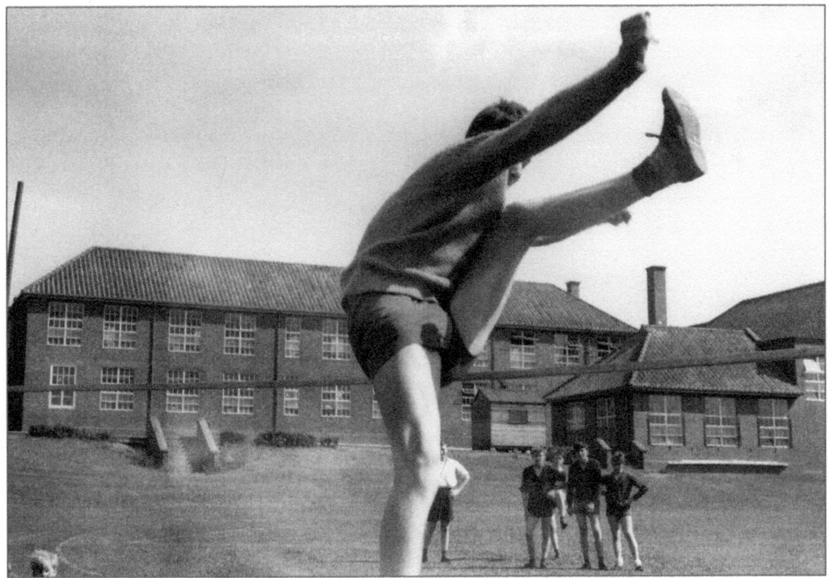

Pictures that show the Coppice Lane buildings at Quarry Bank Secondary Boys' School seem rare. The buildings were demolished in 1974 after a fire, and from the following year secondary education in Quarry Bank was provided by Thorns School. In this picture the 1932 buildings of the Boys' School form the backdrop to a sports day picture taken in 1963. (*Thorns School Archive*)

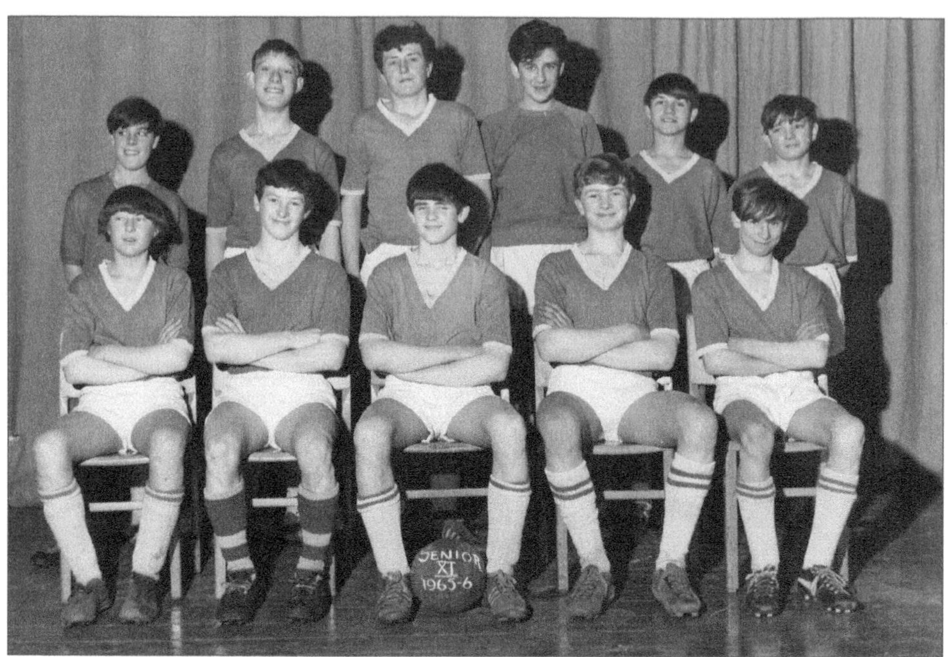

Unidentified members of Quarry Bank Boys' Secondary School football team of 1965/6. (*Thorns School Archive*)

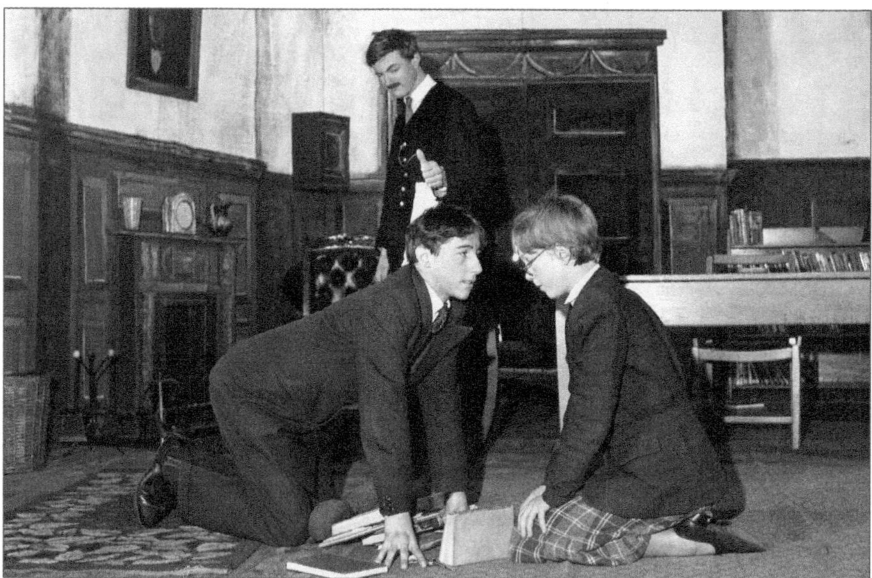

Sport and drama both seem to have been important at the Quarry Bank secondary schools. The Boys' and Girls' Schools combined for this production of *The Happiest Days of your Life* in 1966, produced by teacher Stuart Burton. Frank Martino plays a headmaster in this scene, joined by Christopher Brookes and Elizabeth Dobson in the foreground. (*Thorns School Archive*)

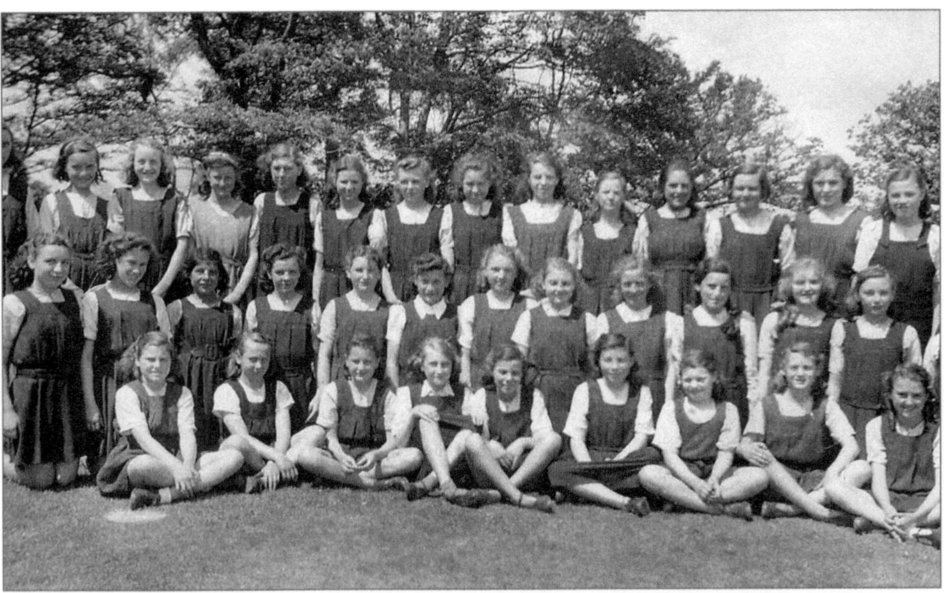

Some of the girls at Quarry Bank Girls' Secondary School in June 1945. Back row, left to right: Cissie Hill, Mary Ledham, Iris Cartwright, Olive Whitehouse, Pauline Symonds, Brenda Green, Jean Evans, Betty Guest, Gladys Fisher, Joyce Ashmore, Jeanne Bedford, Margaret Patrick, Beryl Bloomer and Jean Dwyer. Middle row: Margaret Atkins, Hazel Hamblett, Jean Sidaway, Ethel Hingley, Jean Weaver, Barbara Dunn, Jean Hollis, Phyllis Priest, Mary Parkes, Margaret Gill, June Bowen, Betty Guest and Irene Davies. Front row: Eva Webb, Corbett Poole, Mary Scott, Marjorie Pearson, Beryll Chell, Fanny Cartwright, Gladys Williams, Beatrice Tibbetts, Brenda Haden and Mavis Harold. (*June Bowen*)

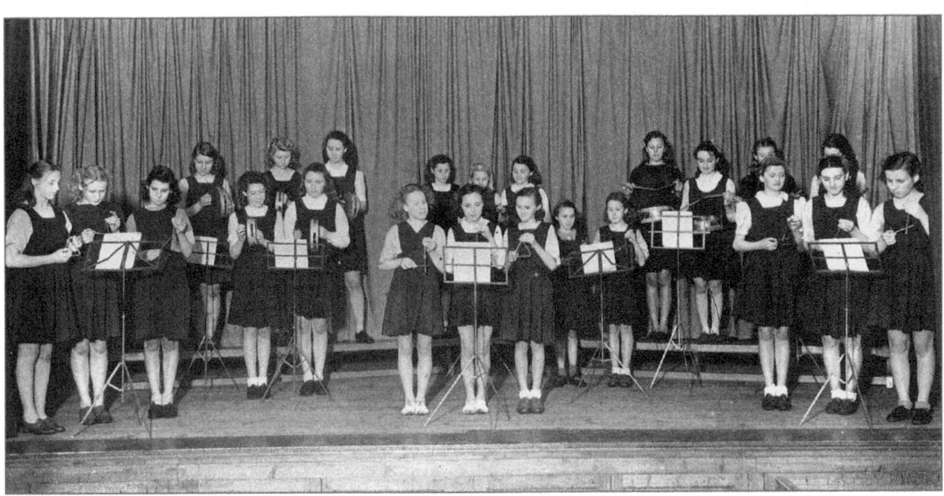

Quarry Bank Girls' Secondary School's Percussion Band, photographed in 1948. (*Betty Priest*)

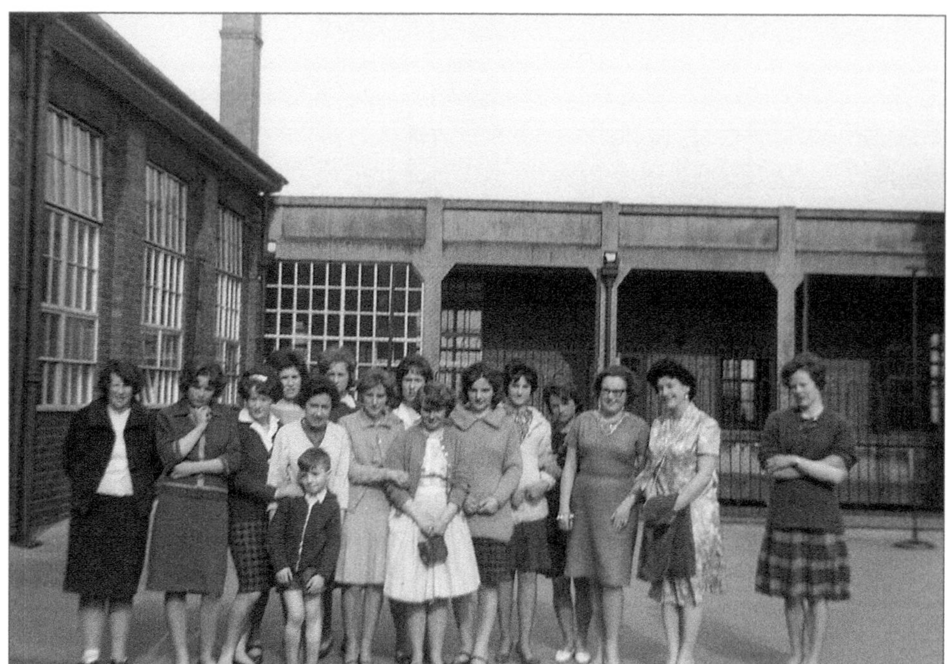

This 1962 picture of Mrs Forest's class at the Quarry Bank Girls' Secondary School is unusual in that it also shows us part of the school building, demolished when the schools combined and moved to Thorns. Housing now occupies the Coppice Lane site. (*Hazel Payne*)

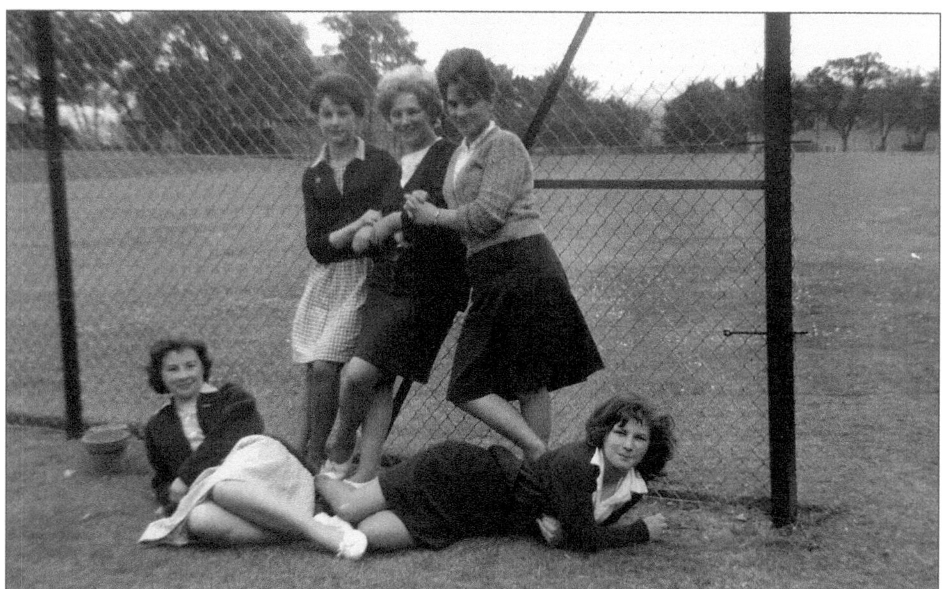

The Girls' School playing fields in 1962. Rosalie Raybould, Diane Surtees, Cheryl Jasper, Margaret Potts and Rita Knowles pose for the camera. (*Hazel Payne*)

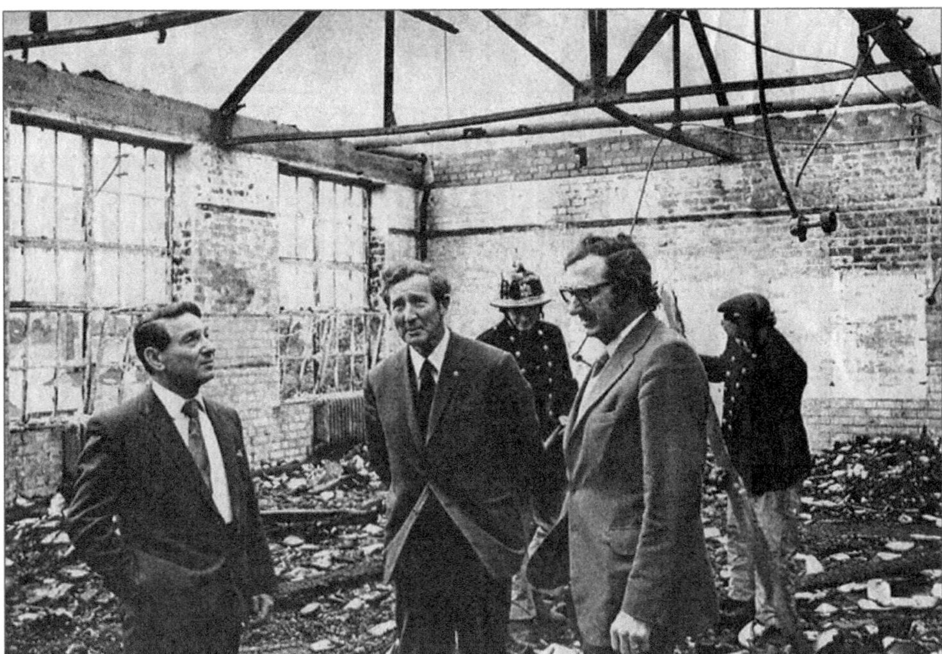

In June 1974 headmaster Mr J.J. Martin shows Councillor Wilson and Director of Education Mr J. Buck around the smouldering remains of the Boys' School section of Quarry Bank Secondary School. The fire hastened the reorganisation of local secondary education at Thorns School (later Thorns Community College), although building the latter was delayed by open-cast mining on the proposed site. (*Express & Star*)

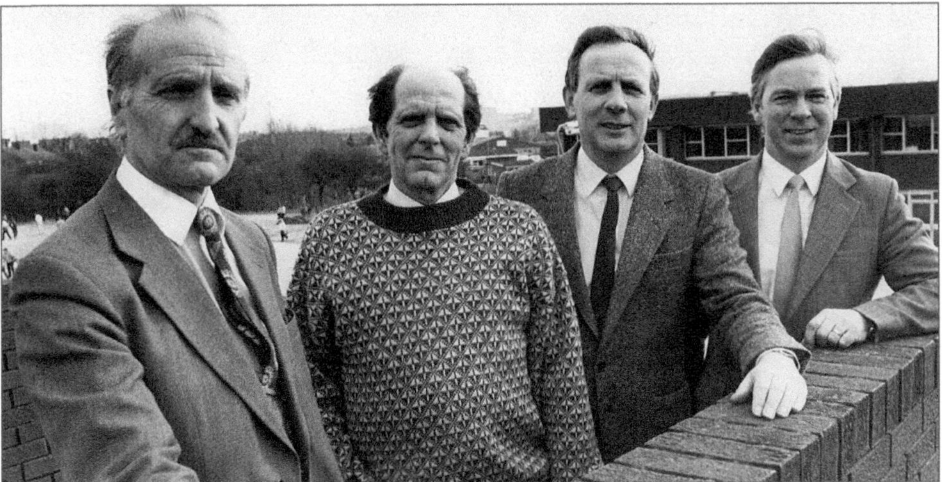

Some teachers moved from the former secondary schools to the new Thorns School. Vice-Principal Jack Siddaway, left, had completed thirty-two years' local service when this picture was taken in 1987 and was joined by Tony Brake, Philip Millward and Geoff Attwood, all of whom had completed twenty-six years' service. (*Express & Star*)

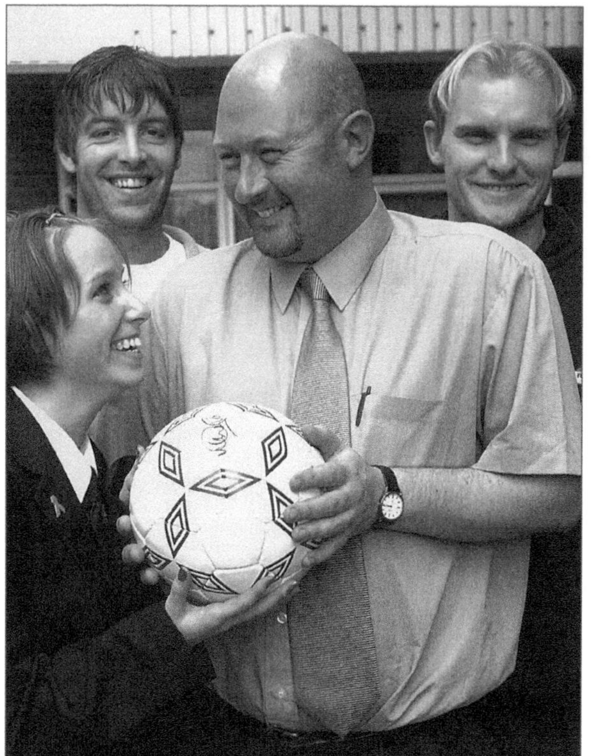

In May 2002 Year 11 pupils at Thorns School and Community College presented Adrian Wilkes, their form teacher, with a farewell present. The school's head girl, Cheryl-Ann Smith, is seen here making the presentation, joined by Paul Butler and Michael Oakes from Wolves – Adrian's favourite football team. With the assistance of the headmaster, Dave Mountney, this presentation was a surprise addition to the school leavers' assembly of that year. (*Express & Star*)

Below: Thorns School and Community College has been famous for the quality of its dramatic productions presented in its studio theatre. Kevin Dunn appears as Fagin in a Thorns production of *Oliver Twist* in 1989. (*Thorns College Archive*)

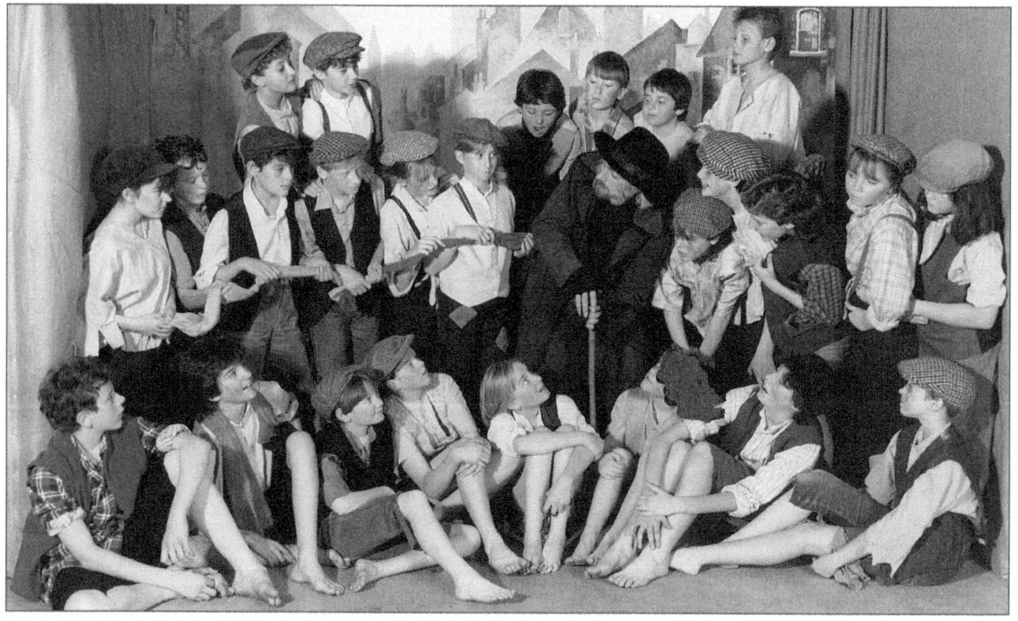

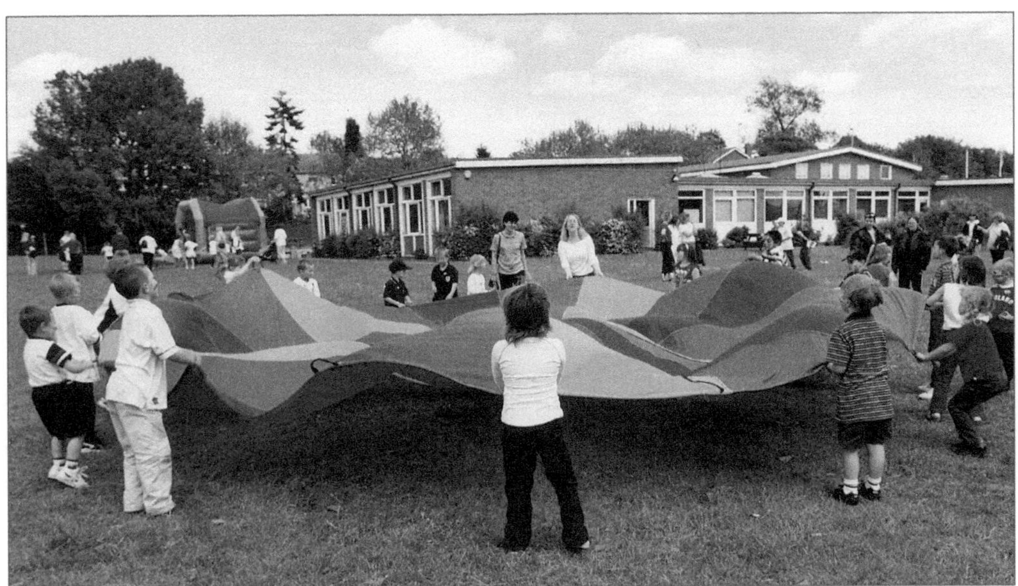

Thorns Primary School, in Thorns Road, is Quarry Bank's newest primary school, having opened in 1969. Here the school building and surrounding field are seen as the children play parachute games to celebrate the Jubilee of 2002. (*John James*)

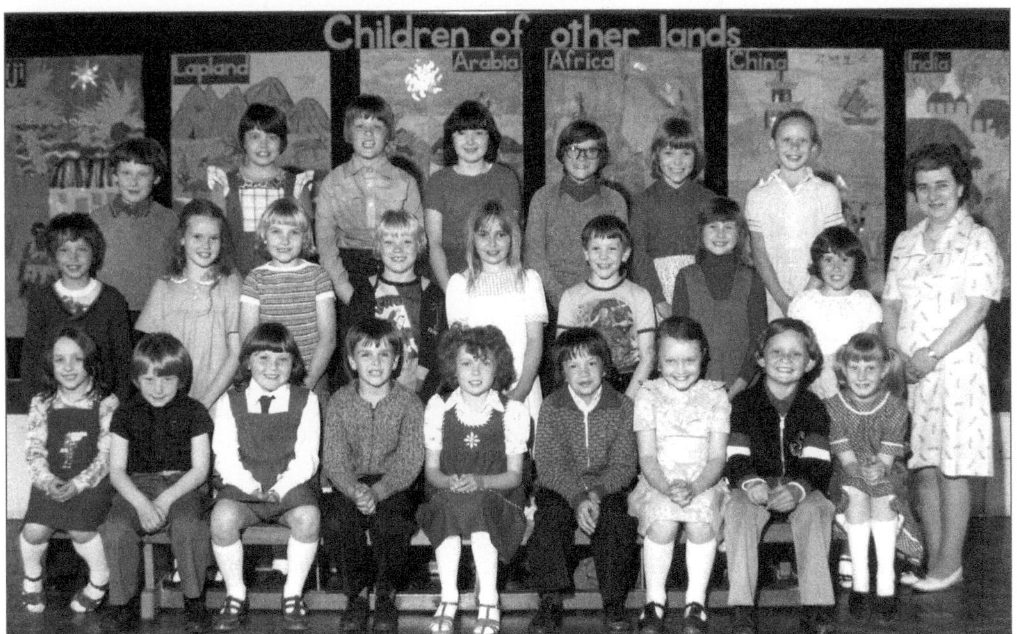

Mrs Marjorie Jenkins and class F1 celebrate the International Year of the Child Frieze at Thorns Primary School in May 1979. Mrs Jenkins taught at the school from 1969, when it opened, until 1980. (*Thorns Primary School Archive*)

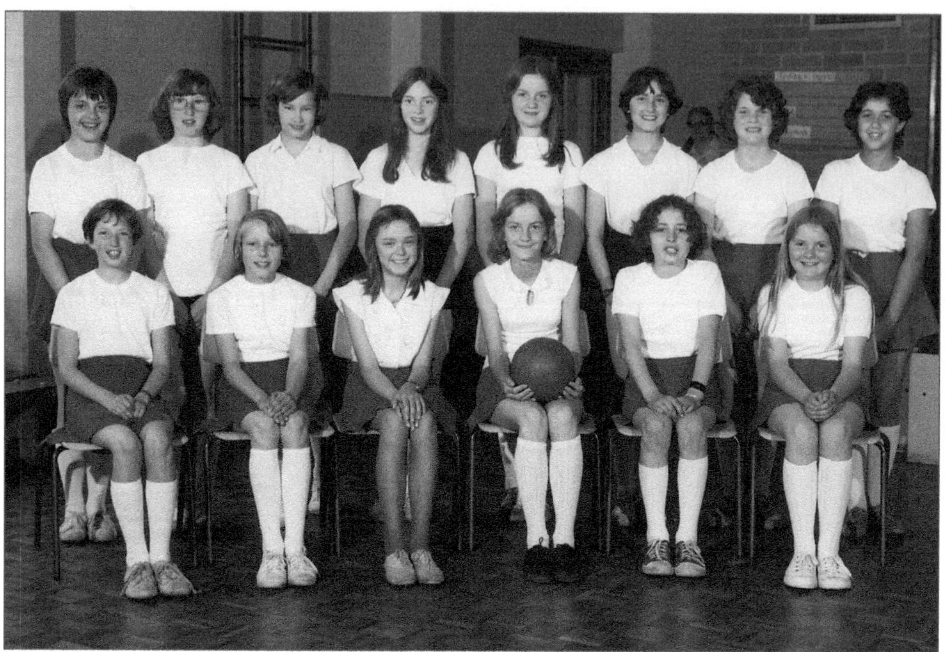

The Thorns Primary School netball team in 1982. (*Margaret Priest*)

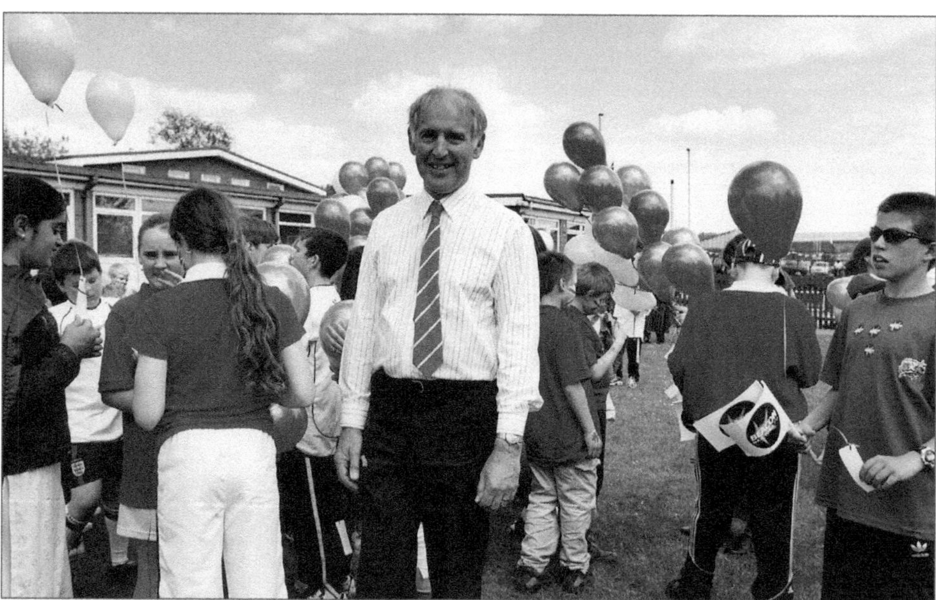

The first head teacher at Thorns Primary School was Miss Sturman, who came to the school from the Girls' Secondary School in Coppice Lane when that was merged with the Boys' School. She was followed by Mr David Howell, seen here in Jubilee Year 2002, during which he retired. (*John James*)

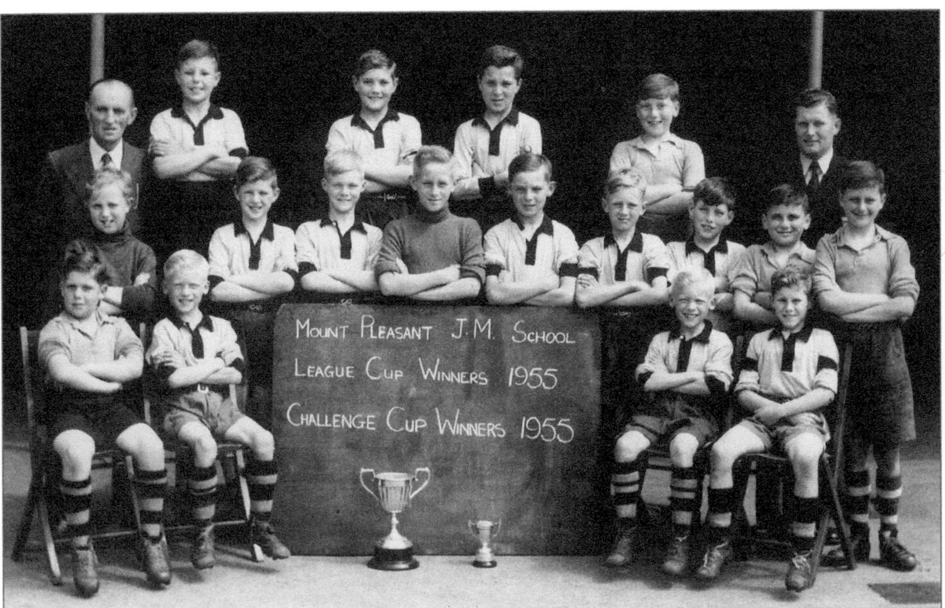

Mount Pleasant footballers, 1955. Back row, left to right: Mr Owen, headmaster, Terry Breese, Barry Herrington, Barry Marsden, Walter Allen and Mr Anslow. Front row: Tony Martin, Robert Ganner, Norman Westbury, Alan Jones, Robert Sidaway, Martin Hill, Terry Allen, Paul Robinson, -?-, Paul Jones, Peter Jones and Robert Tilley. (*Collection of Ossie Biddle*)

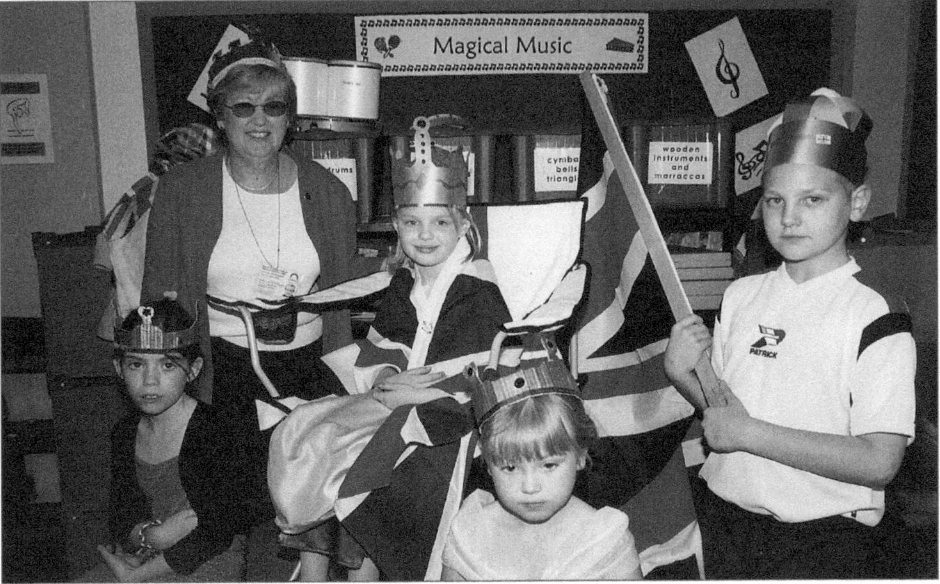

Mount Pleasant head teacher Mrs Gail Bedford and children dressed to celebrate the 2002 Royal Jubilee. The 'Jubilee Queen', Philippa Coley, is attended by Claire Hampton, Natasha Redfern and John Barnsley. (*John James*)

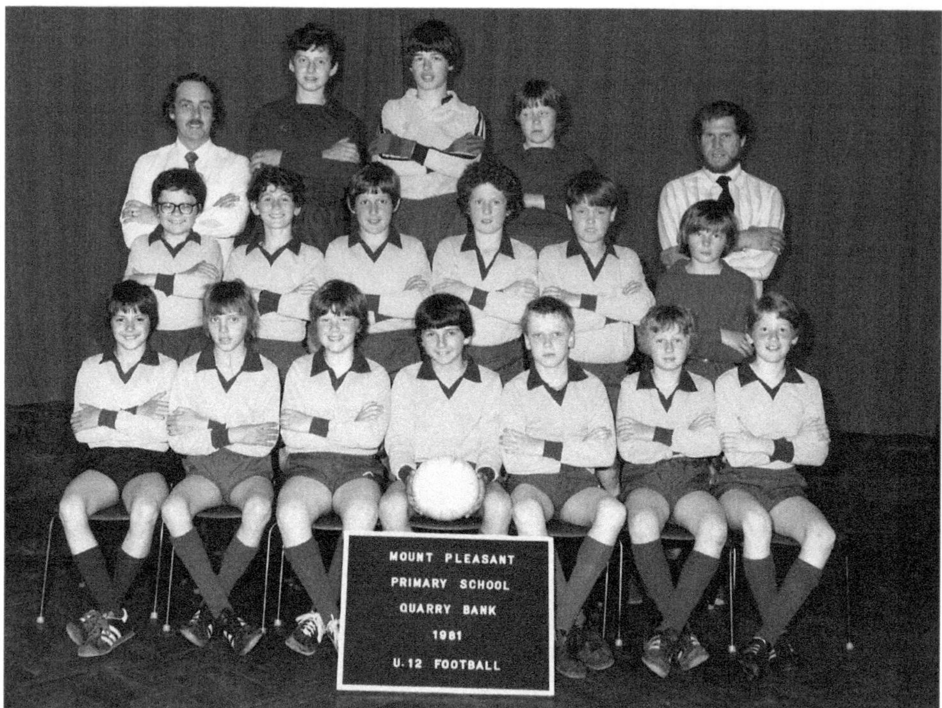

Mount Pleasant team, 1981. Back row, left to right: Graham Nunn (headmaster), Simon Worsley, David Harris, Neal Skidmore, Mr Studd. Middle row: Steven Hollies, Jason Grinell, Adrian Pargeter, Martin Bevan, Grant Batham, Gavin Davenport. Front row: Tony Guest, Chris Pardoe, Clark Griffin, Ellis Fulward, Mick Bolton, Julian Adkins, Glyn Dudley. (*John James*)

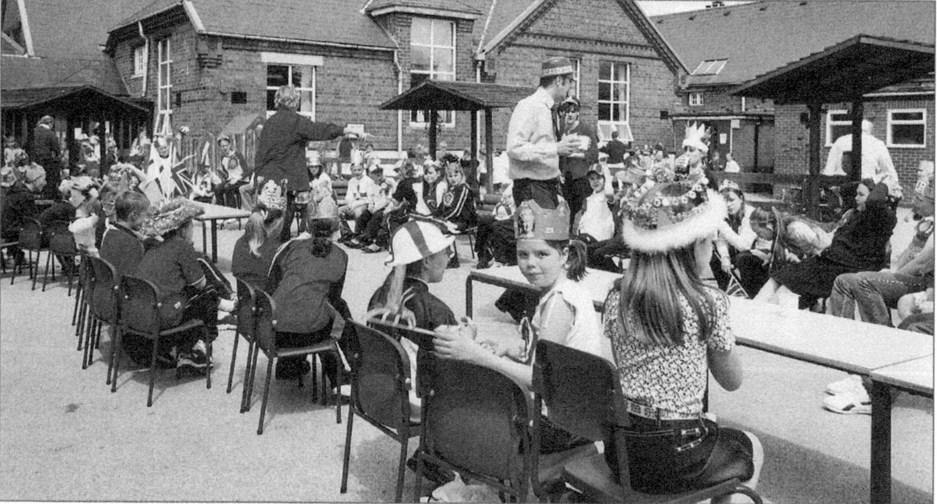

Mount Pleasant Primary School celebrating the 2002 Royal Jubilee with a tea party in the playground. (*John James*)

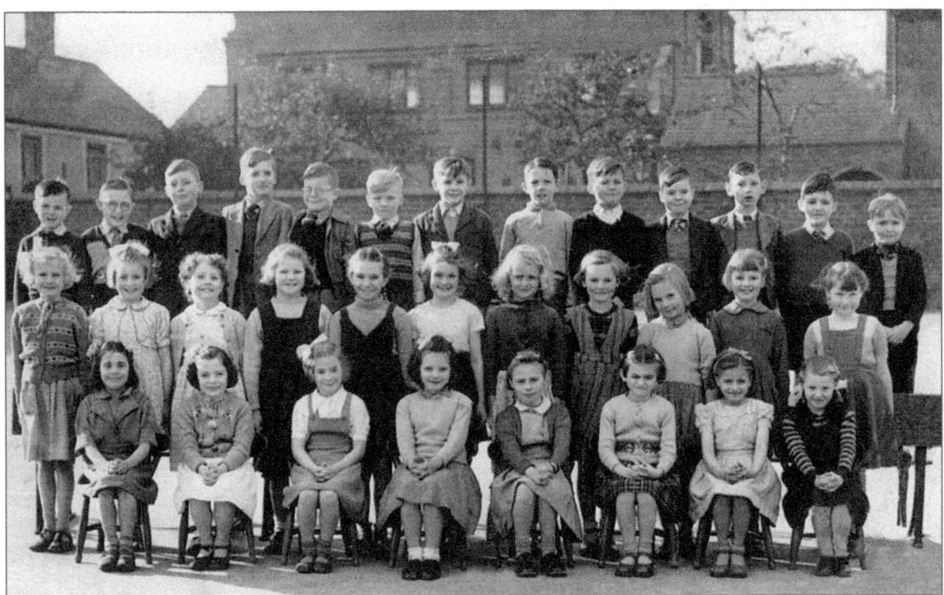

Mount Pleasant Primary School, 1955/6. Kathleen Day (née Homer), second from left in the middle row, supplied the photo and remembers some of her friends in the picture: Sylvia Dillard and Virginia Hastings on either side of her, plus Marlene Brettel, Janice Harvey, Jill Brett, Janet Fulford and Pearl Billingham. The picture is taken looking across the playground, with the hall behind the Wesleyan chapel in the background. Mount Pleasant School began life in that building while the School Board building was being built. (*Kathleen Day*)

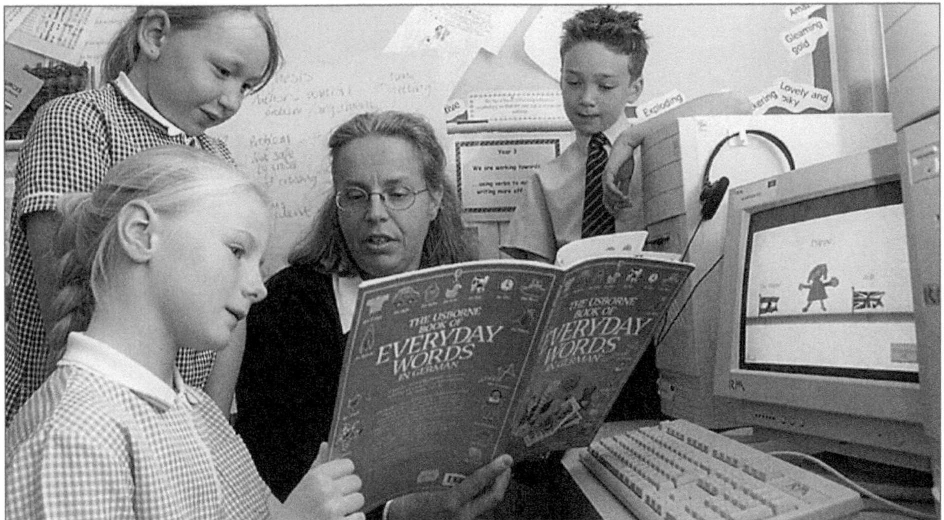

Half a century later pupils at Mount Pleasant discuss the possibilities of video-conferencing with schoolchildren in Germany, learning European languages and computer skills. Left to right: Hannah Thomas, Kate Mills, Brigitte Klingenberg from Germany and Ashley Bourne. (*School Archives/Express & Star*)

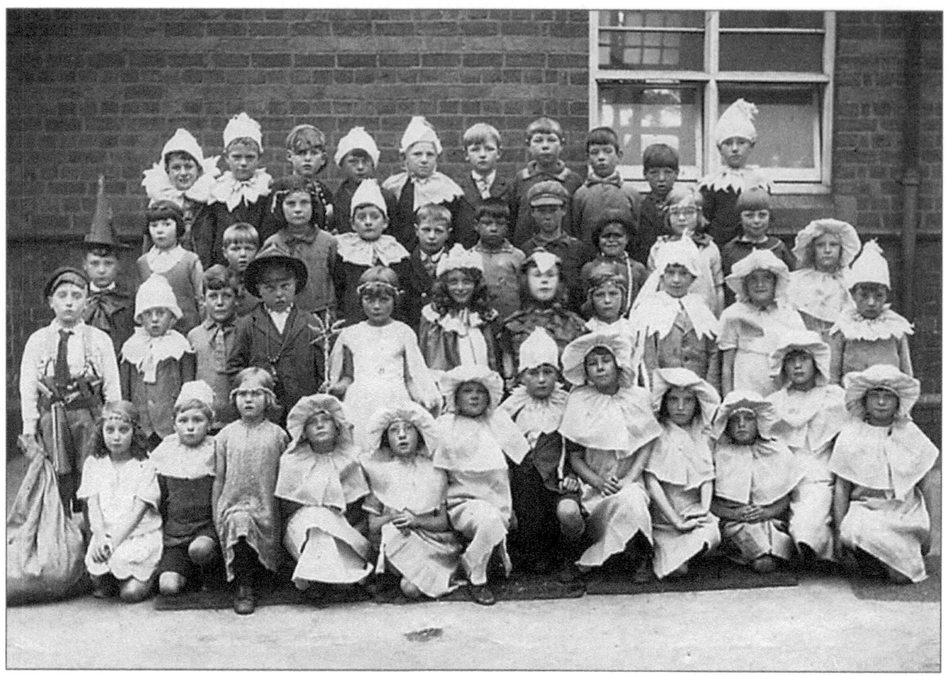

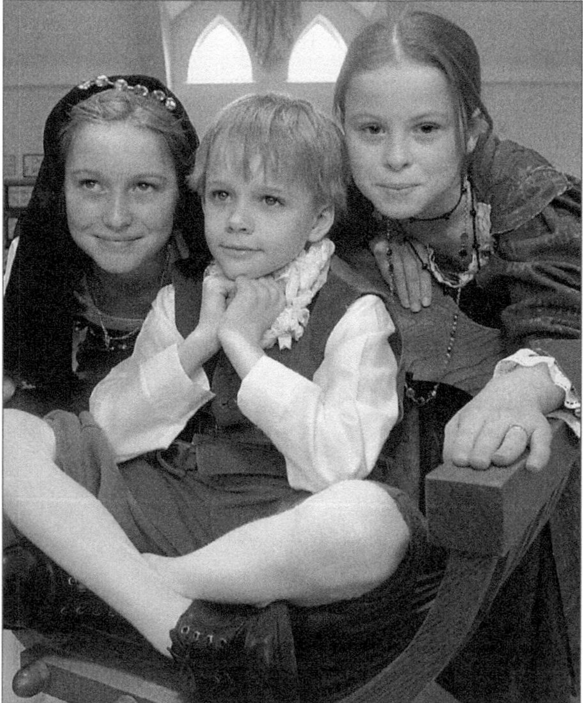

Dressing up at Mount Pleasant. *Above*: Children dressed for a Christmas play at Mount Pleasant School, *c.* 1928.

A king and queen, assorted fairies, and a postman seem to be featured in this play. *(Joyce Parkes) Left:* Three children at Mount Pleasant School dress in Tudor costume as part of a programme about life in Tudor England. Robert Bloomer, Laura Mann and Naomi Wale use costumes provided by the Stourbridge-based Gloriana touring company in 2003. (*School Archives/Express & Star*)

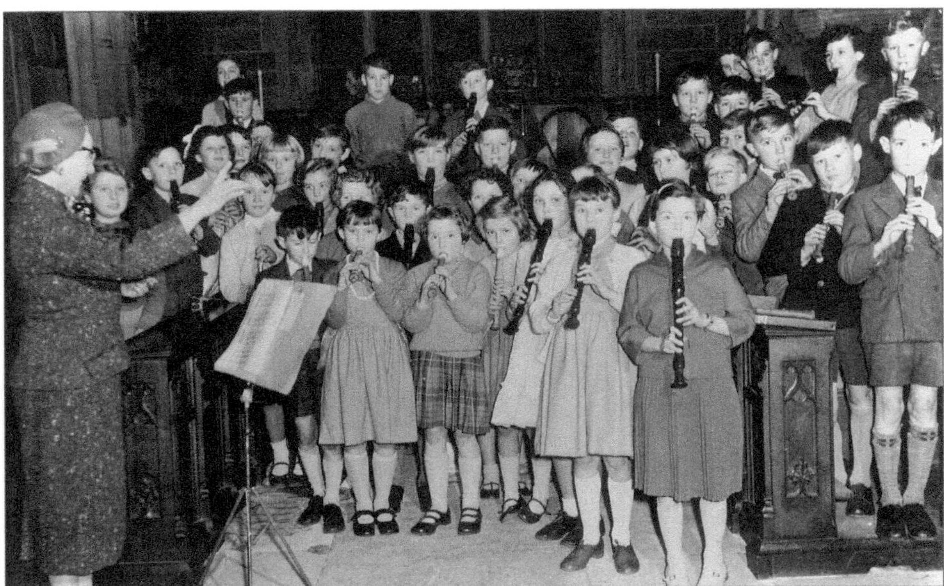

Miss Mantle (left) conducts her recorder group from Mount Pleasant School at a Christmas service at Kinver Church in 1956. Miss Mantle joined the staff in 1945 and stayed at the school until her retirement – then came back part-time to teach the recorder groups! (*MPLHG*)

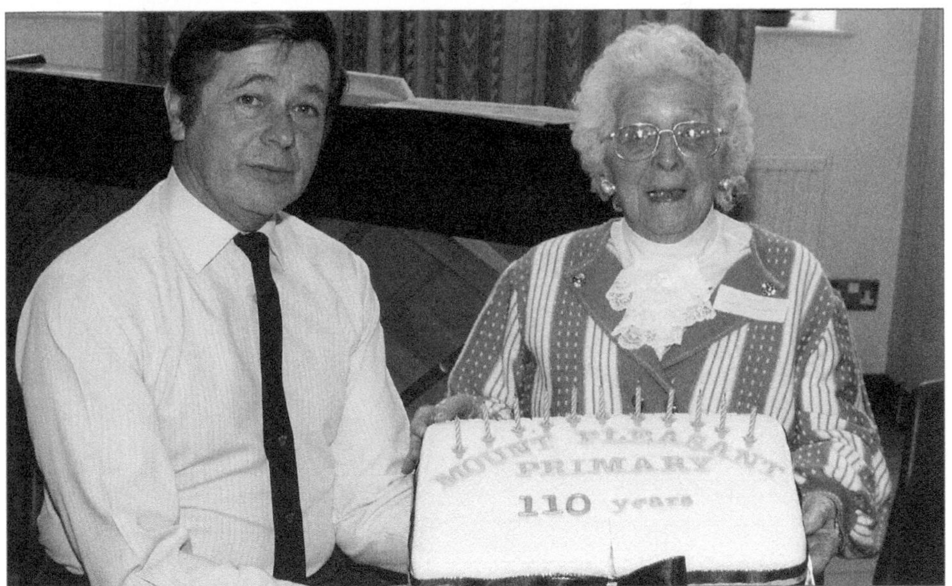

In 1998 Mount Pleasant Primary School celebrated its 110th birthday, and published a history of the school to mark the occasion. Hilda Mantle, then ninety-nine, came along to join the festivities and is seen here, with John James, ex-pupil of the school, with the birthday cake. Miss Mantle died on 27 June 2002. (*Ned Williams*)

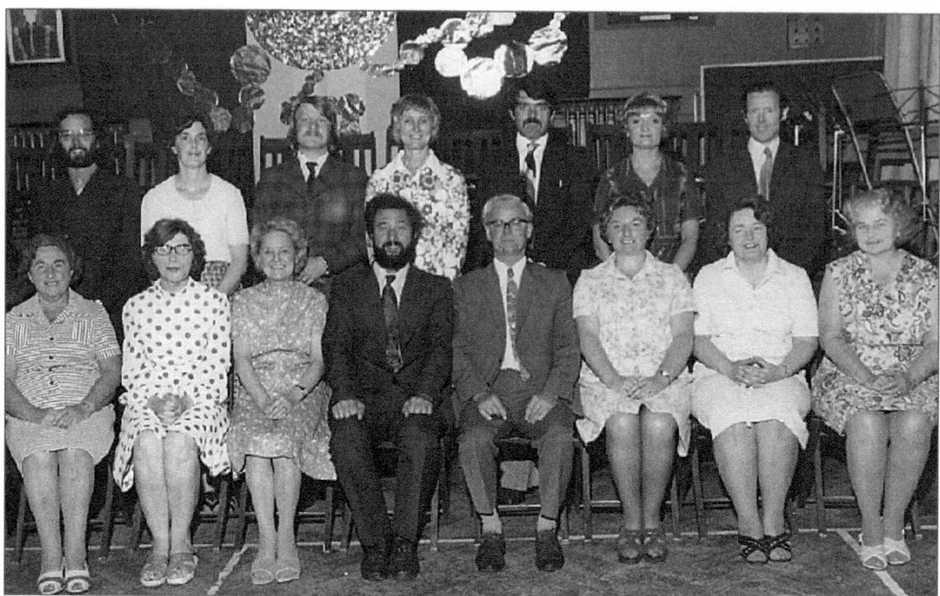

Teachers past and present. For a time, when this picture was taken in about 1975, Quarry Bank Primary School ran as a middle school. Back row, left to right: Mr Moody, Mrs Williams, Mr Weston, Mrs Willetts, Mr Pepper, Mrs Judge and Mr Mundon. Front row: Mrs Hunt, Mrs Davies, Mrs Parkes (school secretary 1952–87), Mr Eric Walker (head teacher), Mr Davies, -?-, -?- and Mrs Hancox (school pianist). (*Joyce Parkes*)

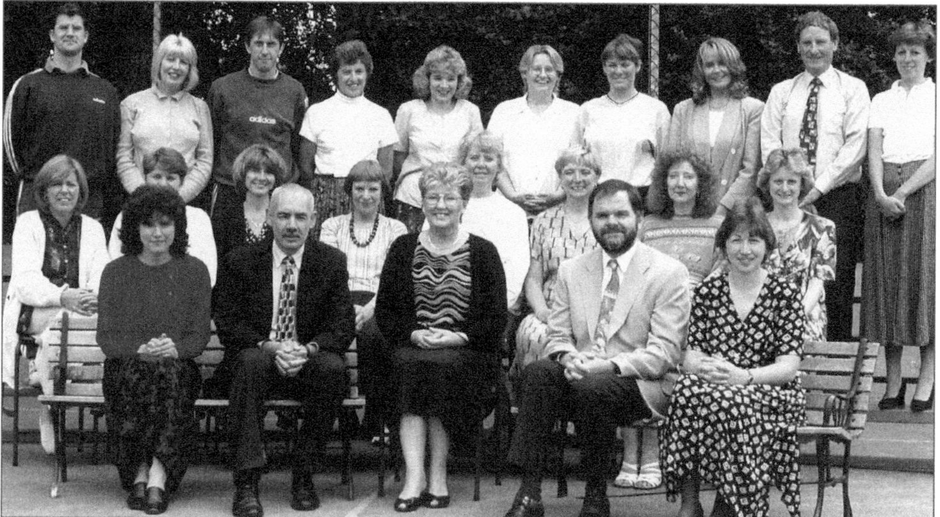

Staff at Mount Pleasant Primary School, 3 July 1998. Back row, left to right: R. Walker, D. Harris, D. Rudge (site manager), M. Smith (secretary), S. Tudge, S. Darbyshire, A. Jones, C. Humphries, P. Thomas and G. Bird (secretary). Middle row: H. Hemsley, J. Hartill, E. Newton, L. Price, V. Nash, H. D'Arcy, J. Roberts and N. Fletcher. Front row: G. Stone, J.B. Davies, G. Bedford (head teacher), Dr S. Tucker (chair of governors) and Jane Geddes. (*Ned Williams*)

QUARRY BANK AT WORK

Like many Black Country towns, Quarry Bank developed industries that were specialised aspects of 'metal bashing'. The nail and chain trades were widespread in the area until machine-made products created the long decline of hand-made products. The hollow-ware trade was also a big employer, and many Quarry Bank folk worked at 'The Jury' in Thorns Road, or 'The Judge', and Tubular Hollow-Ware in Oak Street. Meanwhile many small metal-working firms and engineering workshops existed.

The pictorial record of Quarry Bank at work is thin, and therefore this section of the book looks at the workplaces that have been part of the local landscape, rather than portraying the processes once to be found there. As Quarry Bank becomes increasingly residential, industry becomes concentrated in one or two particular areas, such as Thorns Road below Stevens Park, and the area around Sun Street and Oak Street.

There is a long tradition of living in Quarry Bank and working elsewhere. In some cases this meant working in Brierley Hill or the Lye. For some it meant working in Birmingham or at the Austin factory at Longbridge.

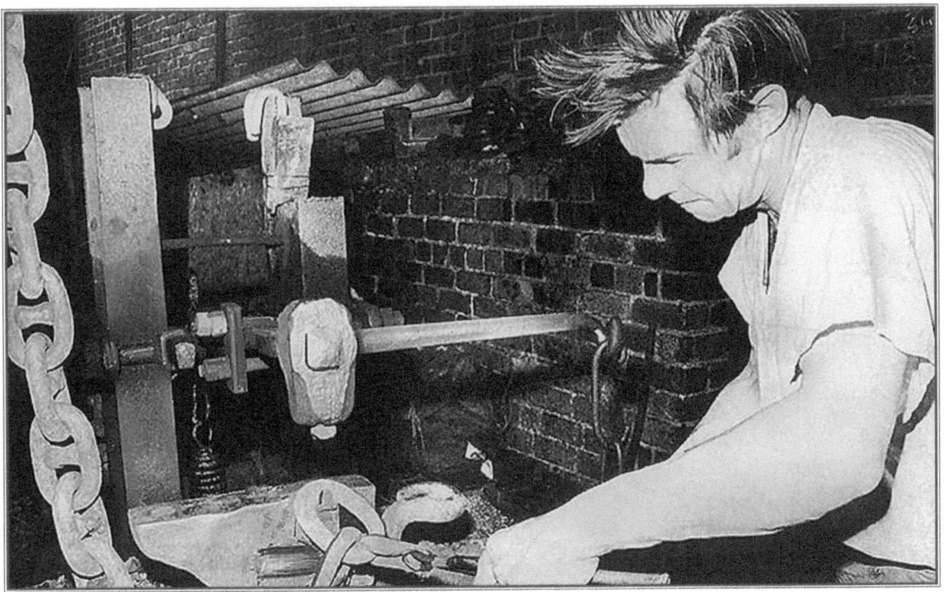

John Brian Williams still making chain the traditional way at Noah Bloomer's chain works in Oak Street in 1974. (*Express & Star*)

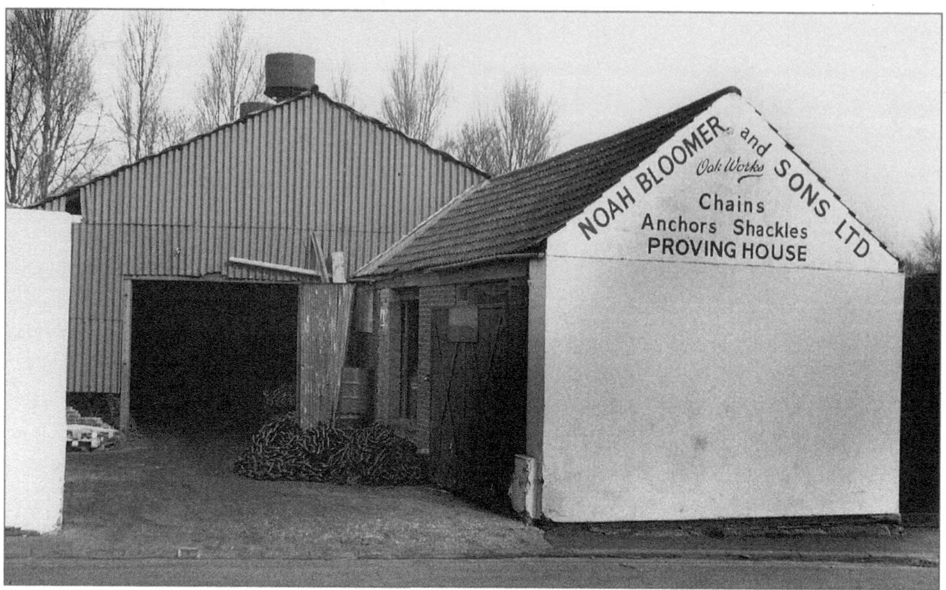

Noah Bloomer's chain works had became a proving house and warehouse for chain products by 1998 rather than a place where chain was made, despite the fact that chain had been made on this site in a traditional manner until the early 1970s. The area around Oak Street still remains one of the industrial areas of Quarry Bank and there is now an Oak Street Trading Estate. These premises currently deal with crashed car salvage. (*Ned Williams*)

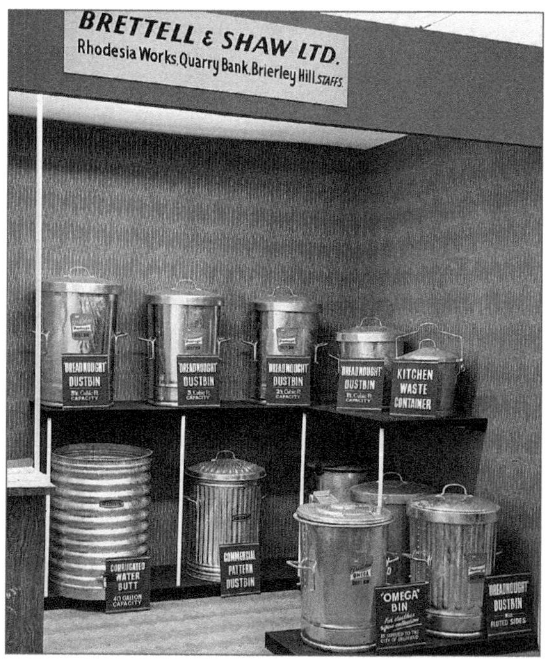

Brettell & Shaw have occupied premises in West Street, Quarry Bank, for many years, but currently want to move production of galvanised ware to Hayes Lane in the Lye. The site will be redeveloped for housing – thus becoming yet another part of the deindustrialisation of Quarry Bank. The Rhodesia Works in West Street was built by local builders Arthur Webb & Sons and was much enlarged over the years. This picture of the company's products displayed at a trade show in the 1950s reminds us of the pride that Quarry Bank once enjoyed in relation to its local industries and products. Dustbins made in Quarry Bank were sold all over the world. (*John Shaw*)

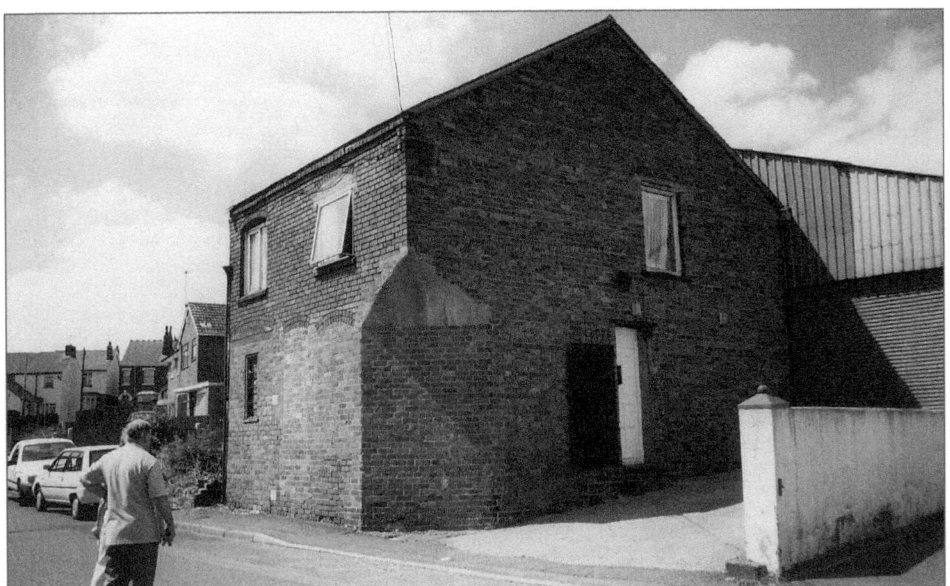

This steel stockholder's building in East Street, photographed in 2001, had once been Nock's Brewery. It has now been demolished and another small part of Quarry Bank's industrial heritage has vanished. Nock's Brewery supplied four very local pubs – which have also vanished. It passed to the Taylor family and then Mitchell & Butler and was closed as a brewery in about 1948–50. *(Ira Hampton)*

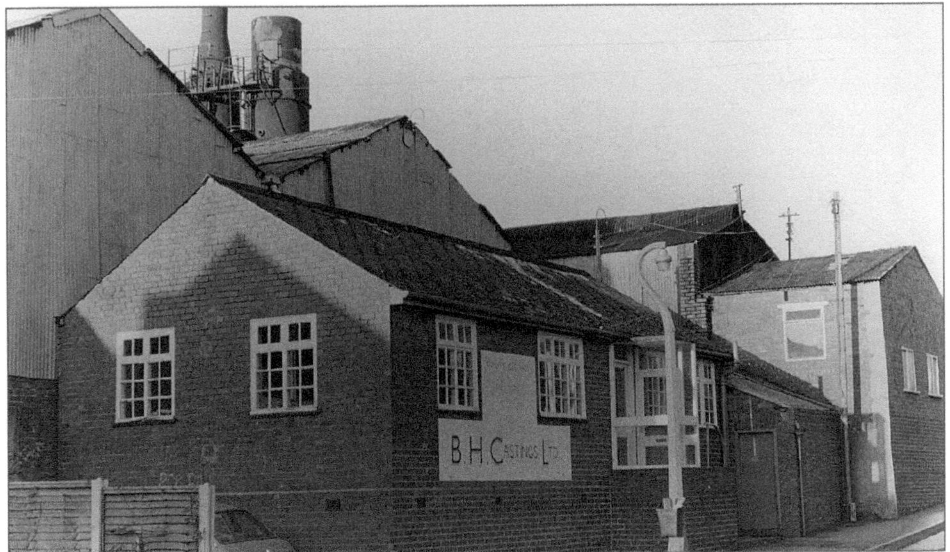

Like the Rhodesia Works of Brettle & Shaw (see opposite), the works belonging to B.H. Castings were surrounded by residential Quarry Bank. This view from Ever Street looks towards the offices, but the factory also bordered New Street. Houses built by Cox's now occupy the site. *(Colin Southall)*

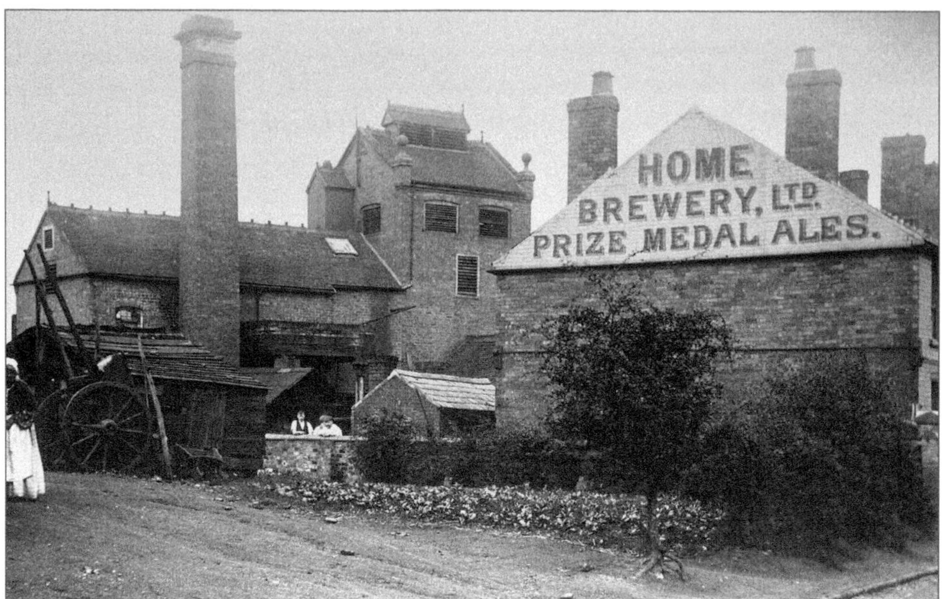

The Home Brewery in Ever Street in 1908, while controlled by Joseph Paskin Simpkiss. He operated the brewery from 1903 until 1916 and ran a few local public houses as well as wholesaling beer. Brewing ceased in 1921, and the buildings were eventually demolished in 1959. (*Keith Hodgkins*)

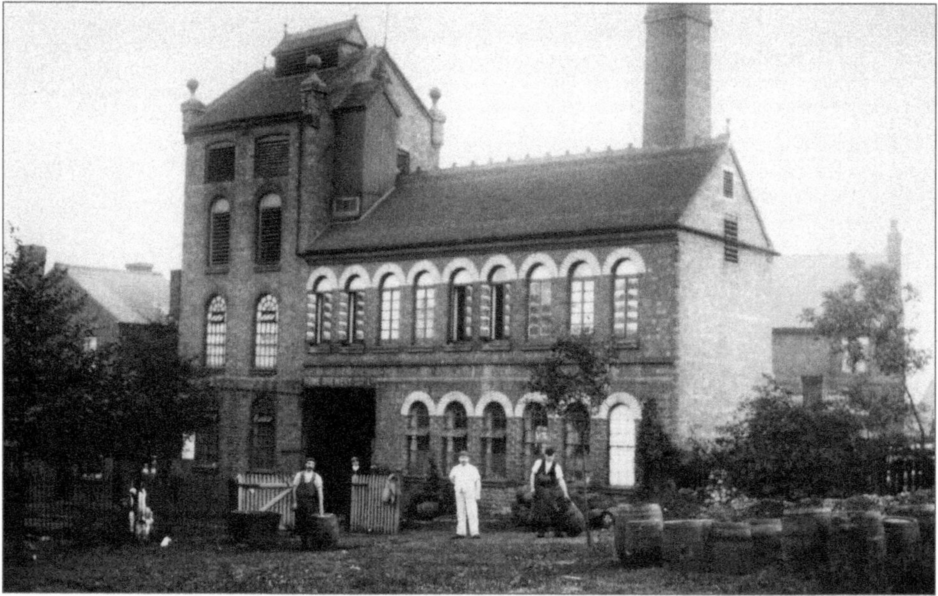

It is difficult today to imagine the brewery buildings occupying part of the Ever Street landscape. Another brewery building in New Street was demolished in 2002, leaving no sign that this was once a local industry. (*Keith Hodgkins*)

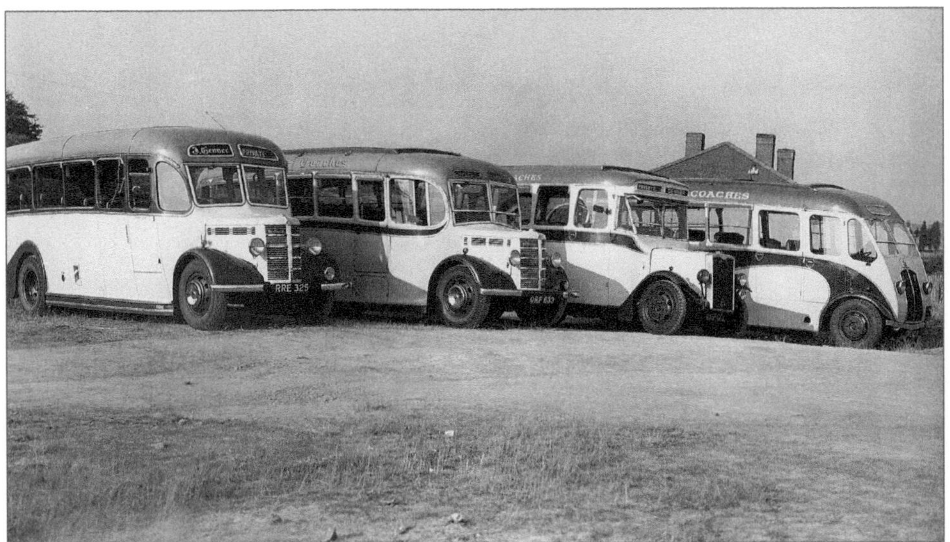

For a small town Quarry Bank produced quite a number of coach operators, although none of them operates from Quarry Bank today. Genner's Coaches used this yard off Sheffield Street during the 1950s. The end wall of the company's garage still carries the name Genner's Coaches, and can be seen from the school entrance below. (*Brian Genner*)

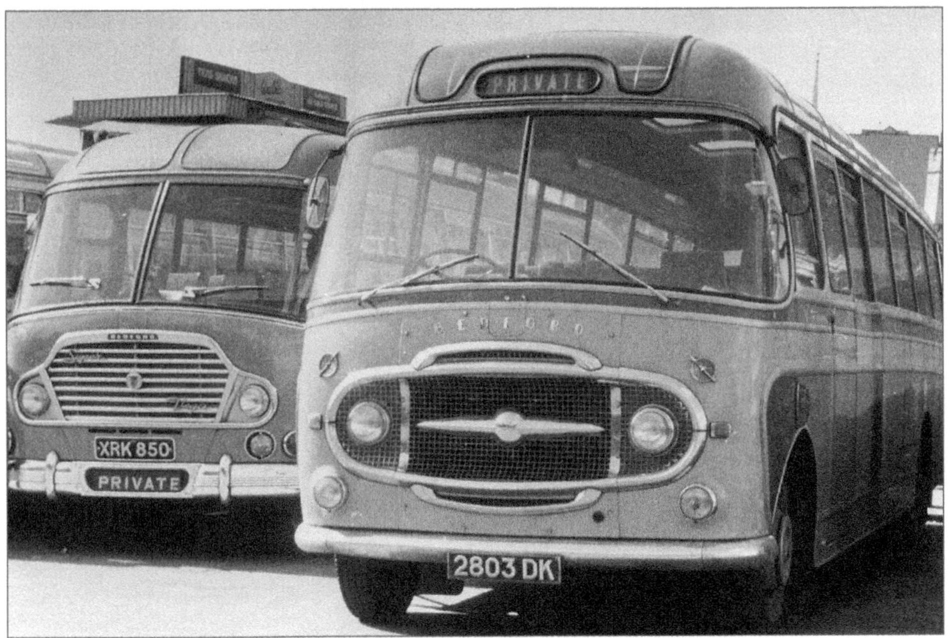

Two Bedford coaches belonging to Homer's Coaches of Quarry Bank, smartly turned out in a red and grey livery. The other well-known coach operators in Quarry Bank were Hadleys, of New Street, and Parkes, of Mount Pleasant. (*Geoff Jones, Hi Life Travel*)

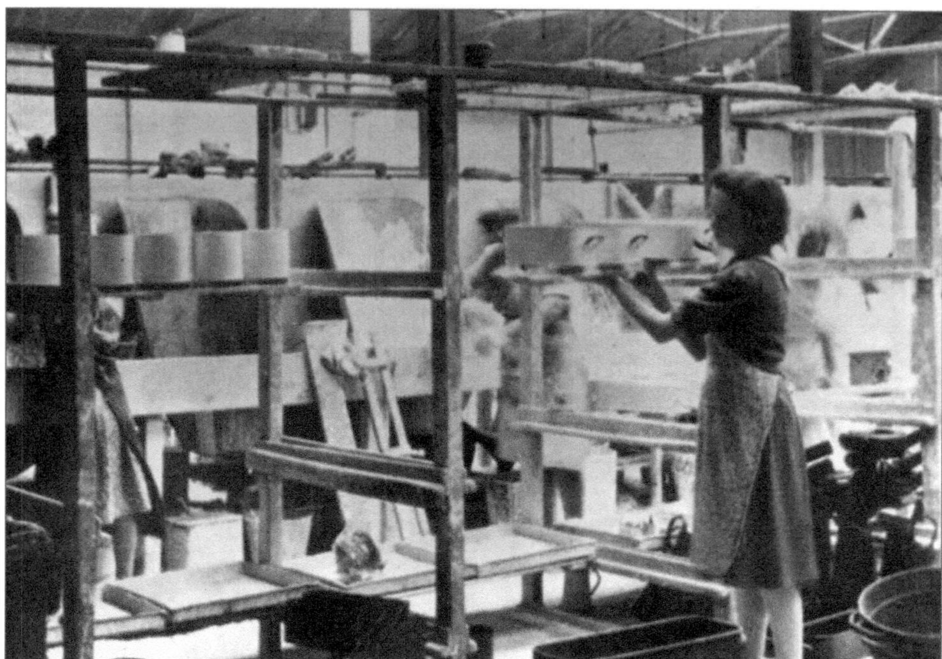

For years the hollow-ware trade dominated the employment scene in Quarry Bank. The Brierley Hill town guide used this picture taken in the 1950s at Tubular Hollow-Ware in Oak Street to represent the industry. Many Quarry Bank folk worked at 'The Jury' in Thorns Road, or at 'The Judge' just across the border in Cradley Heath. (*MPLHG*)

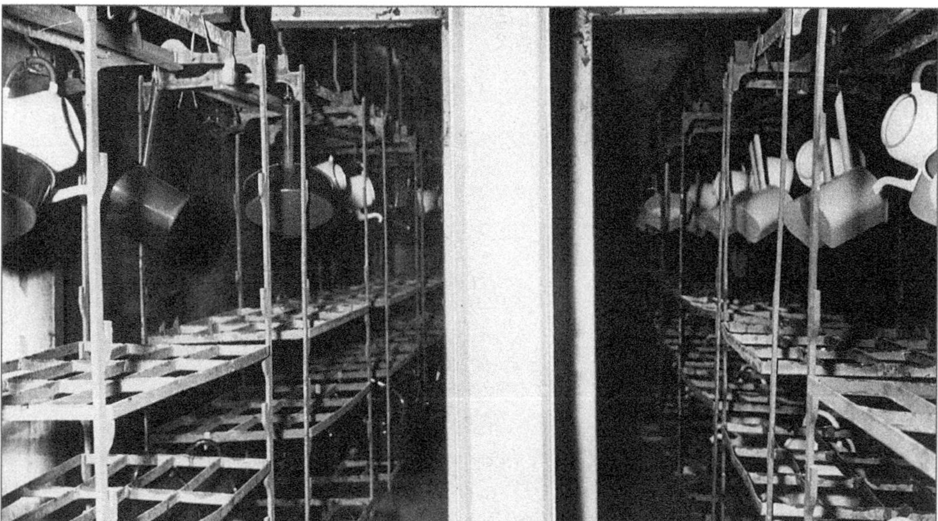

Pictures of Quarry Bank's hollow-ware industry at work seem rare and therefore we have to be grateful for even a glimpse of enamelled pots making their way through the ovens at the Jury Hollow-Ware Works in Thorns Road. (*Marie Willetts*)

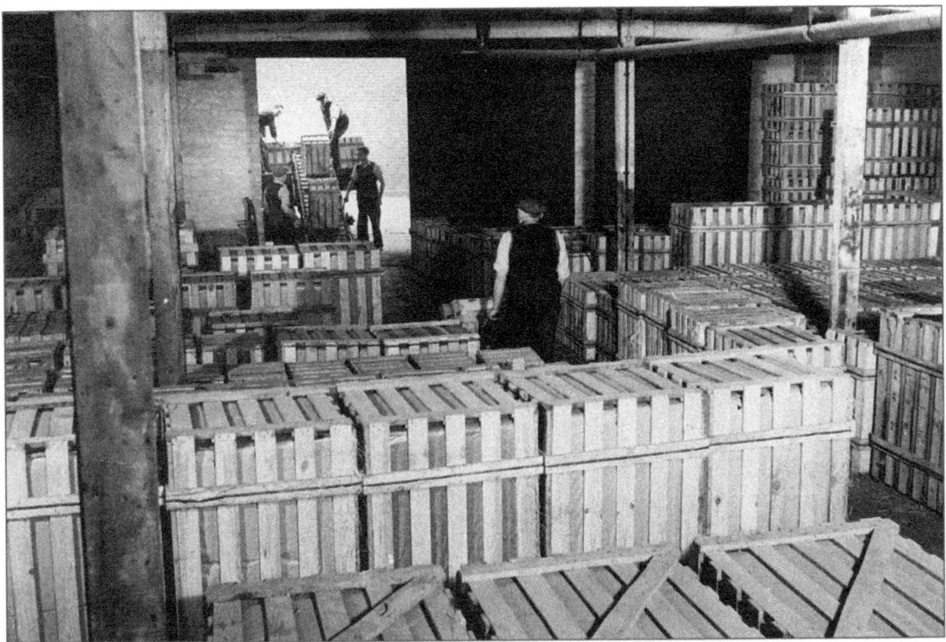

The Jury Hollow-Ware Works in Thorns Road was a large employer, and the works spread over a large area with many departments. This picture shows crates of packed hollow-ware awaiting dispatch from the warehouse. (*Marie Willetts*)

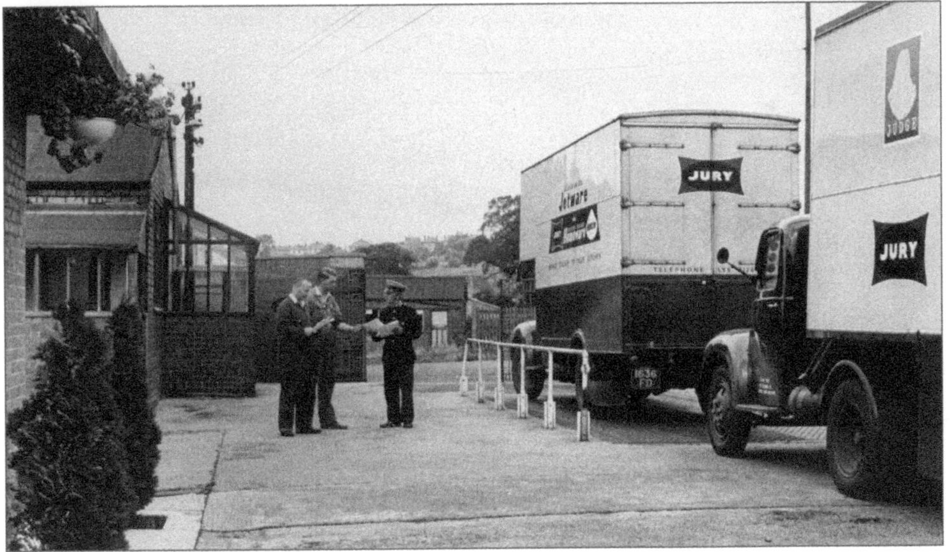

Lorries queue to cross the weighbridge before taking Jury hollow-ware products to their worldwide customers. The area once occupied by John Stevens's Jury Hollow-Ware Works has remained industrialised, but whether this continues remains to be seen. Modern Quarry Bank is much more a dormitory town for people who work elsewhere. (*Marie Willetts*)

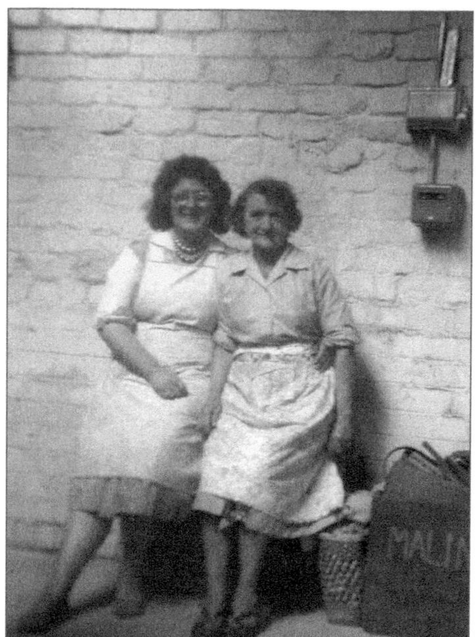

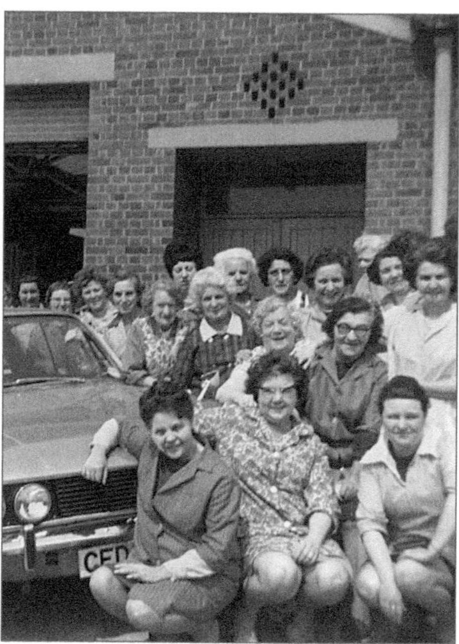

For almost twenty years, until about 1980, the firm of Malins occupied a factory in Thorns Road, where they produced their famous Mamod model steam engines. A large, mainly female, workforce took on the press work, assembly and packing jobs involved – all lost when the firm was sold and production moved to the south of England. Betty Hadlington took a number of photographs of her workmates; the only one to have been identified is Ada James, ace boiler solderer, on the right above left. (*Betty Hadlington*)

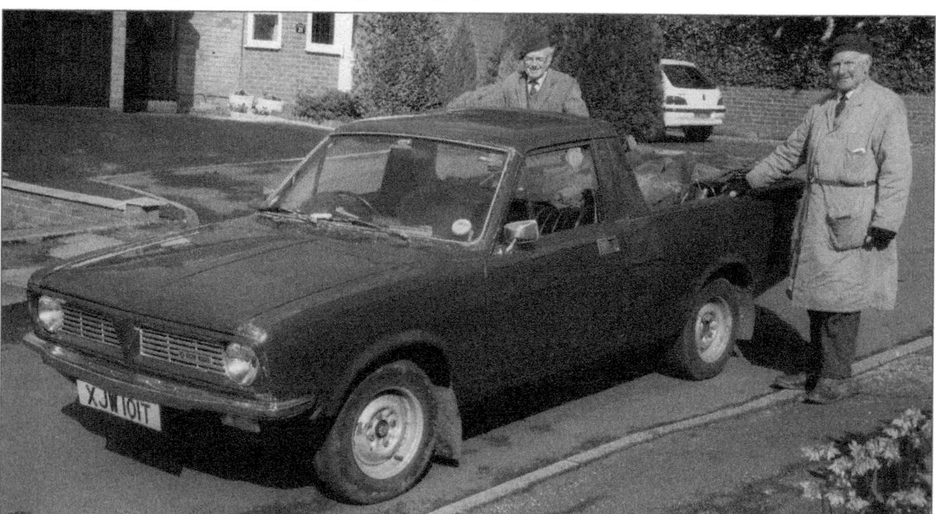

Robert and Harry Chance of Freehold Farm have been delivering milk in Quarry Bank since horse-drawn days – seen here in Aston Close in 2002 with a more modern vehicle. (*Margaret Priest*)

Chapter Seven

The Quarry Bank Carnival

Carnivals have played an important part in the social life of Quarry Bank as a community – no self-respecting Black Country community was once complete without an annual carnival! Before the First World War they were organised by Sunday schools and friendly societies. Between the wars they were organised by a committee raising funds for the Corbett Hospital. After the Second World War the carnival was revived by the Brighter Old Age Welfare Committee – an organisation that had grown out of the War Comfort Fund.

The carnival, or gala, itself was merely the climax of a year-long range of fund-raising activities that raised well over £50,000 over the years. Many well-known local figures gave their time to support the Brighter Old Age Welfare Committee including Councillor Horace Hadley and his wife, Winnie, Mr and Mrs Ewart Bloor, Stan and Madge Grove, Rhea Eyre, Dot Hadlington, Don Manley, Harold Light (the postmaster, who also organised the annual flower show) and May Andrews.

May Andrews served on the committee from 1946, when it was formed, until 1974, when it was disbanded. Her granddaughter, Marilyn Bullock, also served on the committee and was elected secretary. Together they paid out the final payment in 1974. Once again the carnival was revived, this time in support of cancer research, but it has not been held since 2000.

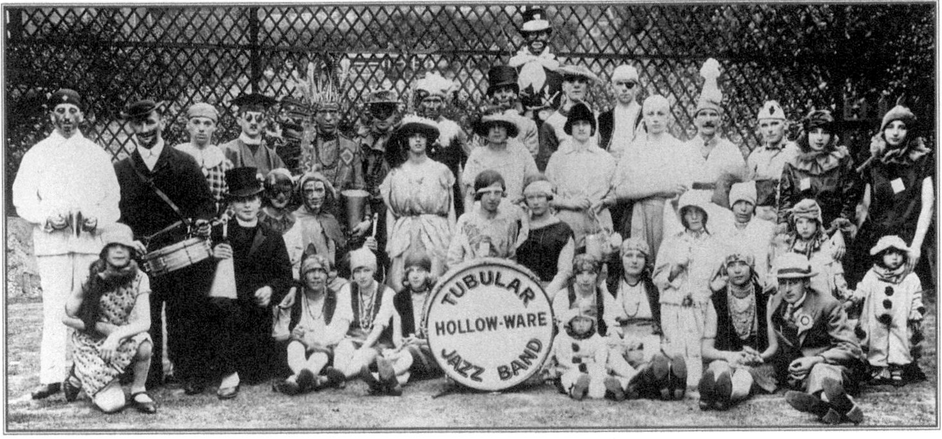

The Tubular Hollow-Ware Works Jazz Band is seen here with everyone in fancy dress for one of the Hospital Committee carnivals of the 1920s. (*MPLHG*)

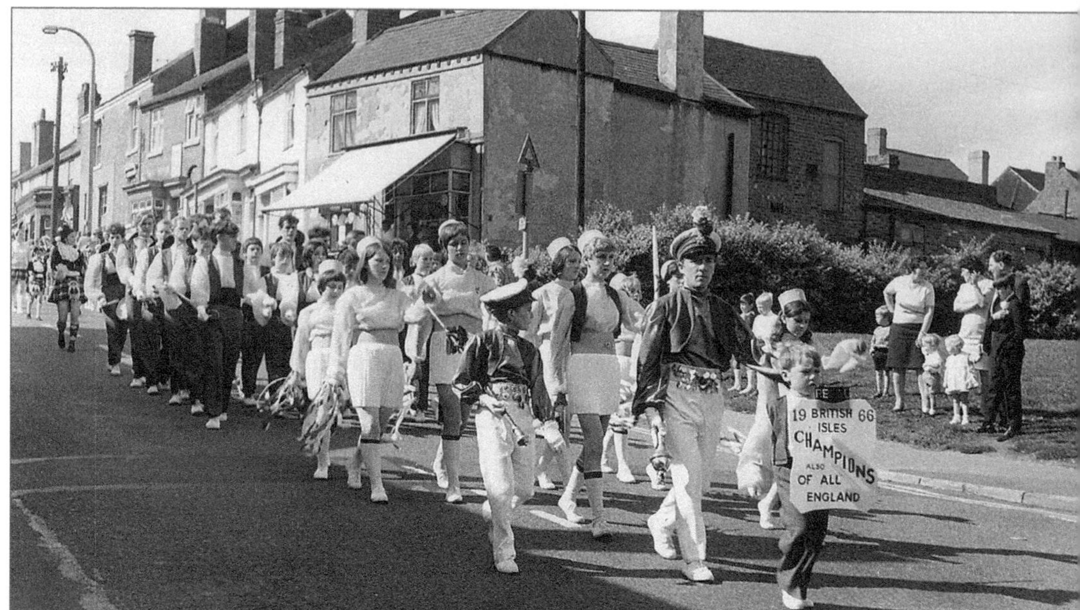

The 1966 or 1967 carnival procession makes its way down Quarry Bank High Street past Grove's butcher's shop and the Sheffield Street Community Centre. (*Marilyn Bullock*)

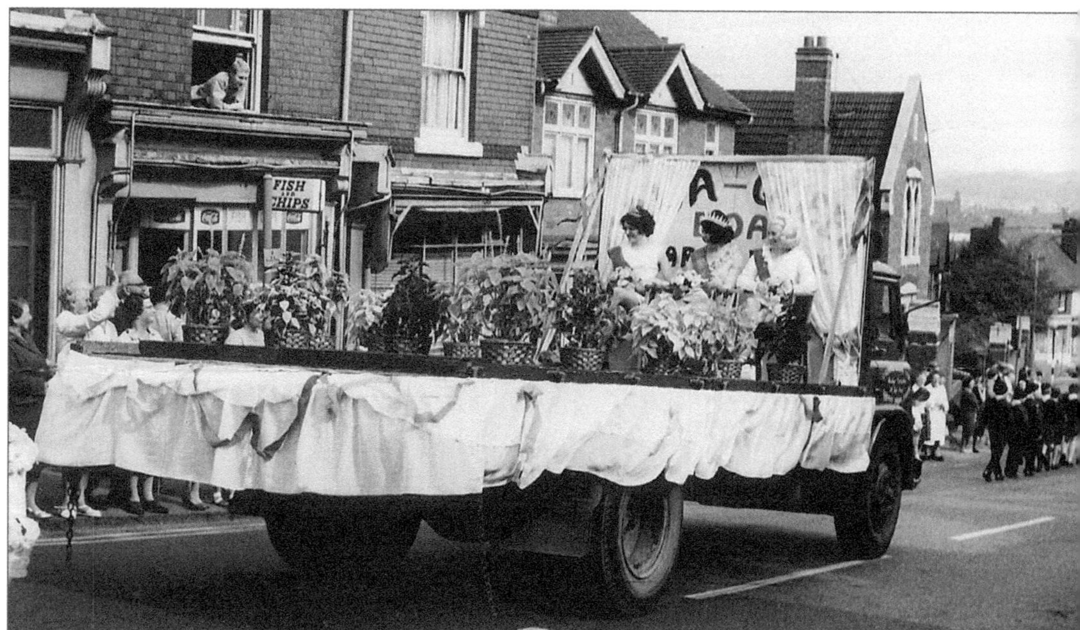

The photographer of the upper picture has turned to record the lorry carrying the carnival queen and her attendants as the procession proceeds past Genner's fish and chip shop into the lower part of Quarry Bank High Street. (*Marilyn Bullock*)

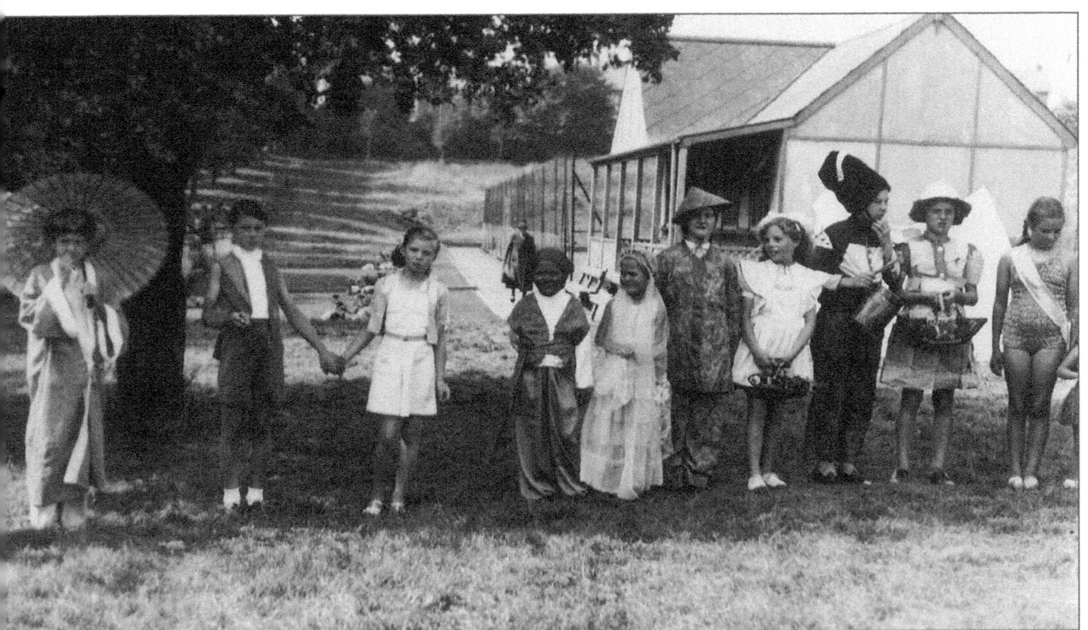

Children line up in Stevens Park for the fancy dress parade as part of a 1950s Quarry Bank Carnival and Gala. Note the old tennis pavilion, once a feature of Stevens Park, in the background. (*Doris Peat*)

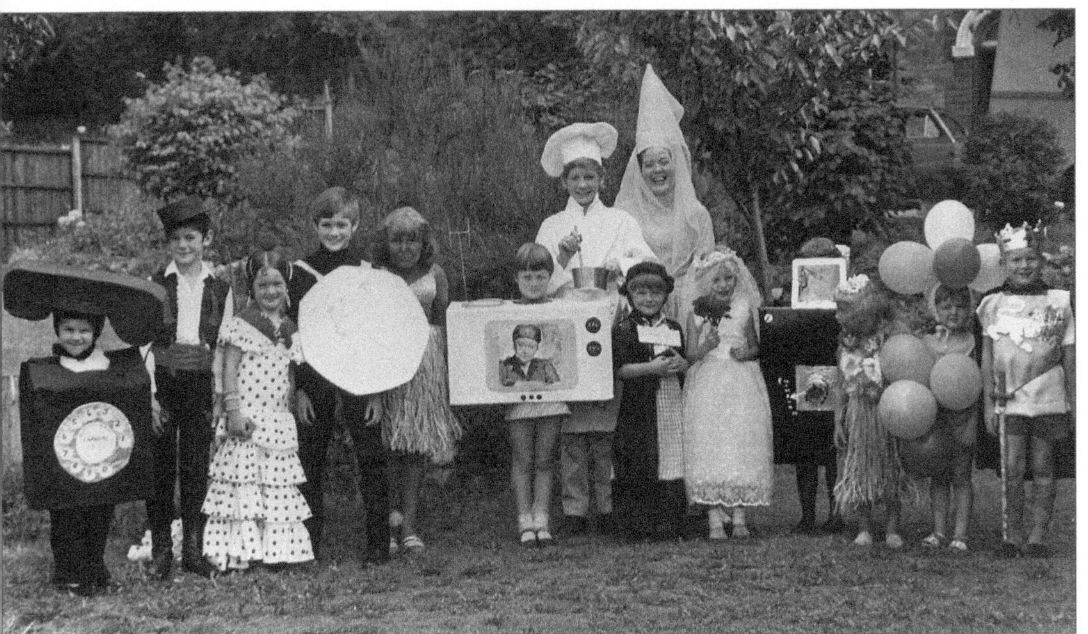

Children from Coppice Close line up for the fancy dress parade at the 1970 Quarry Bank Carnival and Gala. (*Brian Woodridge*)

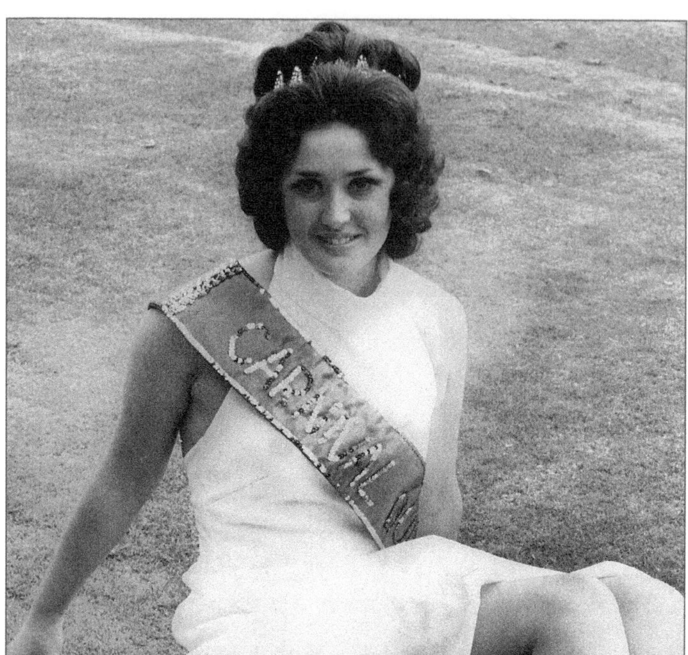

Hazel Payne (née Jones) – Quarry Bank Carnival Queen of 1973. Runners-up that year were Pauline Tromans and Janice Skitt. (*John James*)

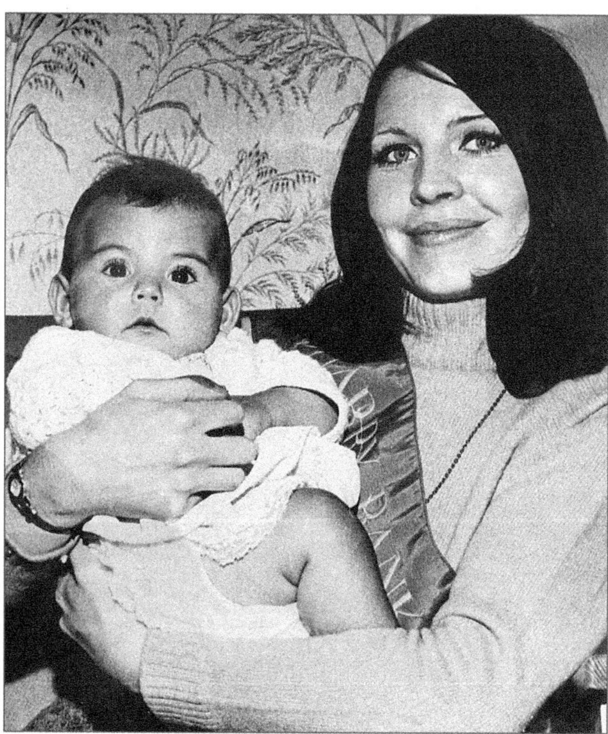

Left: Janice Skitt (née Dunn) seen here with her daughter Amanda, was the Quarry Bank Carnival Queen in 1969. (*Vera Dunn*)

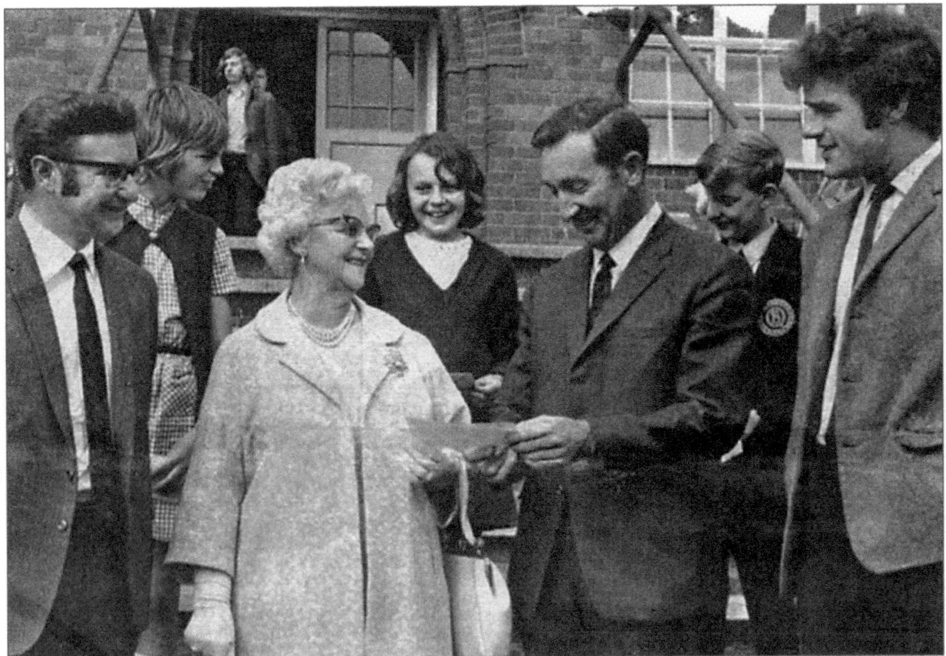

Mr J.J. Martin (third from left), Headmaster at Thorns School, hands over a cheque for money raised by pupils for the Brighter Old Age Welfare Committee in 1970. The latter is represented by, from left to right, Don Manley (chairman), May Fellows (president) and Paul Speakman (treasurer). Pupils include Suzette Harrison, Gail Cox and Philip Hughes. (*Marilyn Bullock*)

Right: In December 1974 the Brighter Old Age Welfare Committee made their final payment and retired from fund-raising and running the carnival, after twenty years. Seated on the left is Marilyn Bullock, the committee's secretary, and on the right is May Fellows, the president. (*Marilyn Bullock*)

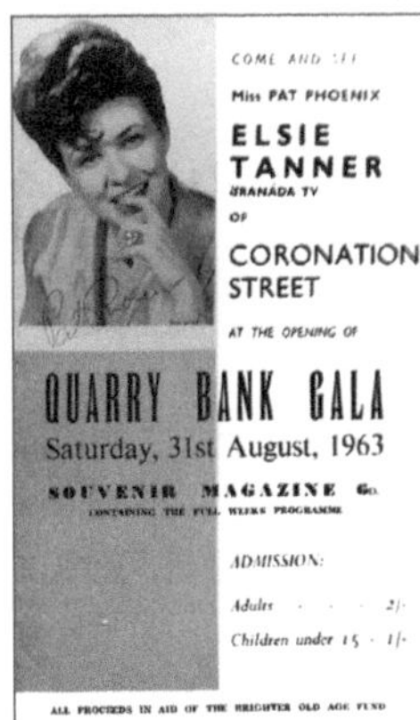

Cover of the 1963 Gala programme.

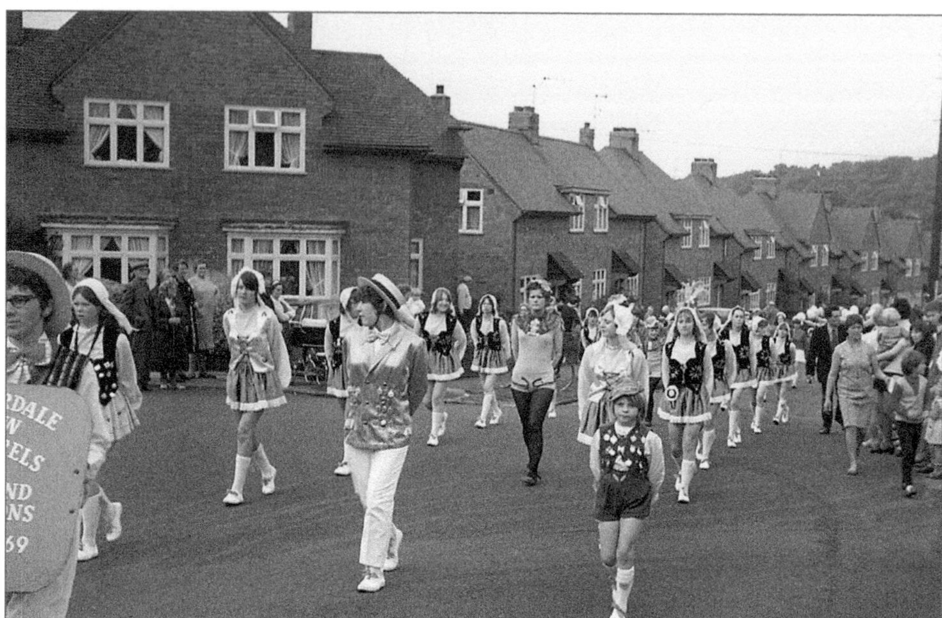

During the 1960s the Quarry Bank carnival procession used to assemble at the bottom of Birch Road before setting off for the uphill walk to Stevens Park. In this picture of the 1969 procession we see the parade setting off up Birch Road. (*Sheila Billingsley*)

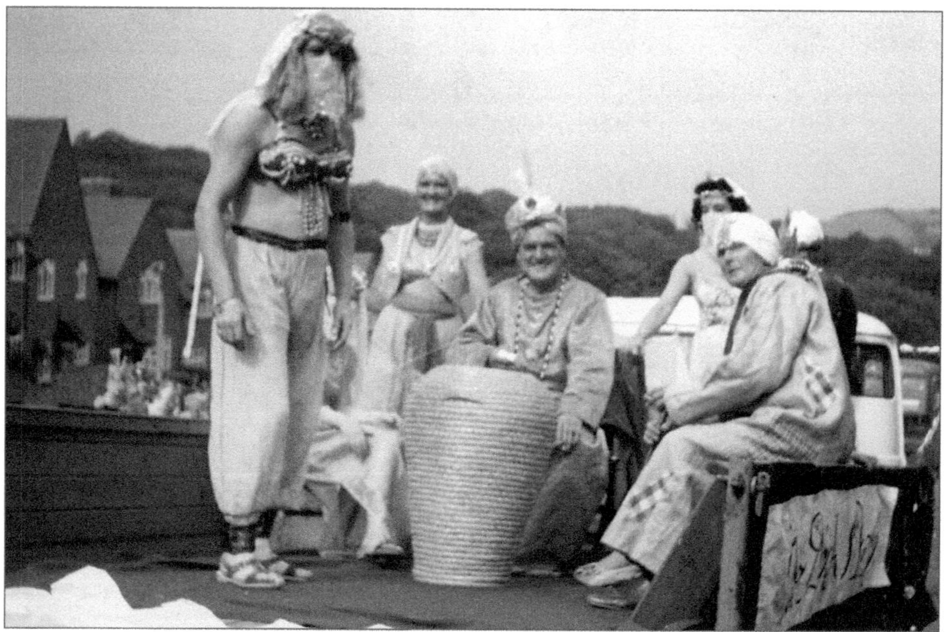

Dressing up and decorating the carnival floats were highlights of Carnival Day. This float is waiting to set off from Birch Road in 1969. (*Sheila Billingsley*)

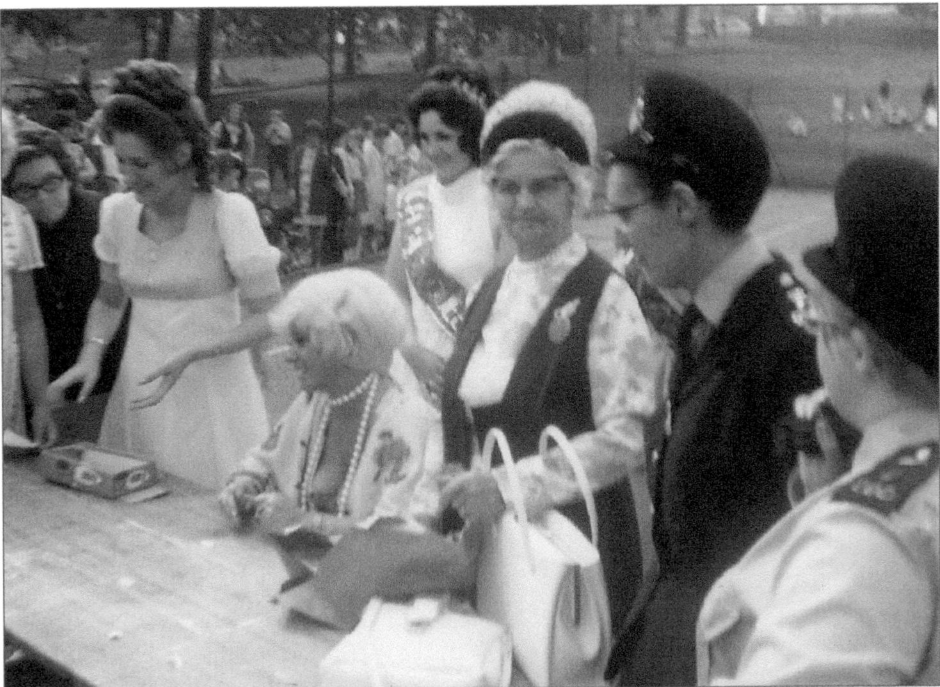

The Carnival Queen, Barbara Windsor and May Fellows, of the Brighter Old Age Welfare Committee, launch the gala at the Quarry Bank Carnival on 25 August 1973. (*Marilyn Bullock*)

Right: Diana Dors chats to Carnival Queen June Greenan, crowned as Miss Industry 1972. High-profile stars like Diana Dors and Barbara Windsor brought huge crowds to the Quarry Bank Carnivals of the period. (*Marilyn Bullock*)

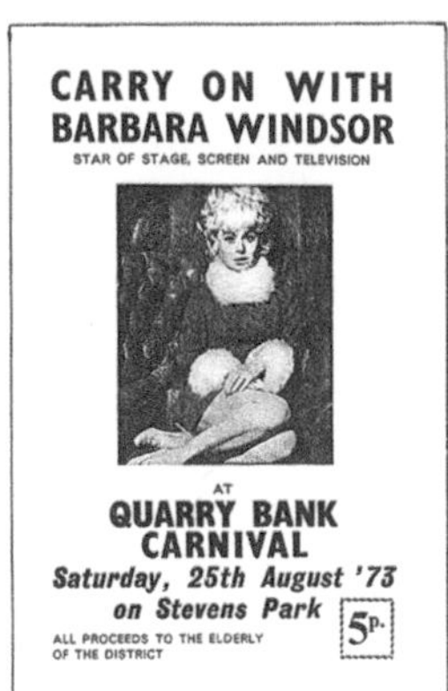

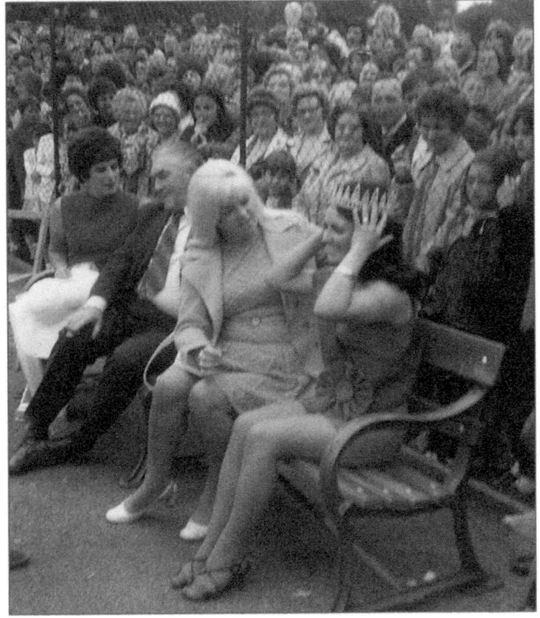

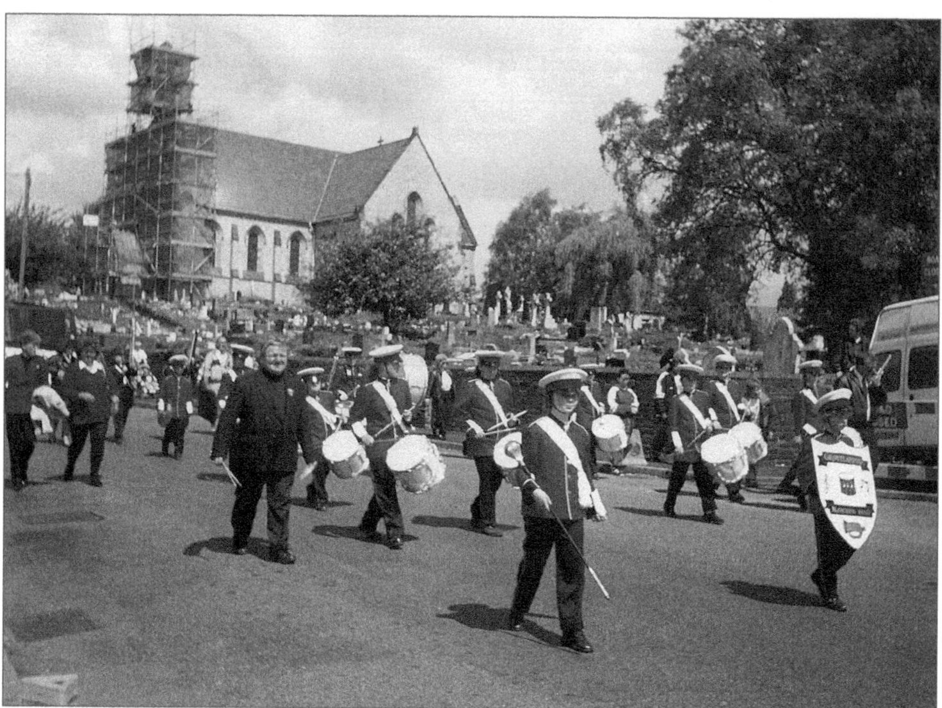

The band leads the procession of the 1991 carnival down Park Road on the way to Stevens Park, with a striking view of Christ Church under repair in the background. (*Shirley Winwood*)

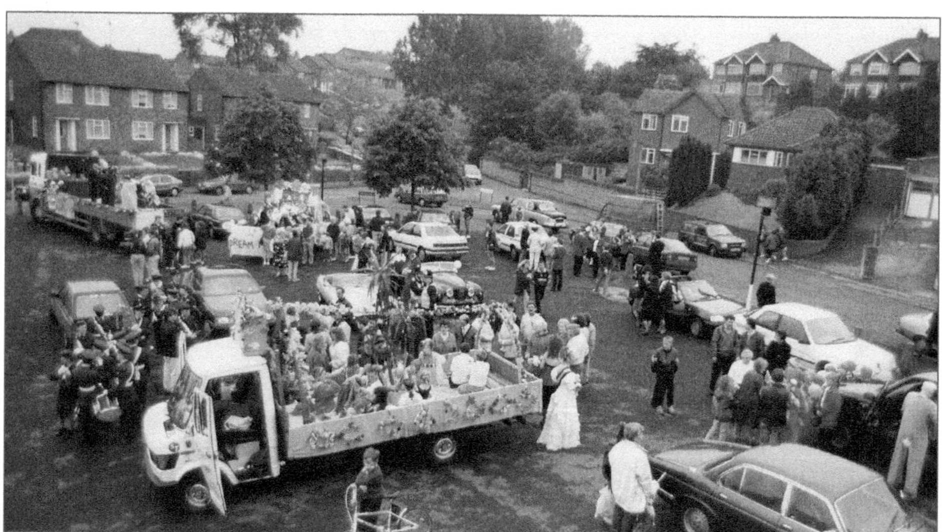

The carnival processions of the 1990s assembled in the car park of The Birch Coppice public house, as seen in this 1991 photograph looking across towards Woodland Avenue. (*Shirley Winwood*)

Ainsley Harriott came along to open the gala in 1995 and is seen here with Shirley Winwood and Vicki Unwin, two of the event's organisers. (*Shirley Winwood*)

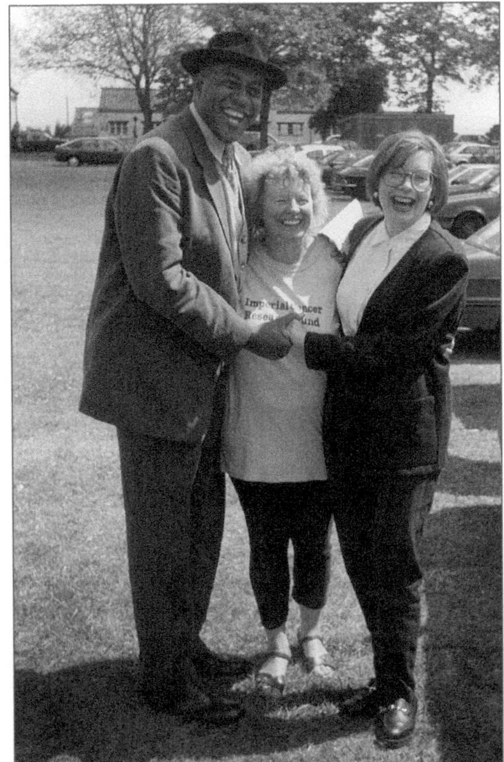

Below: The carnival procession makes its way up Quarry Bank High Street in this picture of the 1989 event. Growth of traffic on Quarry Bank's High Street following the building of the Merry Hill Centre is one of the factors that has made organising the annual carnival more and more difficult. (*Shirley Winwood*)

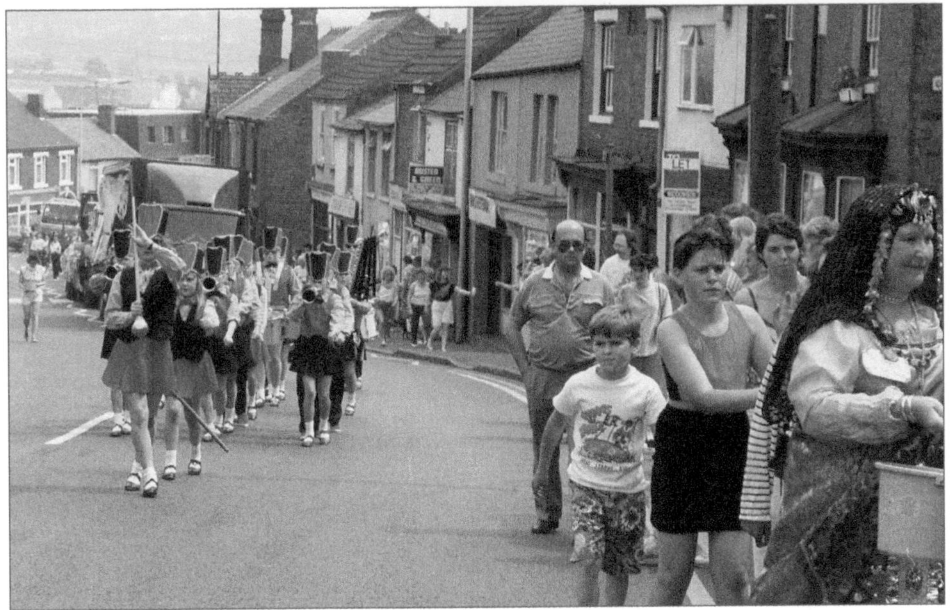

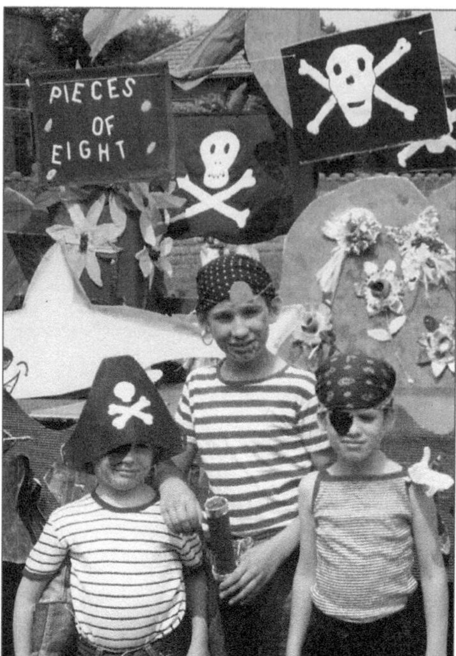
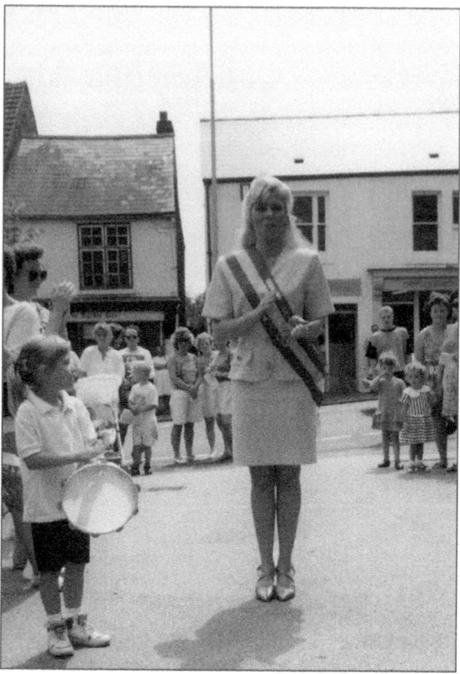

Left: Pupils from Thorns Primary School, Naomi, Peter and Ben Williams, dress as pirates for the 1990 Quarry Bank Gala. (Rose Williams). *Right*: The 1992 Carnival Queen opens the Quarry Bank Primary School Fete and is welcomed to the school by the pupils. (*Liz Cullinane*)

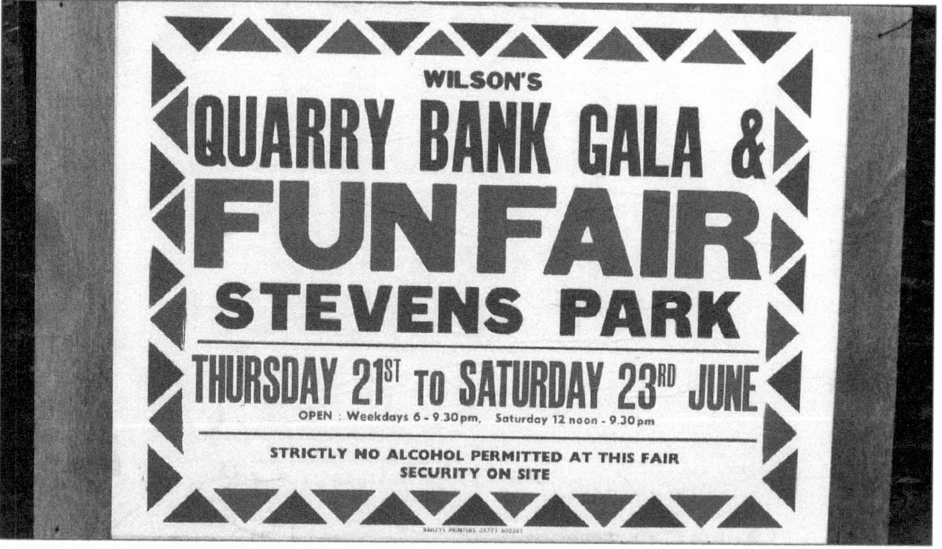

Tom Wilson, the Redditch-based showman, incorporated advertising for the gala into his 2001 funfair poster, but no carnival or gala took place that year, it becoming increasingly difficult to organise such events. The fair still opens in the park twice a year. (*Ned Williams*)

Chapter 8

Around the Pubs

Quarry Bank has its share of pubs, although a number have disappeared over the years. In several instances the pub that exists today is a replacement for an earlier one. The Sun, The Blue Ball, The Thorns, and even The Roebuck on Amblecote Road, all replaced a predecessor of the same name. In other instances the building remains substantially the same but the name has changed. Pubs known today as The Nailmaker and The Corn Exchange, for example, are often referred to by previous names, particularly if they have become a landmark.

In the High Street, The Sun, The Nailmaker – still often referred to as The Church Tavern – and The New Inn all still provide a traditional welcome. Further down the High Street pubs have disappeared: The Queens Head, The Elephant and Castle and The Three Horseshoes. The Fountain Inn in Victoria Street, The Brickmakers Arms in Mount Pleasant, and The White Horse in New Street, still function as excellent 'locals', although their Victorian brethren further from the centre of Quarry Bank such as The Cottage in the Bower have disappeared.

A range of 1960s pubs were built as new housing changed the face of Quarry Bank from the 1960s onwards, and The Round Oak was built very recently on Merry Hill. It is also worth noting that pubs often exist at the points where main roads cross the boundaries of Quarry Bank (such as The Birch Tree, The Robin Hood, The Vine and The Wagon and Horses), technically placing them just outside Quarry Bank or right on the boundary!

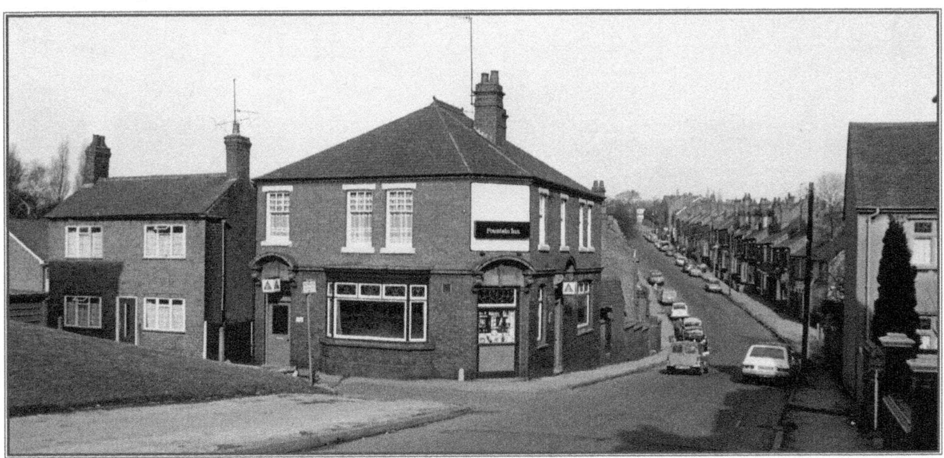

The Fountain Inn in Victoria Street has a good-quality glazed brickwork exterior and has belonged to Atkinsons, Bathams and Butlers over the years with very little change to its appearance, as seen from this 1970s picture. (*Dave Whyley*)

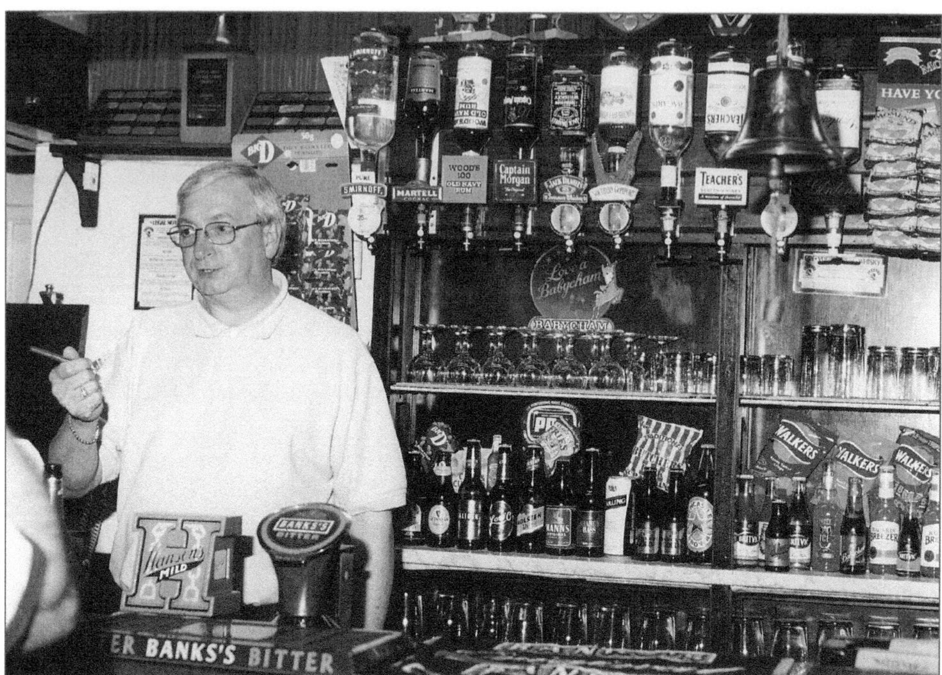

David Cooper, landlord of The New Inn in Quarry Bank High Street, 2003. The first licensee was Moses Stevens (1837–1910). From 1910 to 1932 it was run by Henry Stevens, Moses' son (1862–1950). It was taken over by Simpkiss Brewery in 1932. Many local organisations have used it as a meeting place, and, like all the town-centre pubs, its history is interwoven with the town's history. (*John James*)

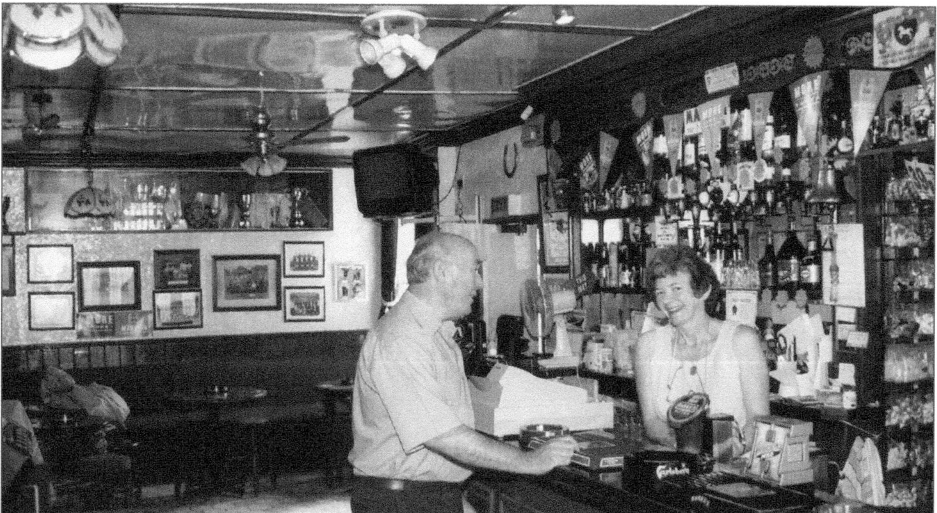

The interior of The White Horse, photographed in 2002, has an excellent traditional feel to it – with photographs and trophies on the wall from darts and bowls teams. (*Ned Williams*)

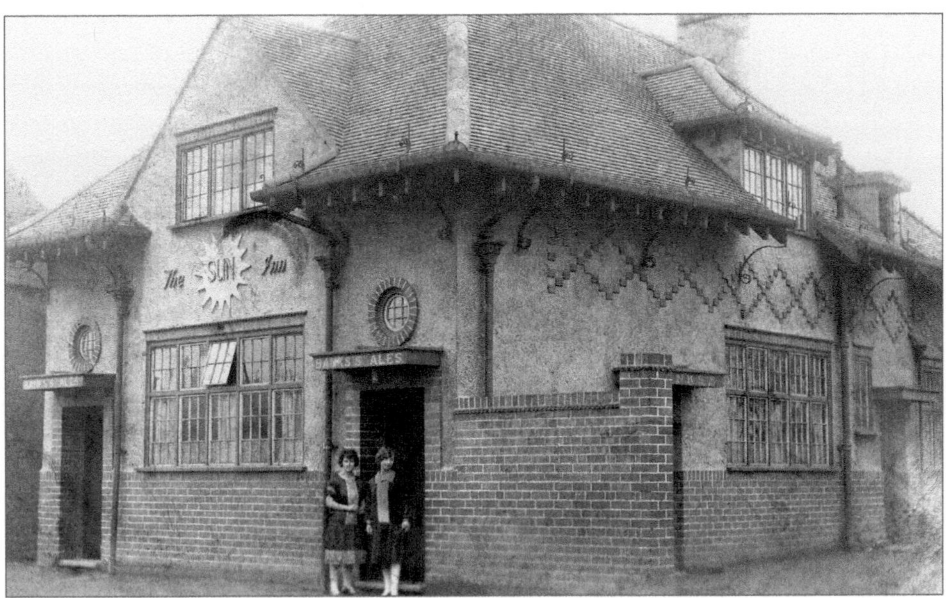

The original Sun public house had just been replaced with a new 1930s building when this picture was taken. (*June Ashmore*)

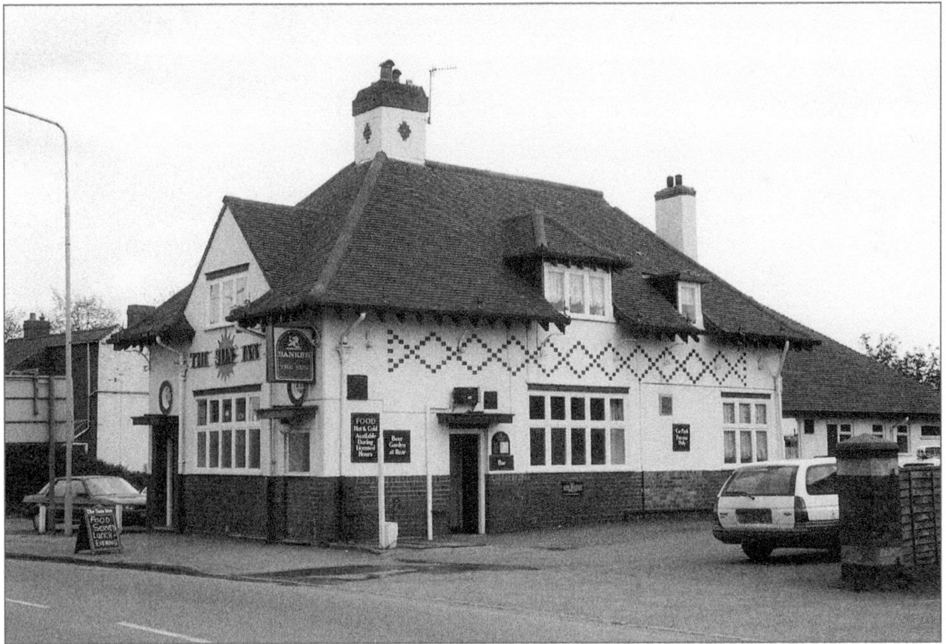

The Sun has not changed substantially since the upper photograph was taken, but the High Street, at the junction with Sun Street, has been realigned and this stretch of road has been christened Old High Street. (*Ned Williams*)

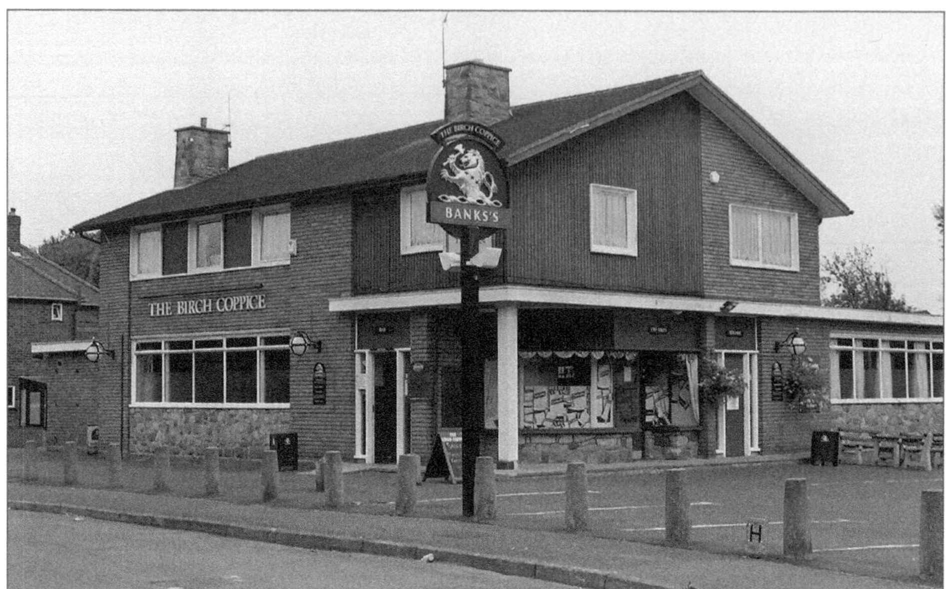

The Birch Coppice public house opened in the 1960s following the extending of Birch Coppice to the new link between Woodland Avenue and Sheffield Street. Its car park later became the assembling point for the Quarry Bank carnivals. (*Ned Williams*)

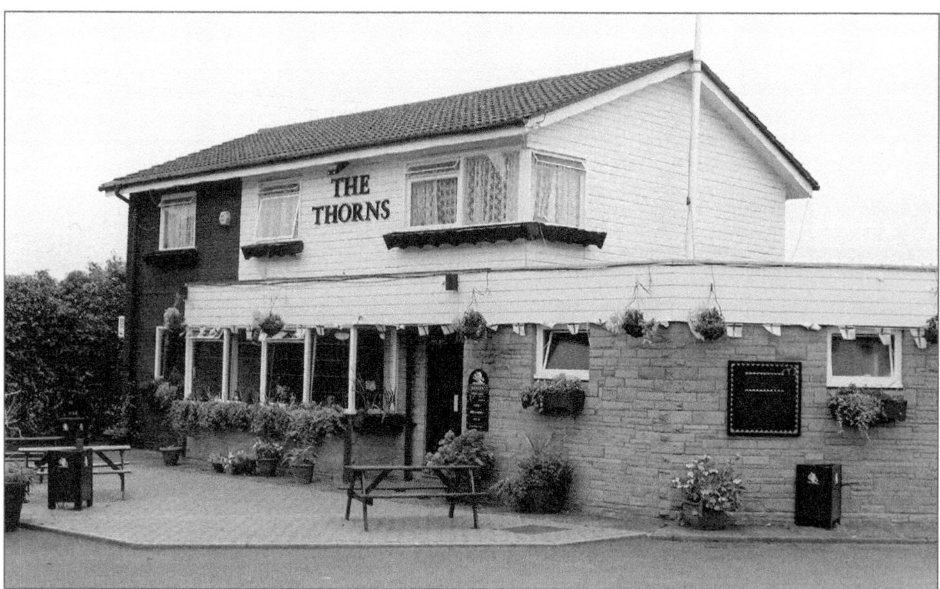

The Thorns public house is another example of a modern building replacing a former establishment of the same name – in this case being built behind its predecessor. Several Quarry Bank pubs just took their names from the communities that they served. The Thorns was quite a distinct little hamlet – on the main Thorns Road, but quite isolated from central Quarry Bank. (*Ned Williams*)

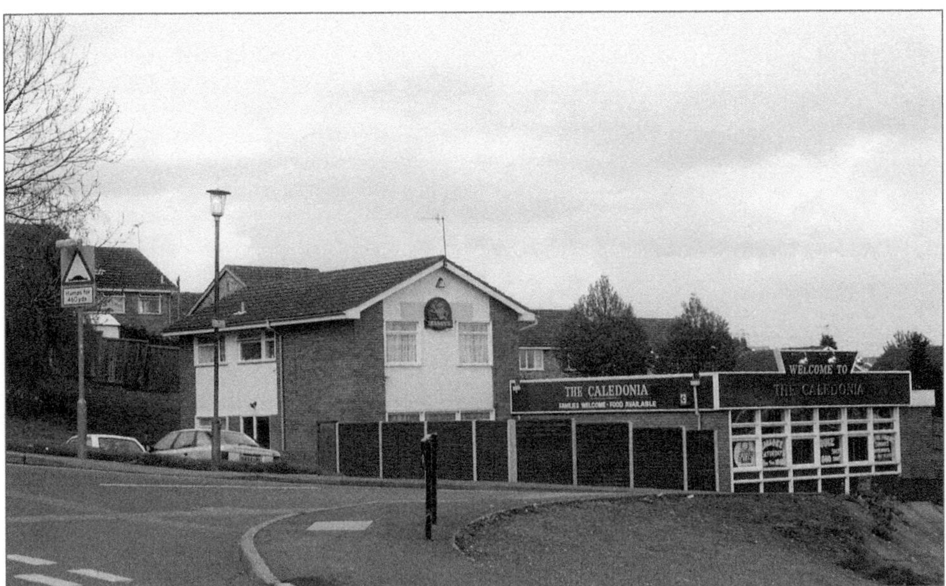

The Caledonia, at the junction of Mousehall Farm Road and Woods Lane, was newly built in the late 1960s to serve the area, which had quickly become covered with housing at the time. The pub, plus the provision of post office and shops opposite, was an attempt to make the estates more of a living community. (*Ned Williams*)

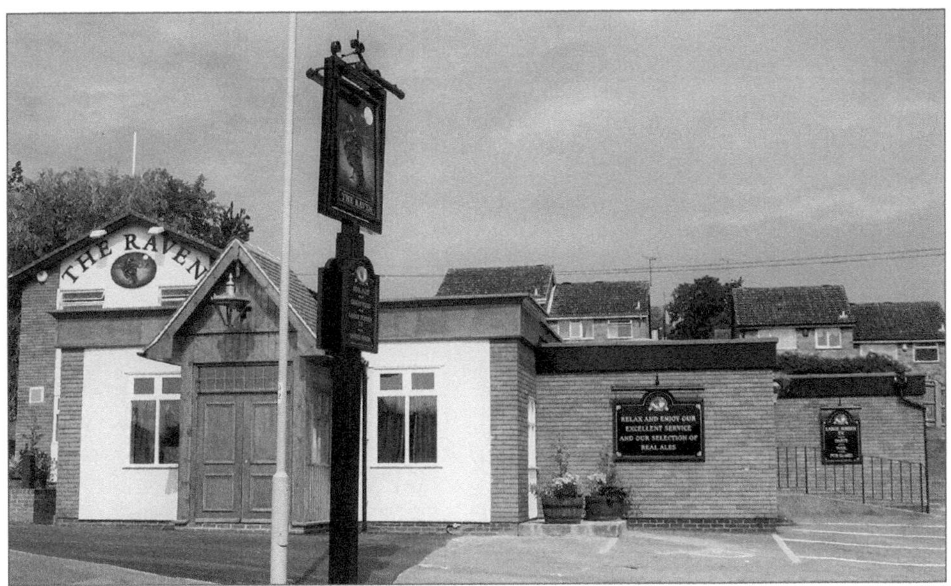

The Caledonia was rebuilt in 2002 and successfully reopened as The Raven. The new name is historically more valid than its old one as this area is close to Ravensitch Farm, whereas Caledonia was really the name of the community at the southern end of this housing development – at the other end of Mousehall Farm Road. (*Ned Williams*)

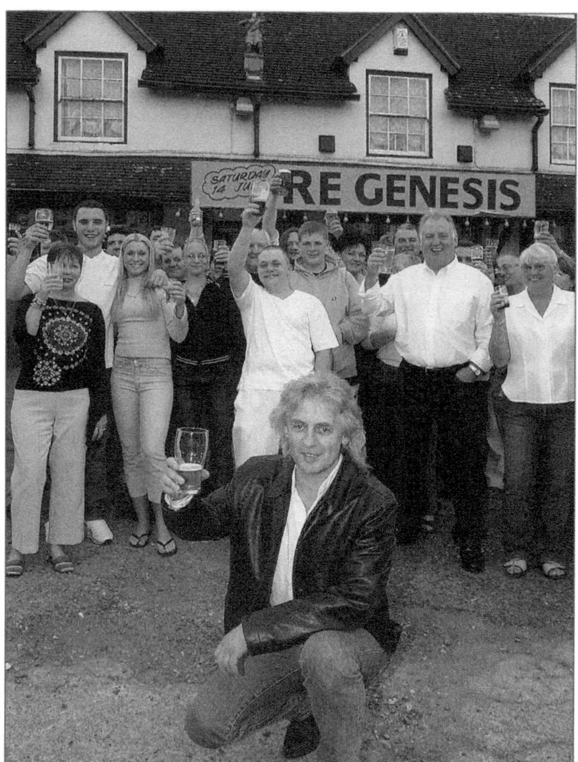

The Robin Hood was built on the old turnpike road from Dudley to Pedmore and was on the boundary of Brierley Hill and Quarry Bank. It was a rural destination for thirsty nineteenth-century working-class visitors from Quarry Bank, Dudley and Brierley Hill and in the 1880s organised its own annual gala. In the 1970s it became associated with Black Country Night Out entertainment, and for eleven years it was the home of the Robin R&B Club. The development of the Merry Hill Complex cast its shadow over The Robin Hood – an eccentric oasis of live entertainment with a wonderful history. In 2003 the owners of the Merry Hill announced that its lease would not be renewed. Mike Hamblett, once a Quarry Bank schoolboy and proprietor of the club, poses outside The Robin Hood on the night of the last show: 23 June 2003. (*Express & Star*)

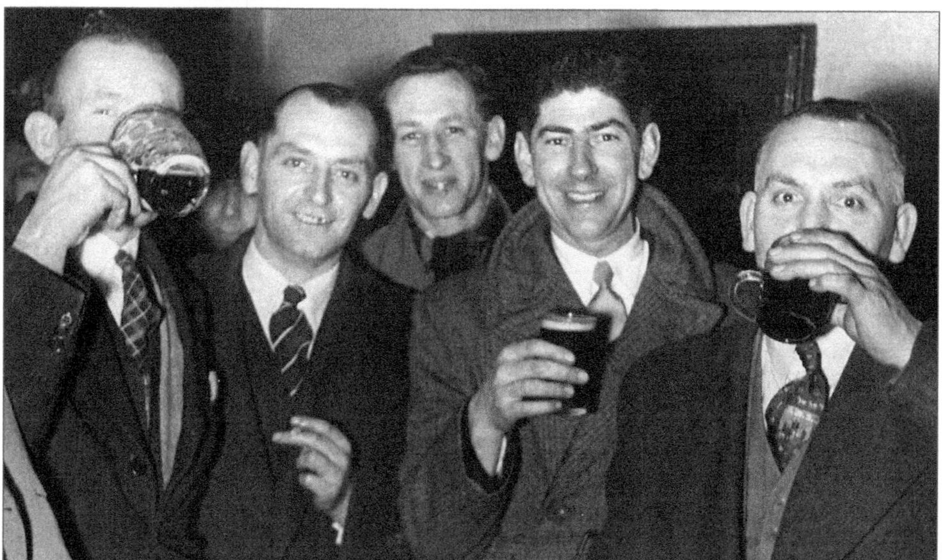

Sam Whiley, George Ingley and friends in the White Horse darts team in the 1950s, when pub closures were unusual and a great deal of community life centred around pubs. (*MPLHG*)

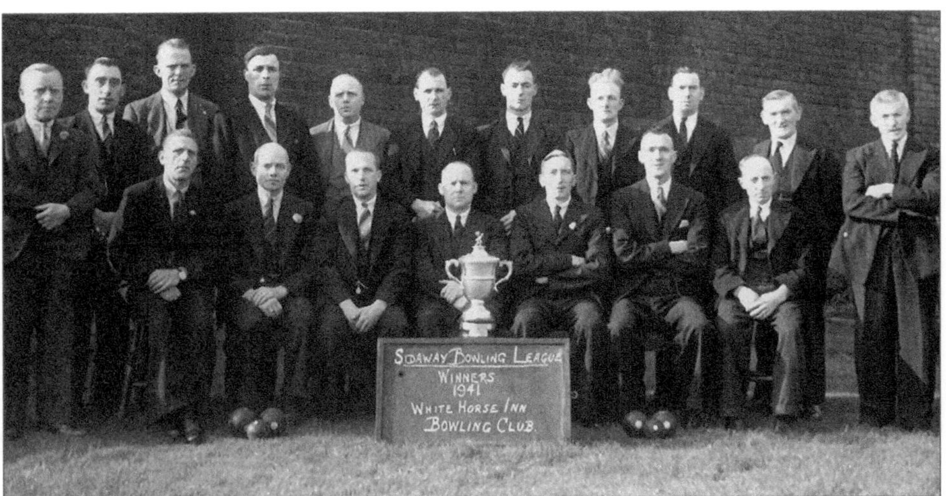

The White Horse has a good quality bowling green just to the rear of the premises – a reminder of the time when many local pubs had bowling greens and flourishing bowling teams. The pub has had a bowling club team for almost a century, and has produced fourteen county players. In 1941 the White Horse Inn's Bowling Club were winners in the Sidaway Bowling League. (*White Horse Collection*)

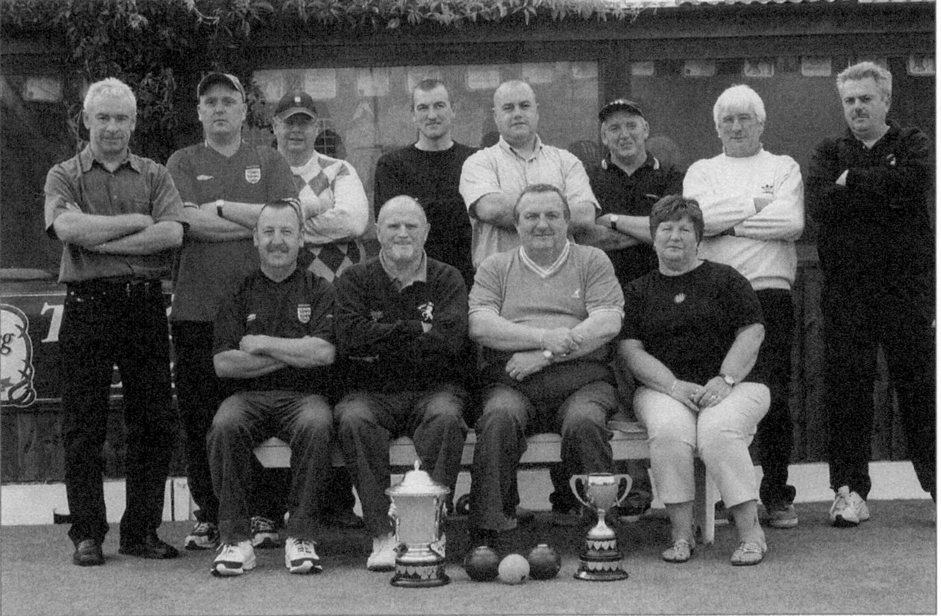

The White Horse Bowling Club is still in the Sidaway League and now enjoys the use of the last bowling green in Quarry Bank. This is the 2002 team. Back row, left to right: Martin Simpson, Alan Parsons, Adrian Ford, Tony Hutton, Andrew Retford, James Hutton, Paul Babbington and Ian Passey. Front row: Paul North, Brian Turner, Malcolm Knowles and Rita Hutton. (*John James*)

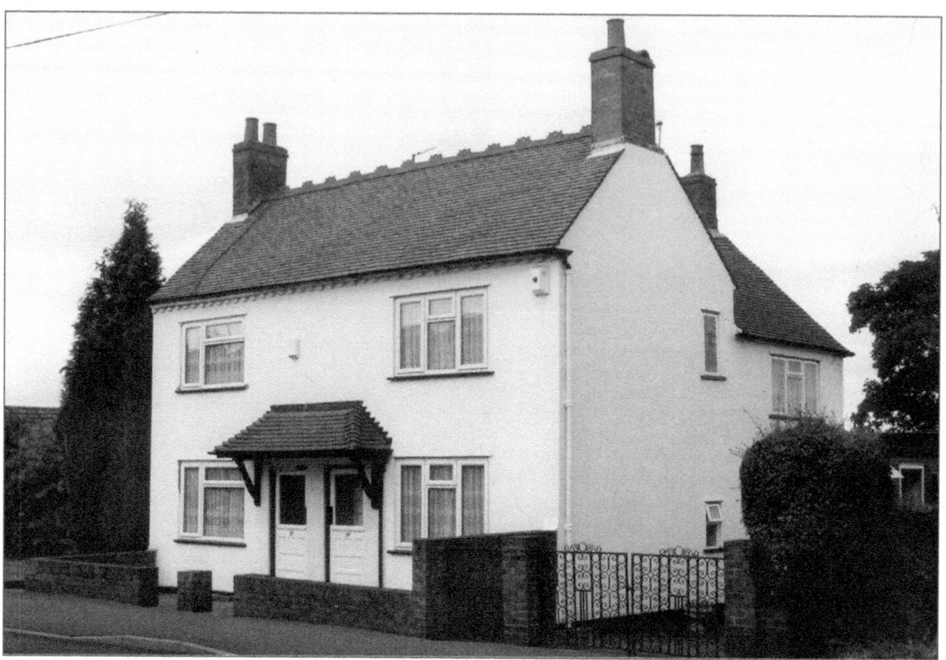

Above the doors of the cottages at 20/22 Amblecote Road is a sign telling passers-by that this was once The Grand Turk – one of Quarry Bank's vanished pubs. Up until about 100 years ago it was an Atkinson's house licensed to Arthur Hobson. He and the licence were transferred to The Black Horse nearby in Delph Road, although this building continued to be the family home and was converted into two cottages. Arthur Hobson's grandson, Ossie Biddle, has lived at no. 20 all his life. (*Ned Williams*)

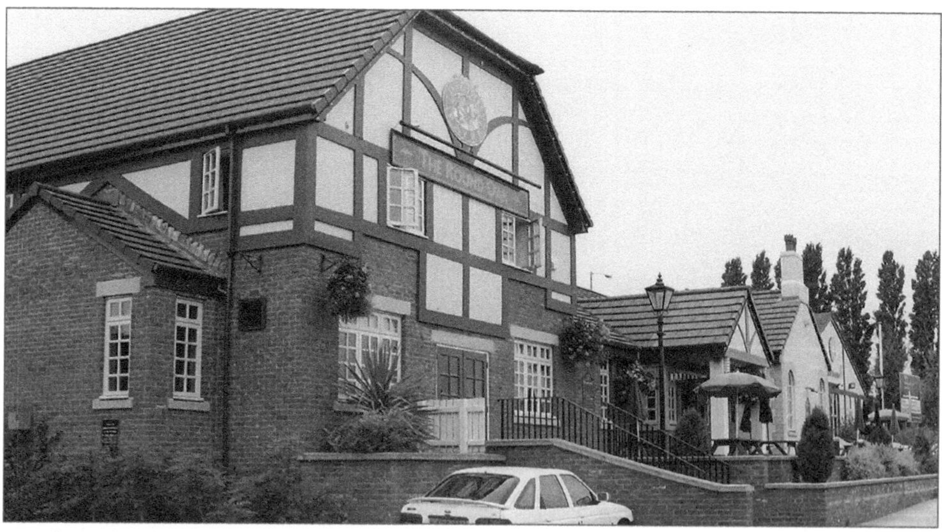

Brand new family pub for the twenty-first century: The Round Oak in Merry Hill. (*Ned Williams*)

CHAPTER TEN

PEOPLE & EVENTS

In both the past and the present Quarry Bank has a record of being a friendly and sociable place to live. In fact photographs of people and of social activities are easier to find than topographical pictures! We certainly have a better pictorial record of Quarry Bankers enjoying themselves than we have of Quarry Bankers at work.

The carnivals, and street parties associated with national events, now seem to be a thing of the past, but there is always something going on down at the Community Centre in Sheffield Street, and around the schools and churches, the three political clubs and the British Legion hall. There are sports clubs and the local Operatic and Dramatic Society. There is Country & Western at the Conservative Club, and rock and roll at the Labour Club since 2002 and brass band music has again been heard from the bandstand in the park. The problem facing a town like Quarry Bank is to find ways of sharing a sense of all this activity and harnessing the activity to preserve a feeling of local identity.

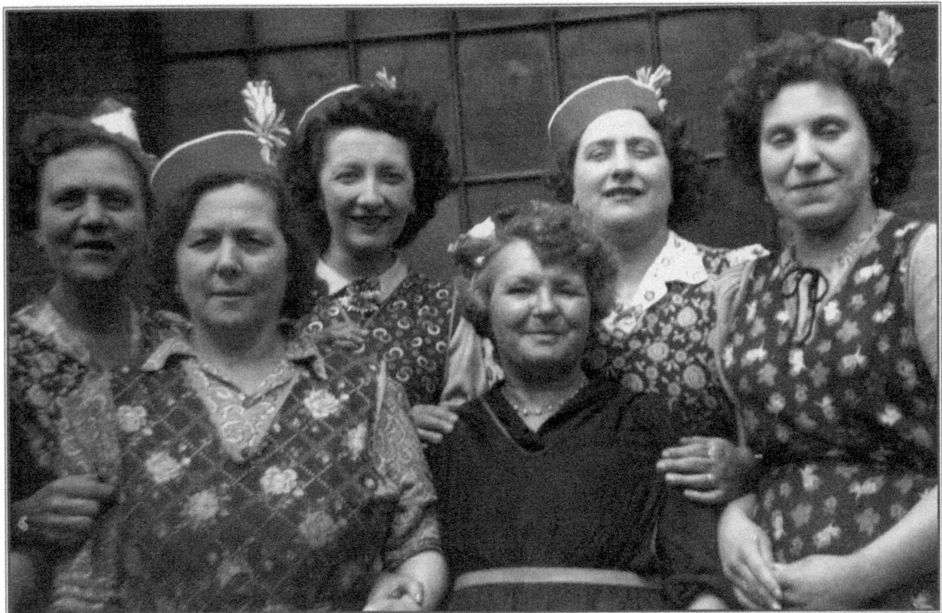

Many pictures of groups of local people celebrating historic events exist – but often with scant information recorded. This 'Coronation' picture from May Whiley's Collection (May is second left on the back row) was taken at Ernest Steven's Hollow-Ware, where many Quarry Bankers worked. In a book like this many people in one photograph are related to someone in another! May's husband Sam appears on page 106. (*Mary Whiley*)

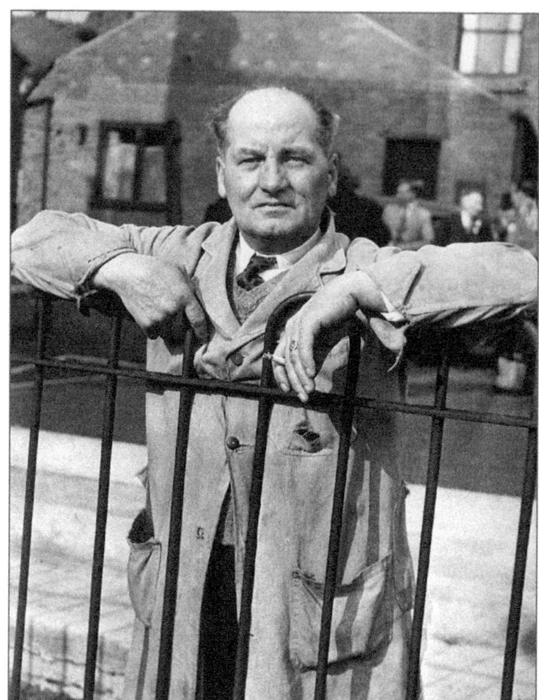

Councillor Sydney Woodhouse: Sydney Woodhouse was born on 22 February 1895 and came to Quarry Bank after his marriage. He joined Brierley Hill UDC in 1934 after Quarry Bank had merged with Brierley Hill and became Chairman of the UDC three years later. He was also steward at Quarry Bank Labour Club for seventeen years. (He is seen here standing by the Labour Club's bowling green.) He died on 17 October 1976, aged eighty-one years. A ward at Dudley Guest Hospital was named after him in 1967, and in Quarry Bank his name is commemorated at Woodhouse Court in Sheffield Street. Woodhouse Court was opened on 4 July 1964 and has since been completely rebuilt. Councillor Woodhouse spent the last years of his life in the accommodation named after him. (*Information and photo collected by Bessie Cranton, MPLHG*)

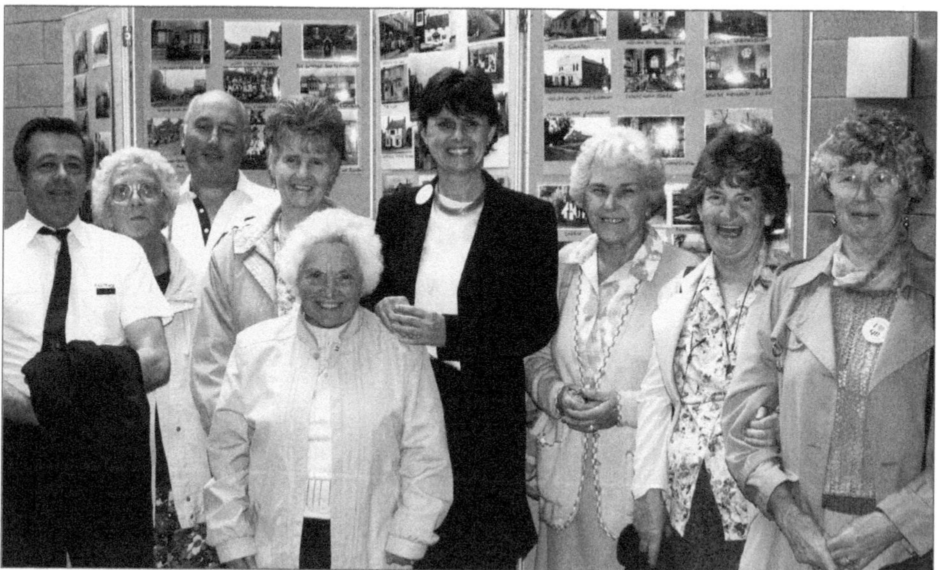

Mount Pleasant Local History Group put on a photographic display at Woodhouse Court. Left to right: John James, Doris Peat, Patrick and Sylvia Shaw, Bessie Cranton (who researched the life of Sydney Woodhouse), Debra Shipley MP, Joan Pearson, Margaret Priest and Marie Billingham. (*Ned Williams*)

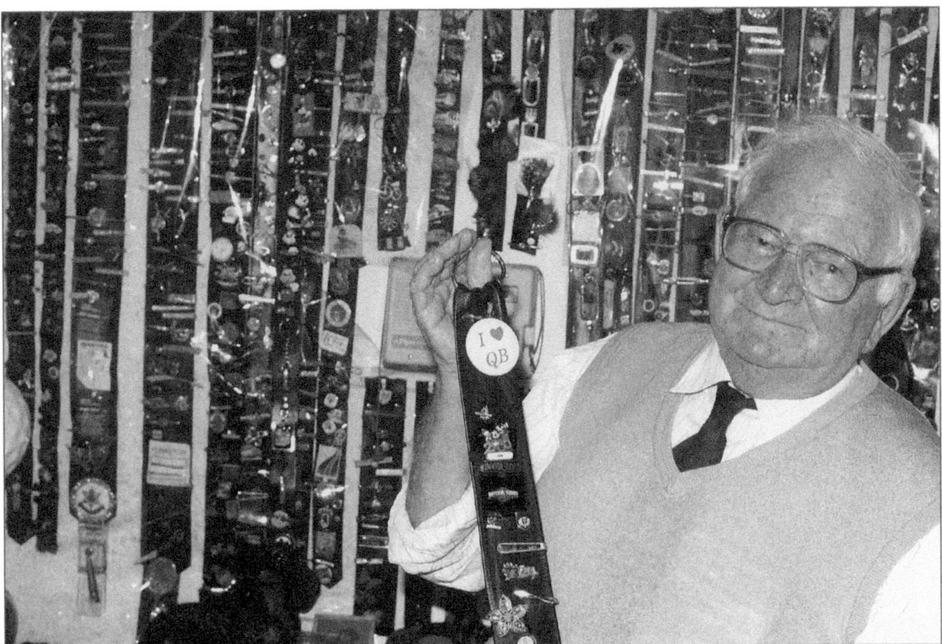

Sam Smith of Woodhouse Court is a collector of tie clips, tie pins and badges, and displays his 'I love Quarry Bank' badge among his collection in 2002. (*Ned Williams*)

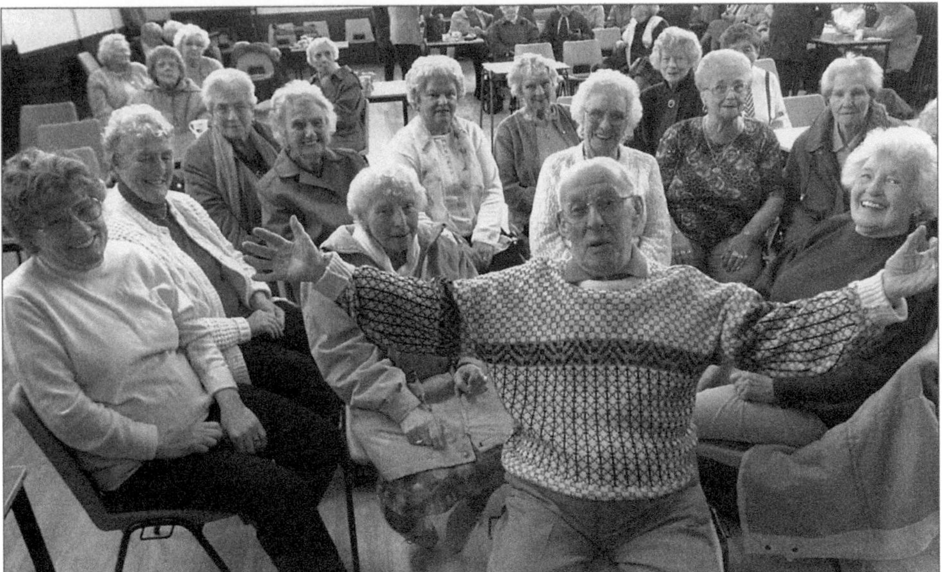

Joe Jones – the last male member of the Quarry Bank Darby and Joan Club – appeals for men to come and join him in 2002. Joe, then aged eighty, joined the club twenty years earlier and was treasurer and secretary for thirteen years. The club meets in the Community Centre in Sheffield Street. (*Express & Star*)

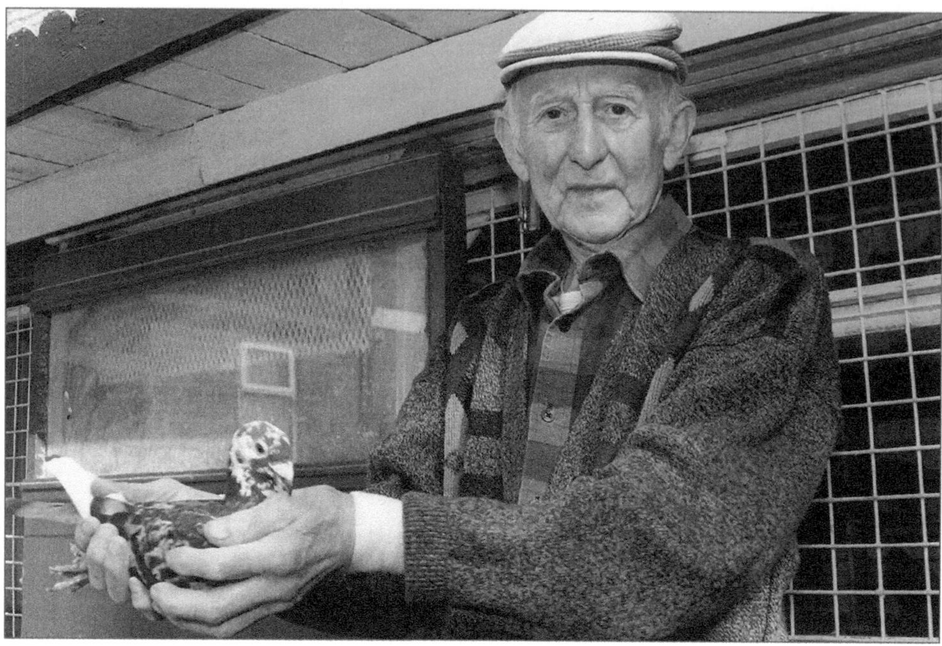

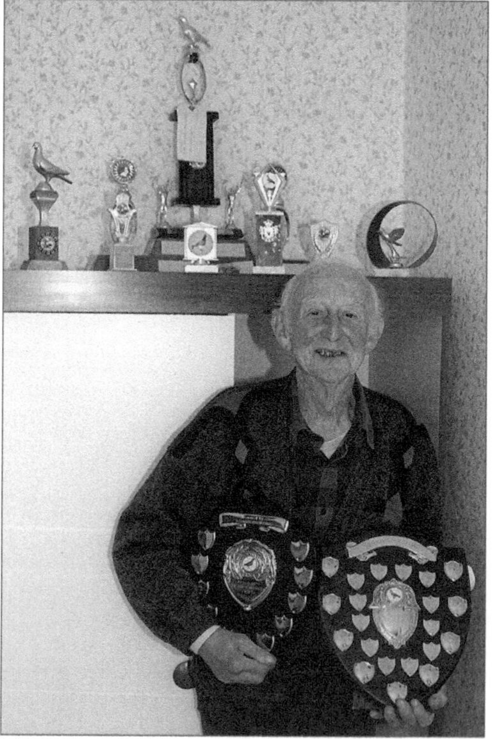

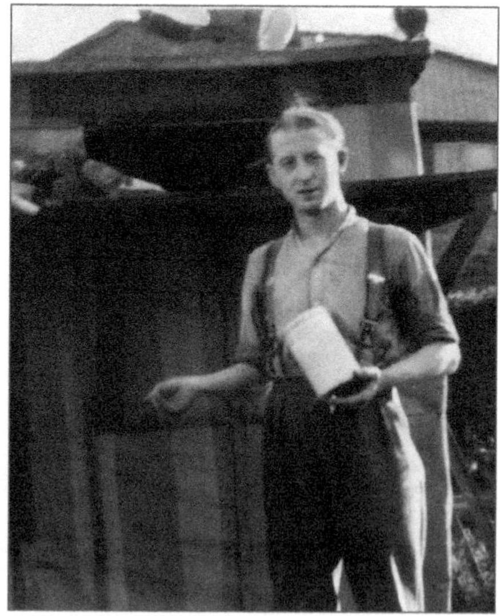

Ron Priest, a Quarry Bank pigeon flyer of Woodland Avenue, seen above outside the pigeon lofts, left with some of his prizes and trophies in 2002, and below as a young man. Once a pigeon flyer always a pigeon flyer. (*Ned Williams*)

This plaque commemorating the first payment of a state pension to a Quarry Bank citizen on 1 January 1909 is on display in the Liberal Club in Quarry Bank High Street. The pension was paid to Mrs W. Shaw (1835–1913), who in 1909 was living on the Amblecote Road. How the 5*s* piece came to be embedded in this brass plate and found its way to the Liberal Club is not clear, but it was already on display at the time of her death in 1913. (The Liberal connection is probably the fact that Lloyd George, the Liberal leader, introduced the pension.) (*Ned Williams*)

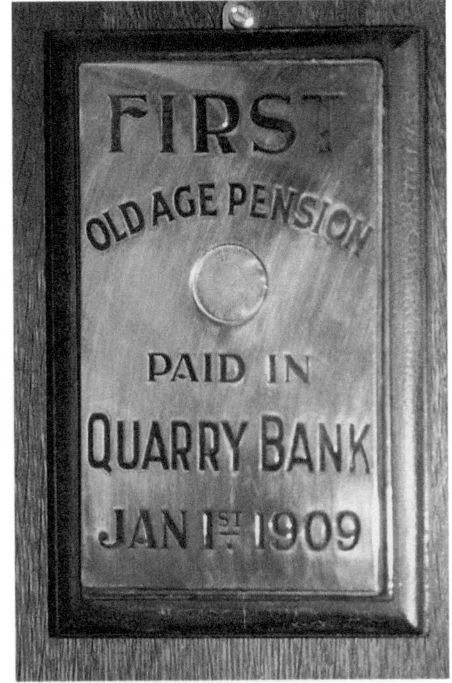

Below: Eddy Mattocks, accompanied by Pat Mattocks, collects his first pension payment from the post office in Caledonia on August 2002. The payment of pensions at local post offices and the latter's survival are back in the news. (*John James*)

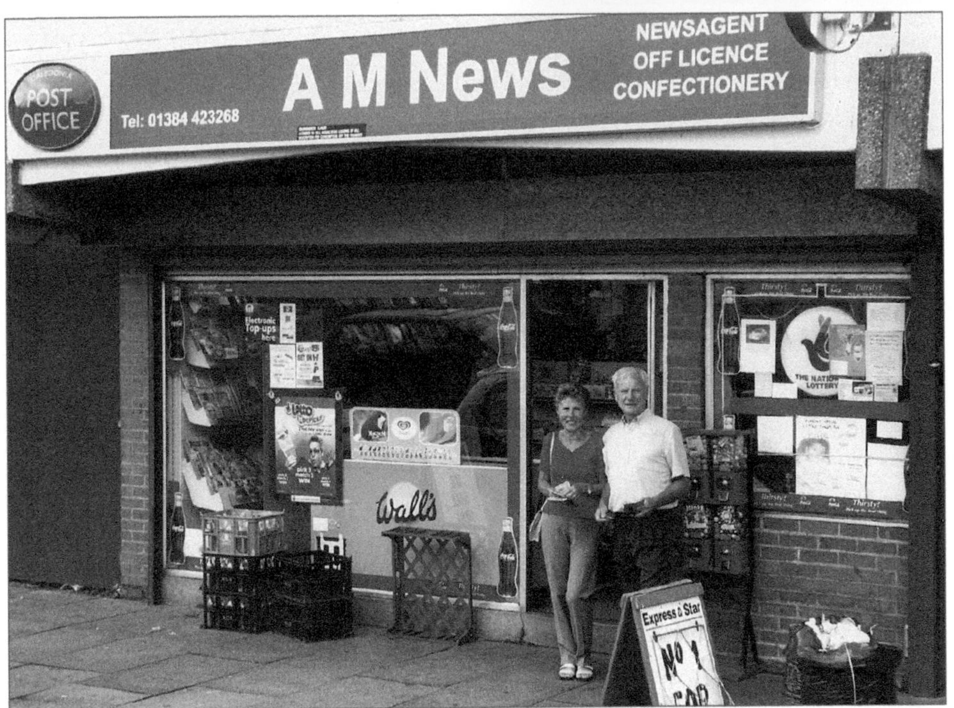

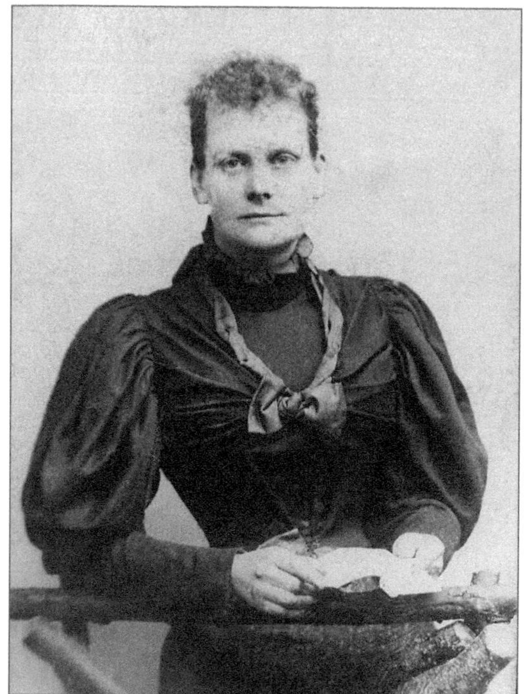

Left: Alice Jones (1868–1958) – Quarry Bank's last corset-maker. Alice was the second wife of Joseph Jones, a chain-maker, and trustee of the New Street Methodist Chapel. Alice worked as a corset-maker from the family home at 52 New Street. She regularly appeared in the Quarry Bank Carnival as 'Pins and Needles'. (*Vera Greatorex*)

Below: Jean James on school-crossing-patrol duty at Mount Pleasant School 2003. School crossing patrols celebrated their fiftieth anniversary in 2003, and Jean will be celebrating twenty-five years of crossing-patrol work in 2004. Over the years Jean has collected a file of local crossing-patrol information. Whether it is a matter of researching the last corset-maker in your area, or building an archive of crossing-patrol information, it's all the stuff of 'local history'. (*Ned Williams*)

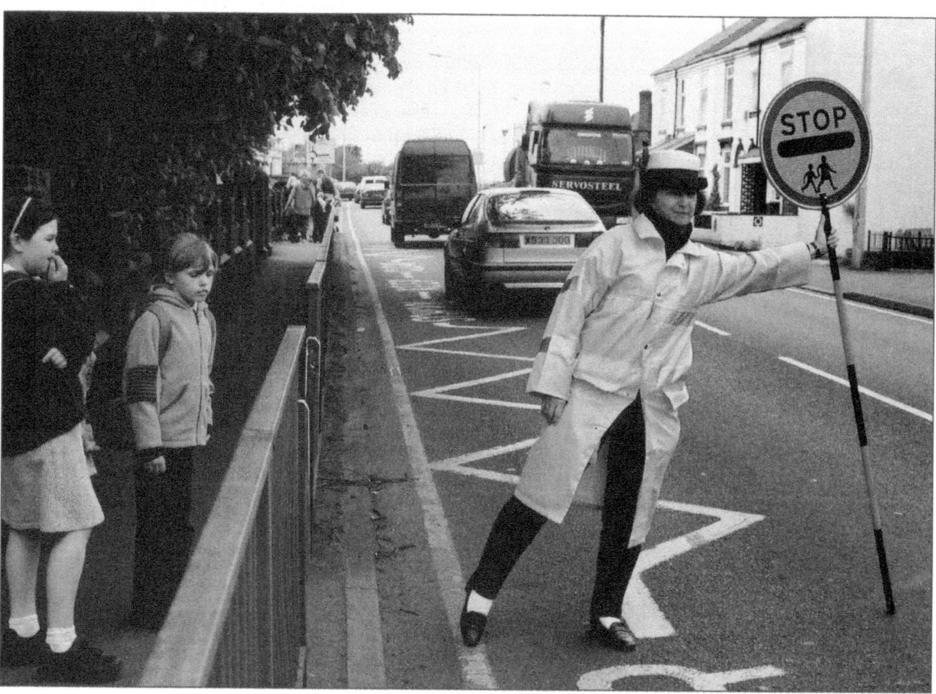

Scouting was established in Quarry Bank just after the First World War and was at first linked to the parish church, using the Victoria Road Sunday school building. Later a headquarters was established in Maugham Street. Harry Hawkeswood ran the 1st Quarry Bank troop from 1923 until 1940, assisted by Enoch Billingham. In 1948 they joined the Brierley Hill Local Association. R.H. Jasper was Scoutmaster at the time, with four scouters, twenty-five scouts and thirteen cubs. In 1970 the troop became Sea Scouts and a new head-quarters was established at Bobs Coppice in the 1980s. Here we see the Sea Scouts taking part in a 1970s Quarry Bank Gala in Stevens Park.
(*Carole Cobb, MPLHG*)

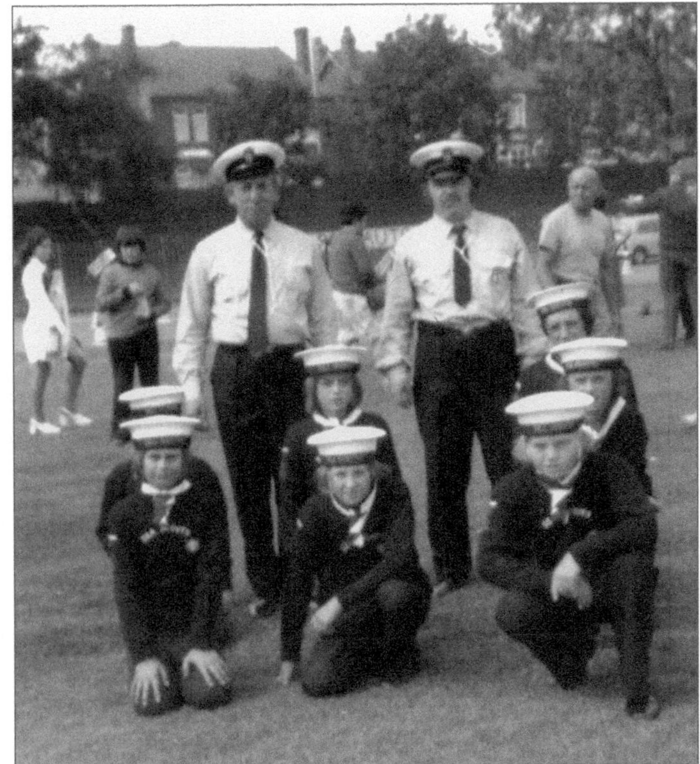

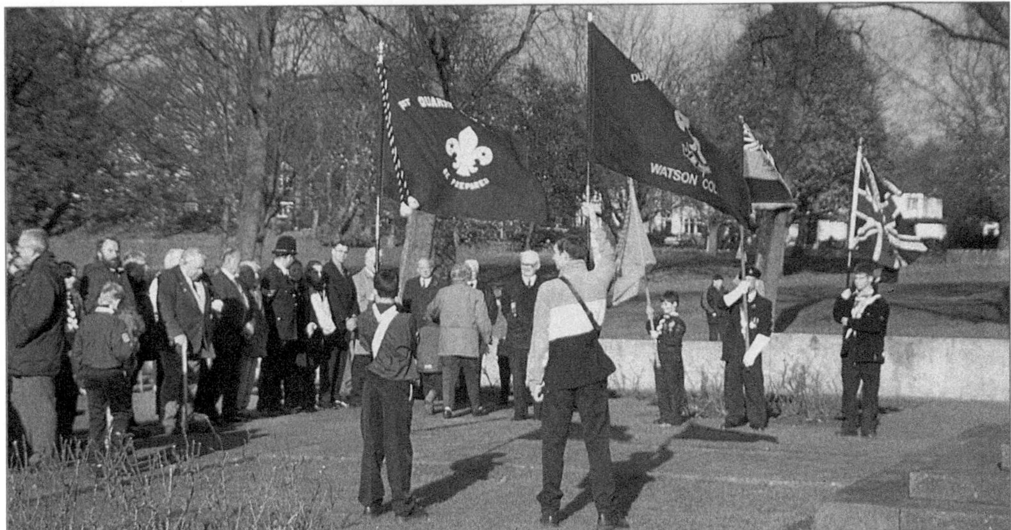

Uniformed youth groups still play a part in public events in Quarry Bank. Here, at the 2000 Remembrance Day Parade, Scouts, Cubs and Boys' Brigade take part in the ceremony at the Peace Memorial in Stevens Park. (*Ned Williams*)

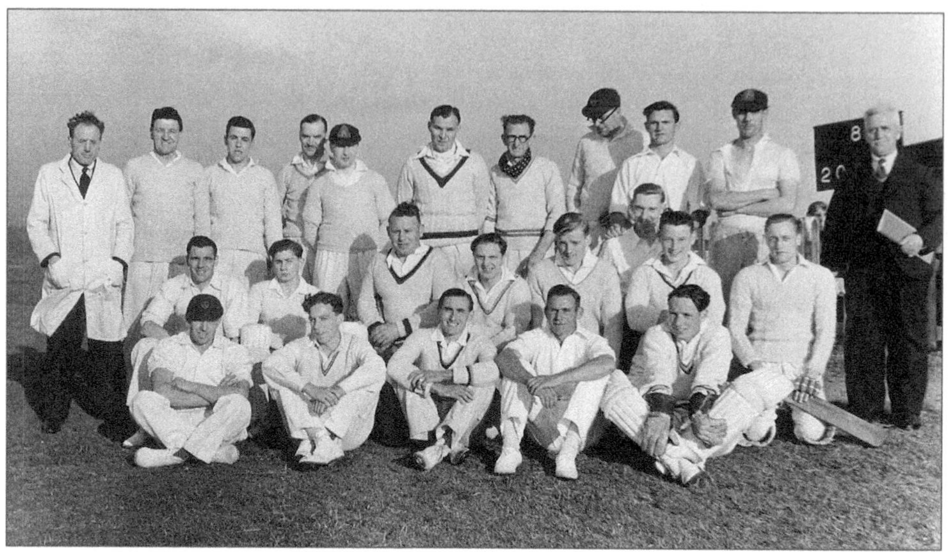

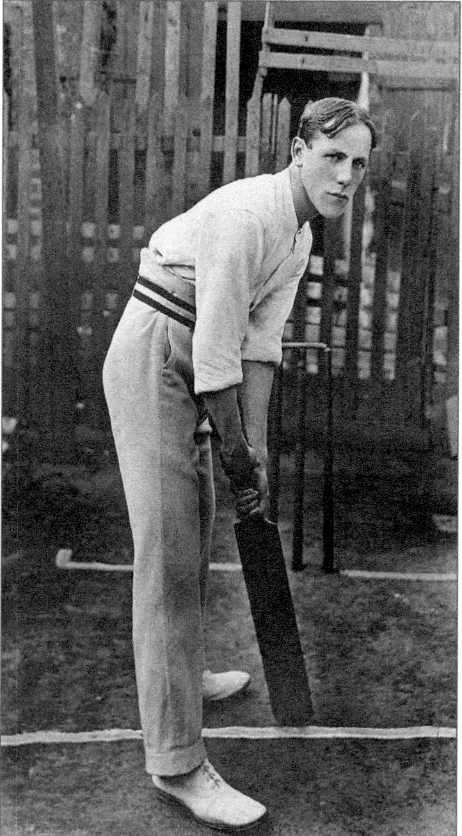

Above: Amblecote Cricket Club, *c.* 1950, included many Quarry Bank players – including Frank and Michael Dunn, Bernard Wood, George Davies, Ron Dovey, Arthur Holt and Peter Greensmith (centre of front row), and secretary Jim Wright. (*Margaret Priest*)

Left: The thought of cricket may conjure up visions of the village green, but cricket in Quarry Bank may have had a more urban style – Albert Dunn, of Quarry Bank Cricket Club, prepares to bat on August Bank Holiday Monday 1911. (*Marie Billingham*)

Below: Trevor Smith, born in Quarry Bank in 1936, who died as this book was going to press in August 2003. Trevor played for Birmingham City Football Club for eleven years and is Quarry Bank's best-known footballer. (*Sheila Marshall*)

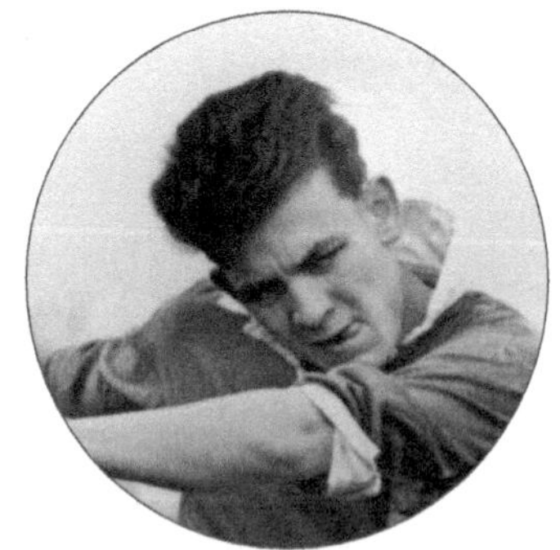

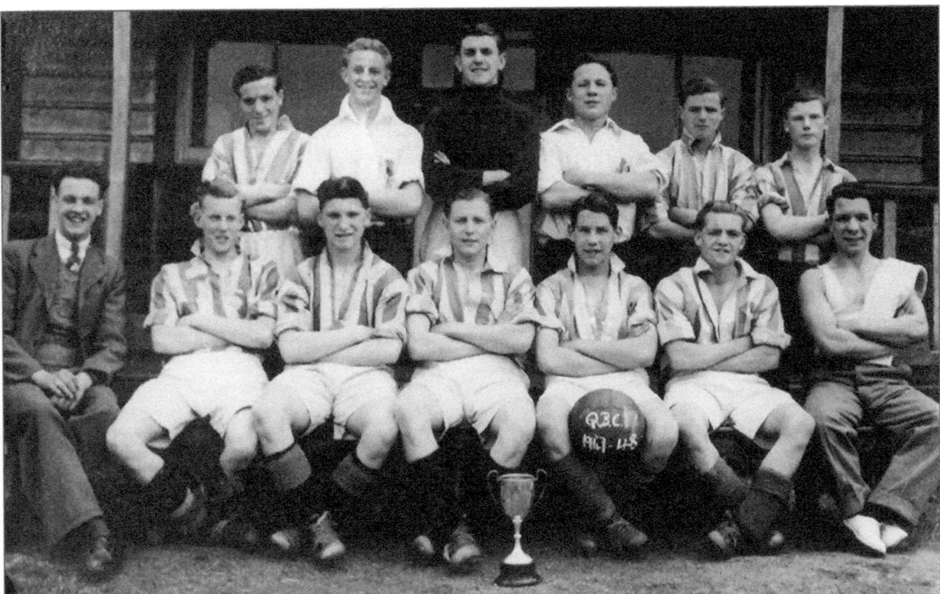

Quarry Bank Celtic Football Team, 1947/8, in front of the pavilion in Stevens Park. Cyril Cartwright, seated left, joined the club when it all began in 1944, and a year later became its long-serving secretary.

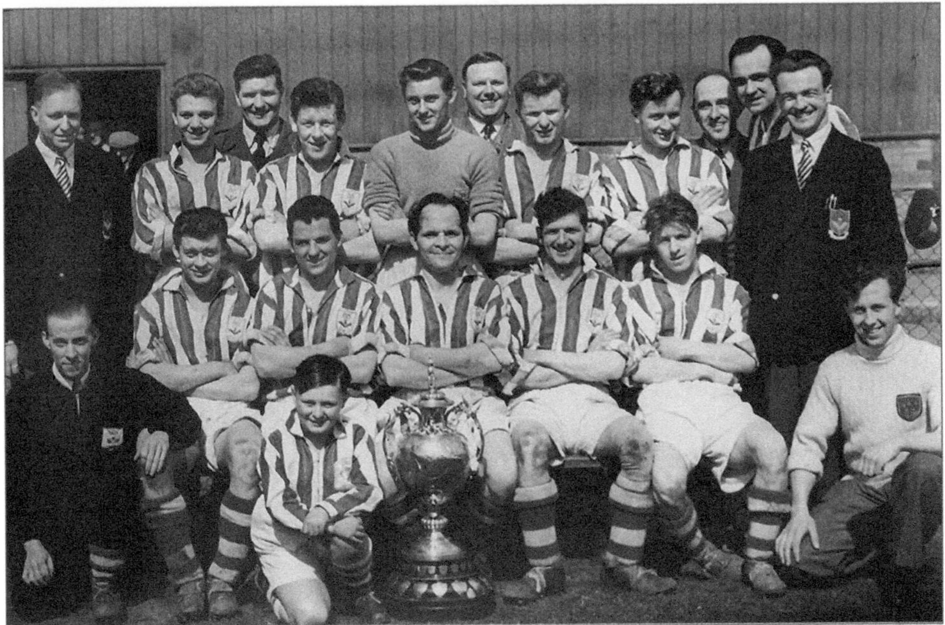

A later photograph of Quarry Bank Celtic, this time with Cyril Cartwright standing on the right. These two photographs are from a small archive of such pictures on display at a barber's shop in Quarry Bank High Street whose provenance is unknown.

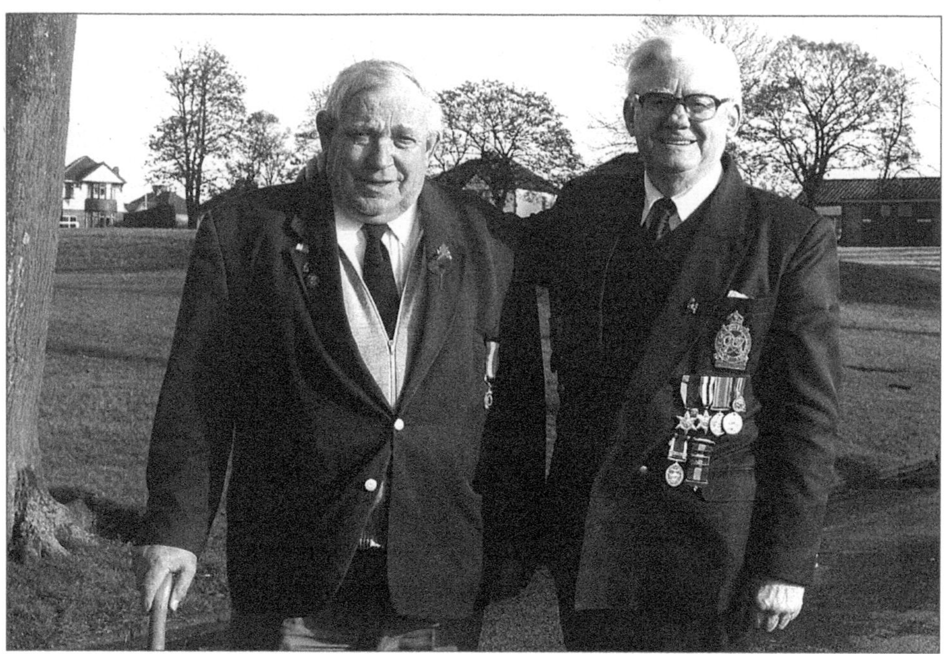

Two stalwarts of the local British Legion, Tom Keeling and Charlie Scott, at the annual Remembrance Day parade in Stevens Park, 2001. (*Ned Williams*)

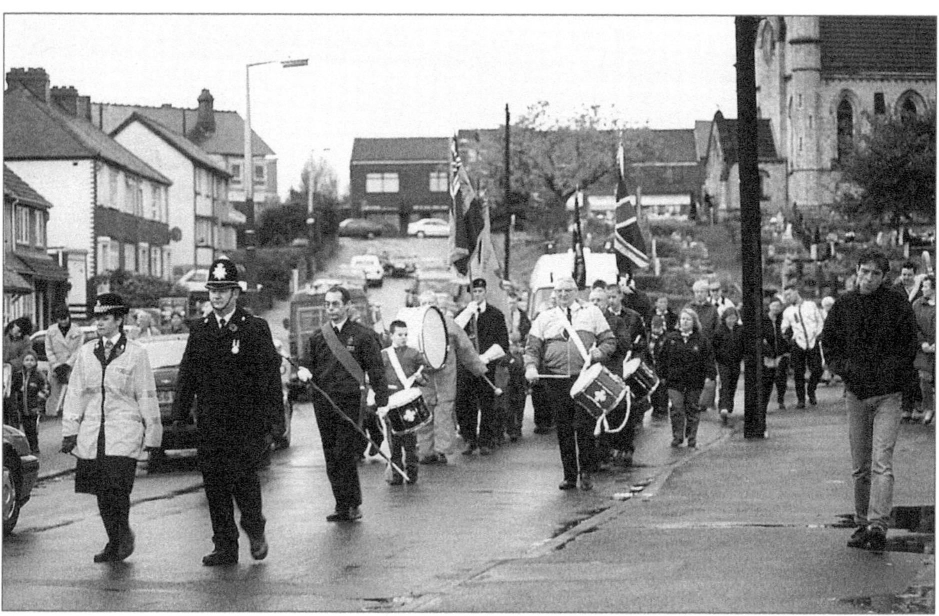

The Remembrance Day parade sets off down Park Road to the memorial in Stevens Park, November 1997. (*Tom Keeling*)

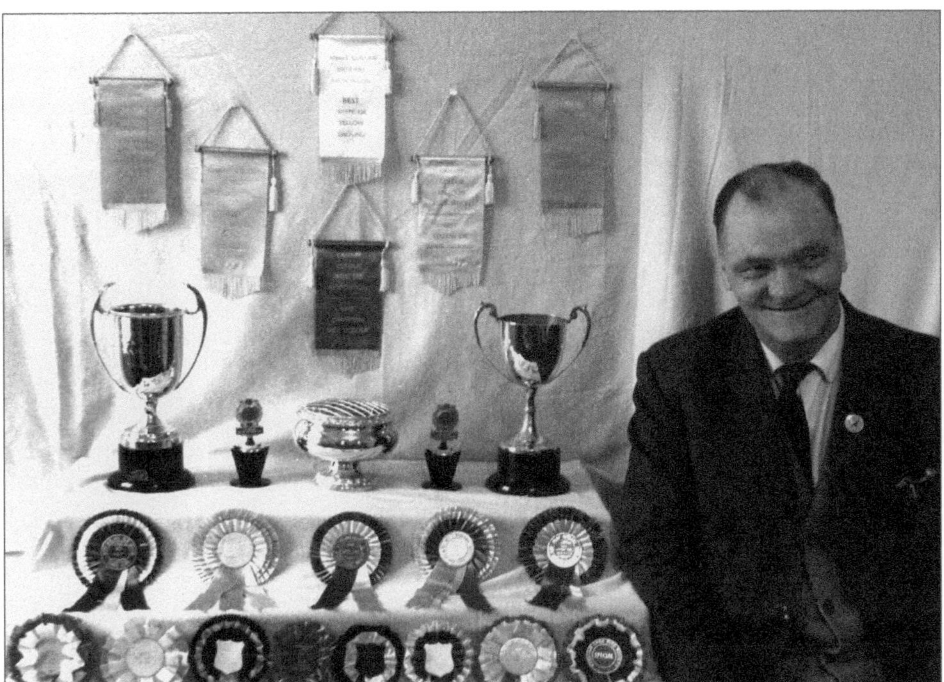

Jack Askins, of Birch Avenue, a member of the Quarry Bank Canary Club, sits at the Community Centre in Sheffield Street with a display of some of the trophies won by his canaries in the 1960s. (*Mrs Askins*)

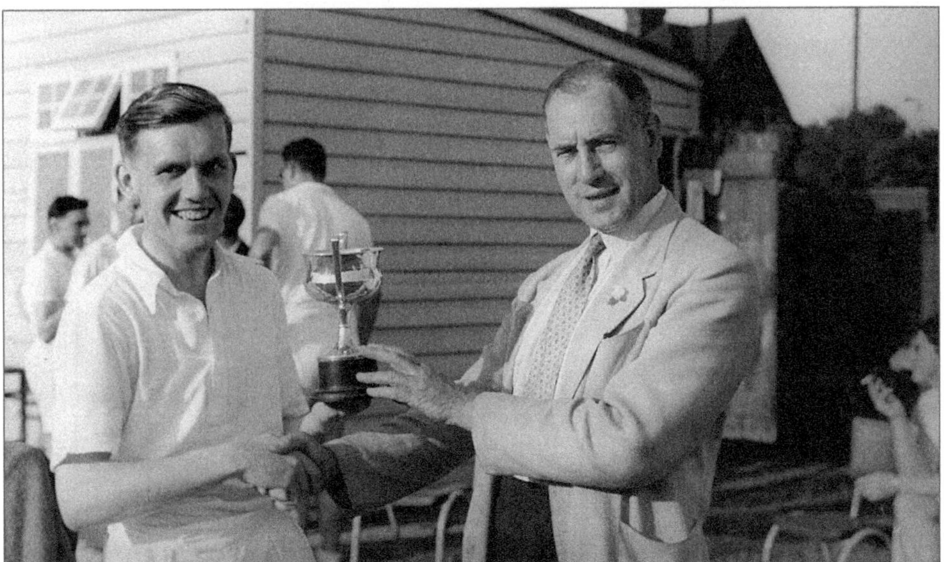

Maurice Stringer wins the Quarry Bank Tennis Club Men's Singles competition of 1953/4 and receives the cup from Arthur Heathcock. (*Maurice Stringer*)

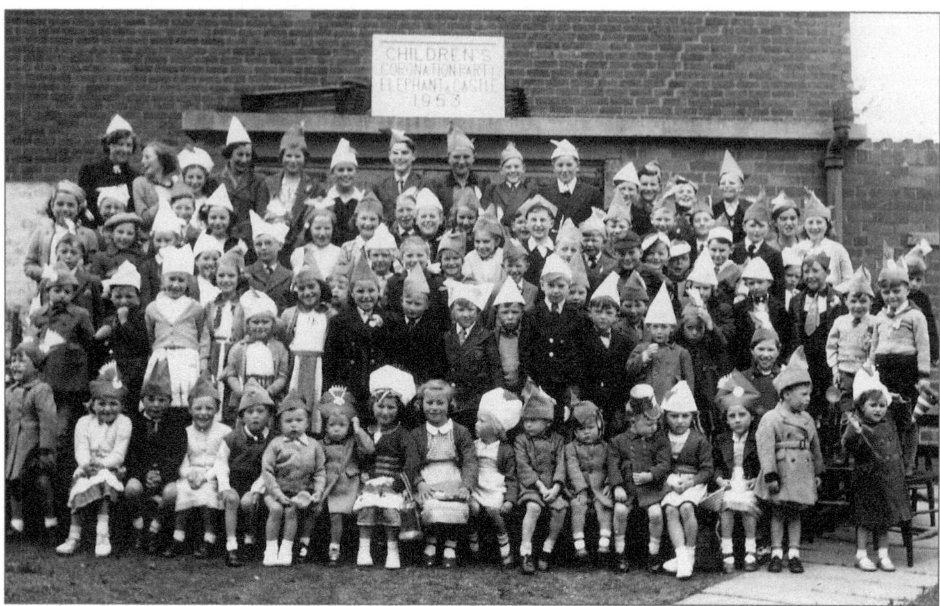

These children took part in a coronation party organised by The Elephant and Castle public house in 1953. (*Brian Harris*)

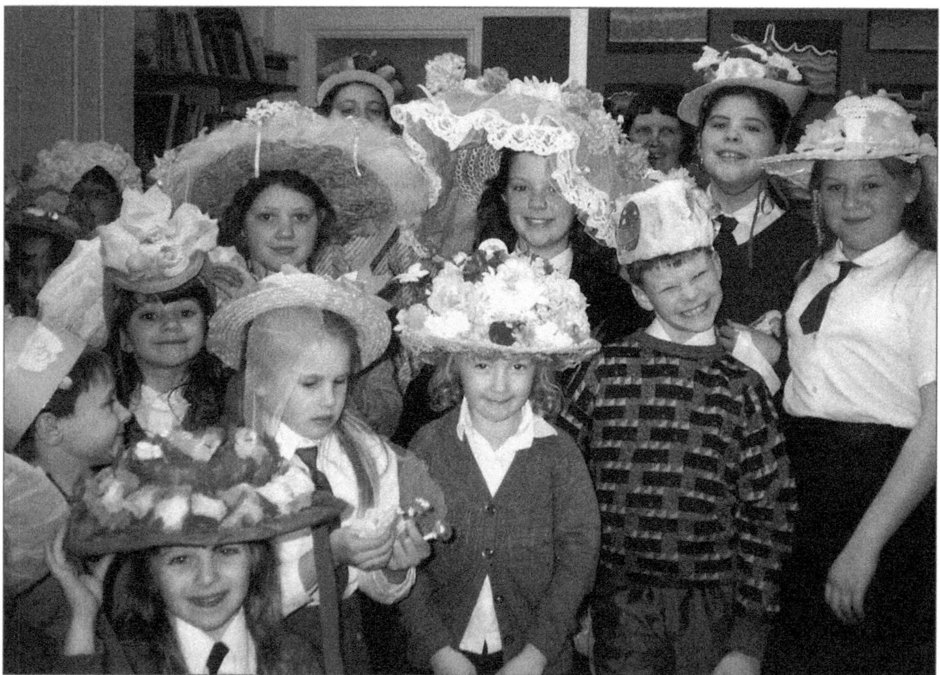

Children in a rather less formal pose are seen here taking part in the fancy hats competition at the annual Quarry Bank Primary School Summer Fayre in 1995. (*Liz Cullinane*)

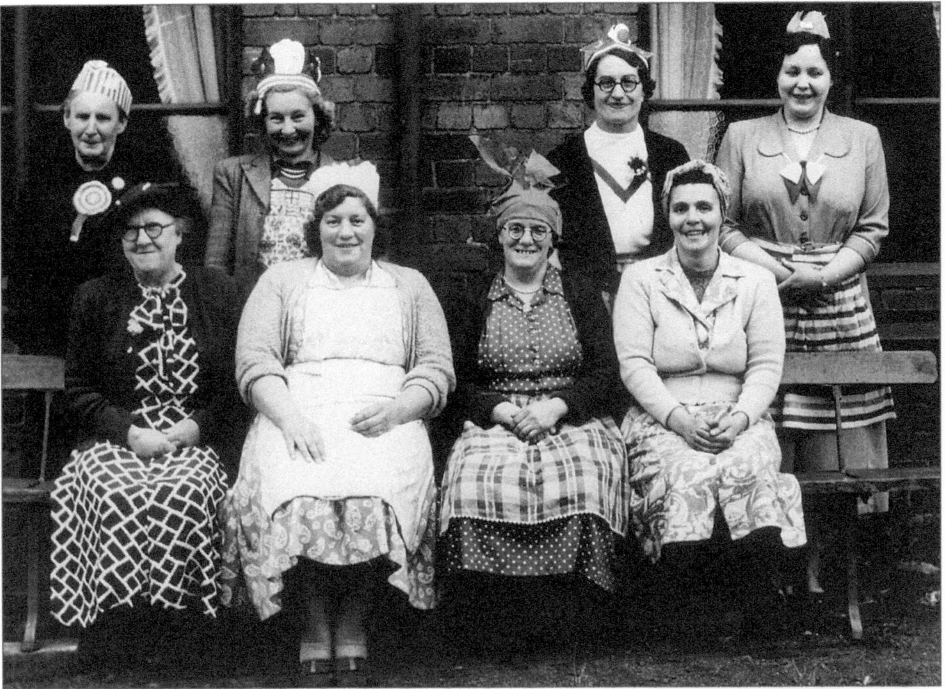

Another coronation party group photographed in Quarry Bank in 1953. (*Derek Siviter*)

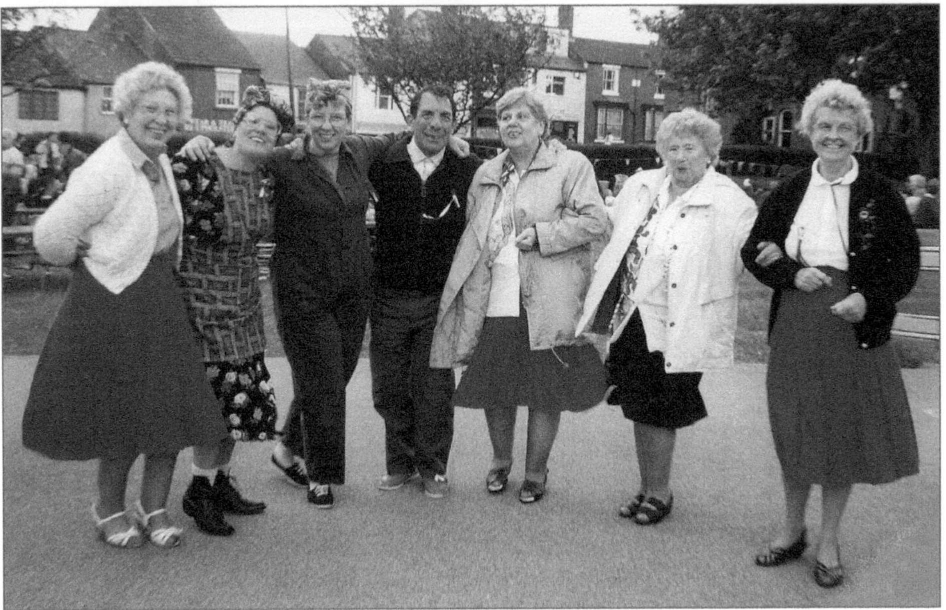

The fortieth anniversary of VE Day was celebrated at Quarry Bank Primary School on 8 May 1995 in both contemporary and period costume. (*School Archives*)

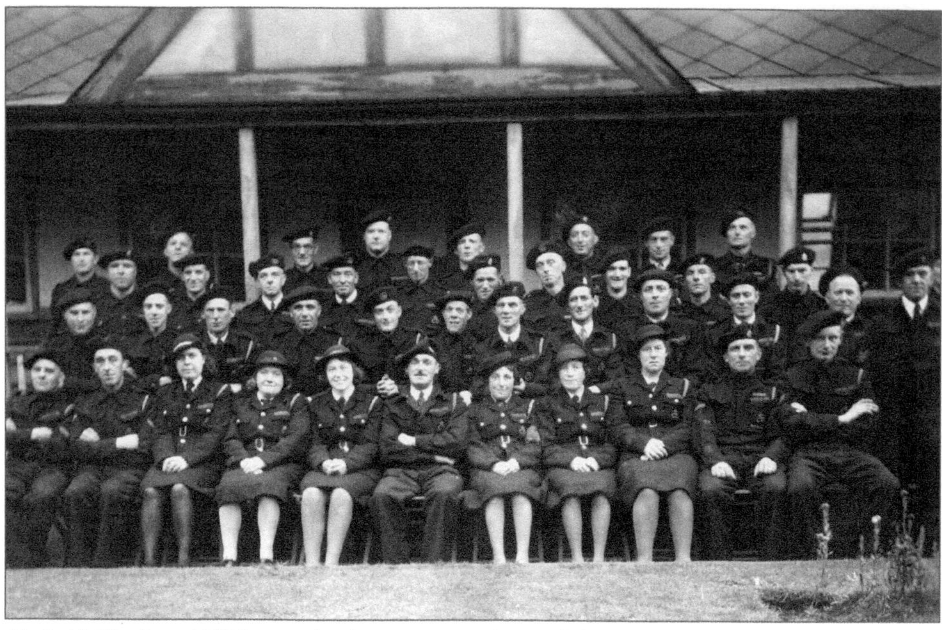

Air Raid Wardens (ARP) pose for the camera in front of the pavilion in Stevens Park, Quarry Bank, early in the Second World War. Leonard Cartwright is on the left in the front row, and his daughter Dorothy has identified some of the other wardens. For example, Ewart Bloor is sitting next to Leonard and Chief Warden Bill Nicholls is in the centre of the picture. The pavilion was one of five ARP posts in Quarry Bank. (*Nancy Marchant/Dorothy Bailey*)

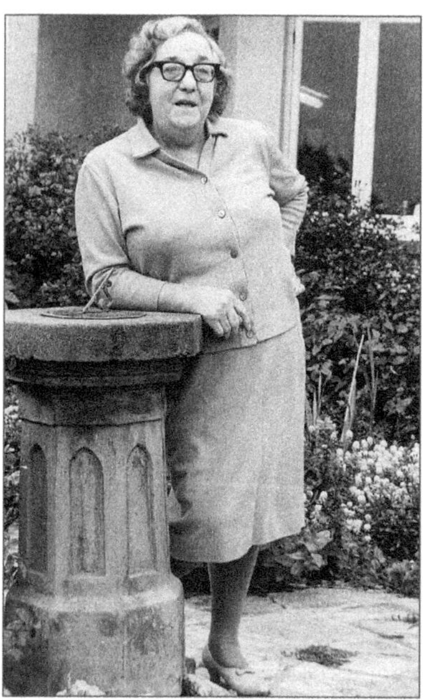

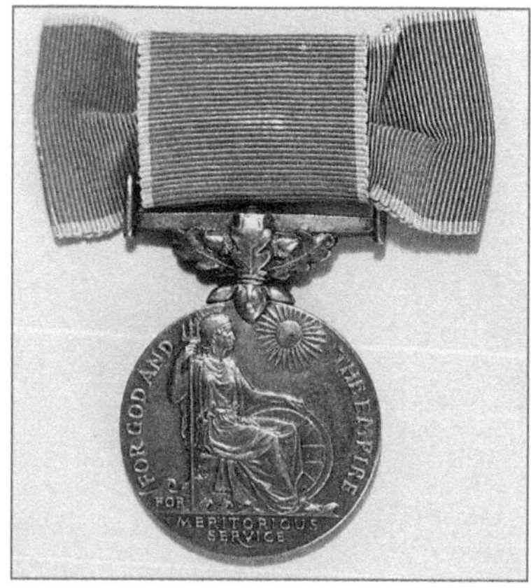

Alice Elizabeth Nicholls of The Limes, Brick-Kiln Street, 1945. Mrs Nicholls was awarded the BEM for her distinguished wartime services. She was one of the pioneers of wartime canteen work. Tireless in her efforts on behalf of Civil Defence and the WVS, she took her mobile canteen to Coventry during the great air raids on that city. (*Patrick Shaw*)

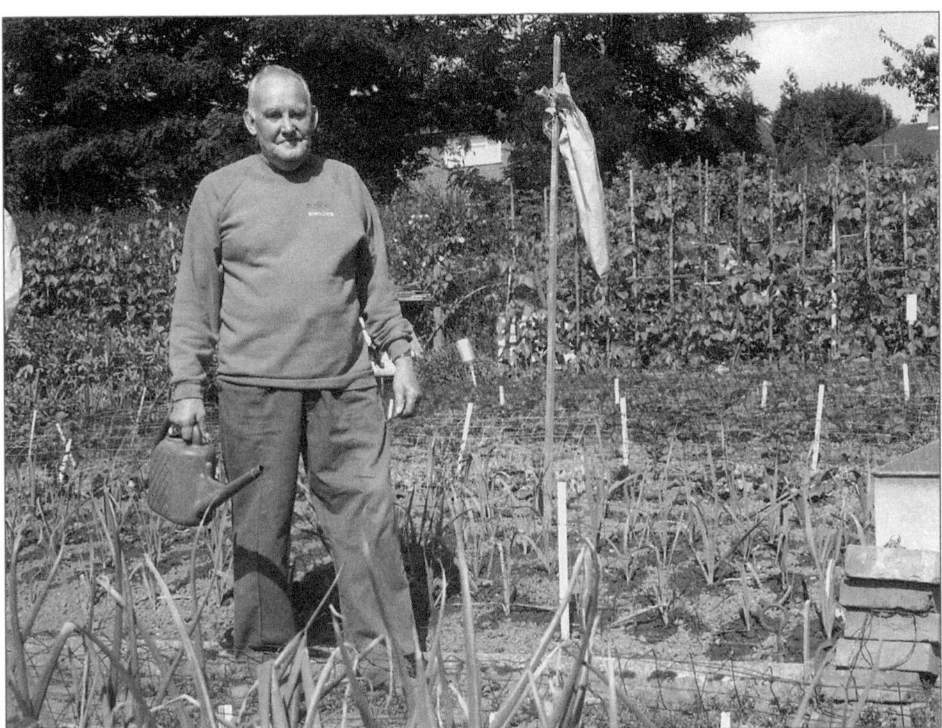

The subject of allotments is often overlooked in local history, and photographs of allotments seem rare. In 2001 two Quarry Bank horticulturists were photographed at work on their allotments at Bobs Coppice: Gerald Dunn, above, and Ern Hill. Mr Hill bred a vermilion rose called 'Royal Visit' to mark the Queen's visit to Dudley in 1994.

The Quarry Bank Gardeners' and Allotment Association promoted horticultural activity in Quarry Bank and used to organise an annual Grand Horticultural Show at the Labour Club from the mid-1960s onwards. At one time a Flower and Vegetable Show was held in a marquee in Stevens Park as part of the galas. (*John James*)

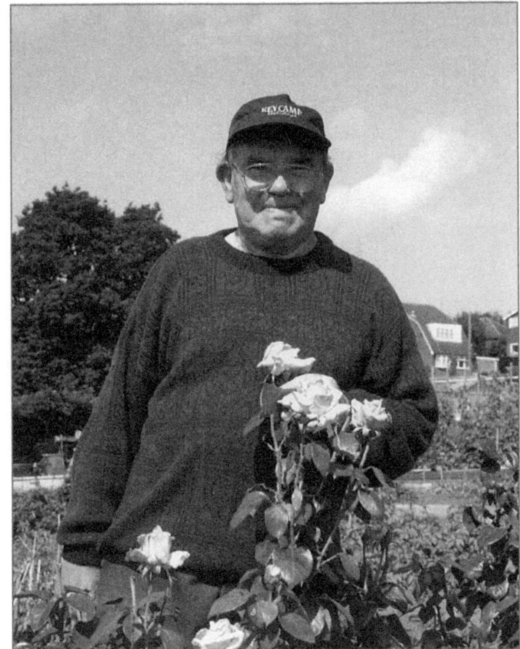

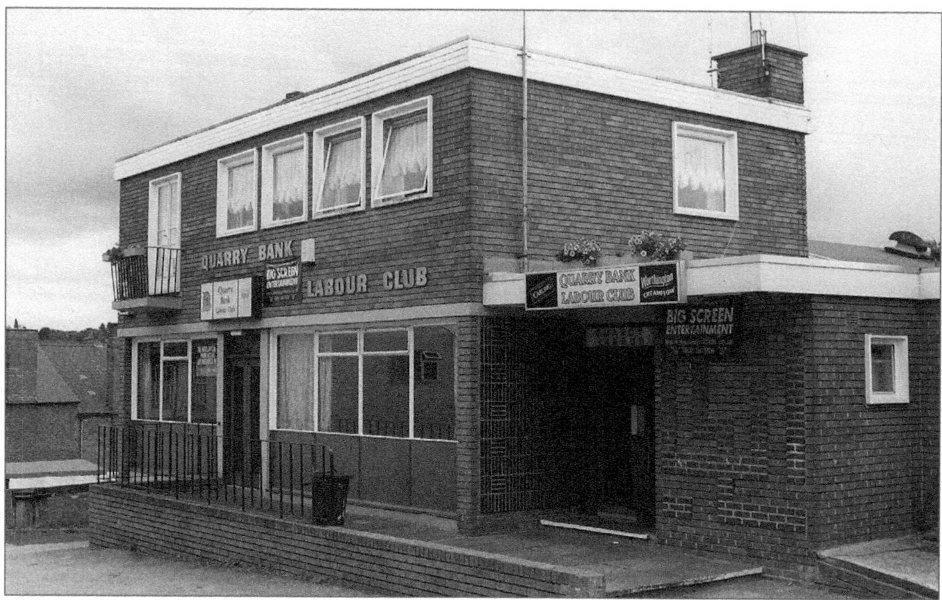

The present Labour Club building in the Lower High Street has replaced an earlier building; like its predecessor the club provides facilities that are used for non-political purposes. (*Ned Williams*)

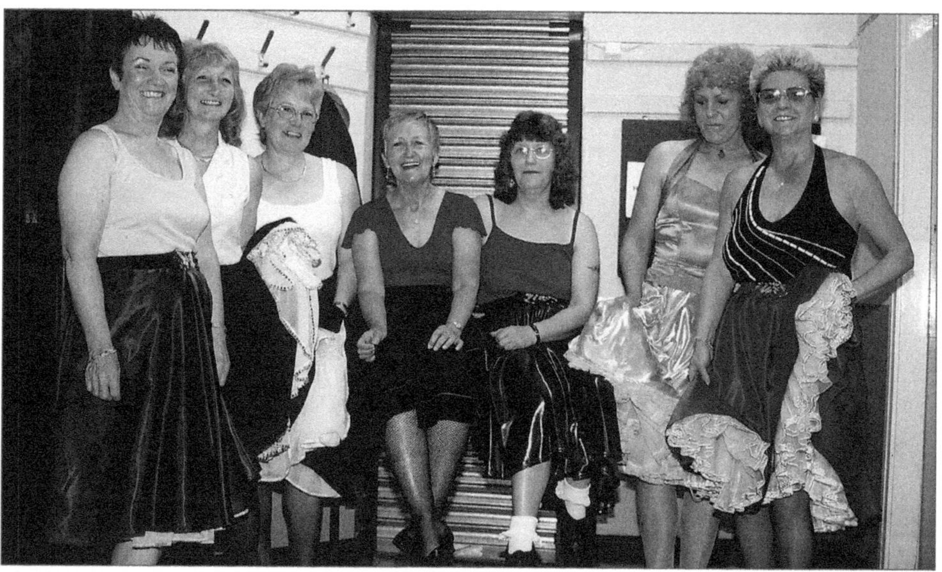

The old Labour Club seemed to be associated with playing bowls and the annual horticultural show – nowadays, on Wednesday nights, it is host to the Quarry Bank Rock and Roll Club. This picture shows Lizzie Edwards, Vera Harris, Jane Griffiths, Ceinwen Powell, Chrissie Shakespeare, Val Styles and June Ashmore at the Rock and Roll Club entrance on 24 April 2002. (*Ned Williams*)

Pat and Eddy Mattocks, married at Christ Church Quarry Bank, 9 July 1955 (*see* page 61), take to the dance floor at a holiday camp in the 1950s. (*Eddy and Pat Mattocks*)

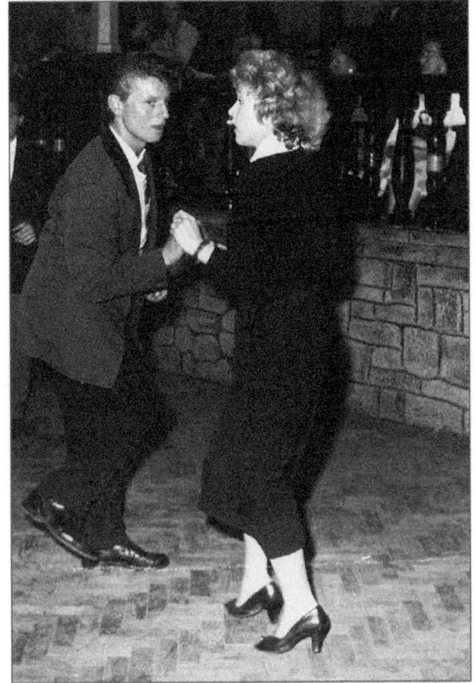

Below: Rock and Roll rocks on at the Quarry Bank Rock and Roll Club in the Labour Club on 24 April 2002. *Left*: Jean James and June Ashmore take to the floor. *Right*: Alan and June – also regulars at this Wednesday night Rock and Roll venue. (*Ned Williams*)

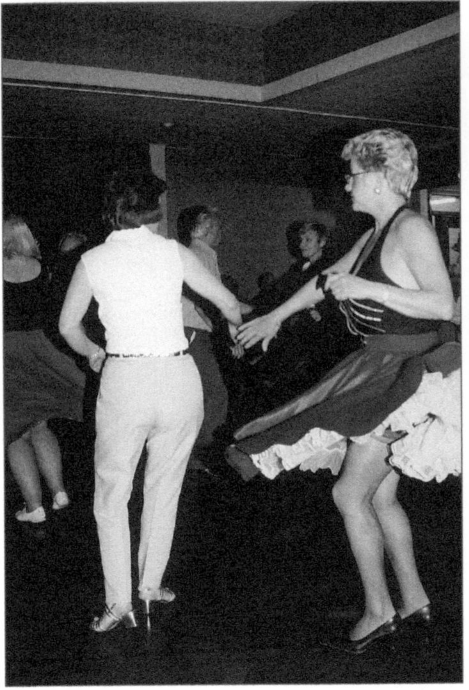

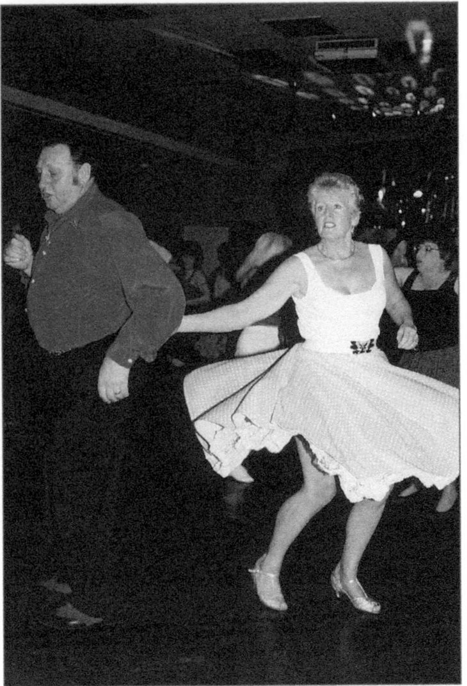

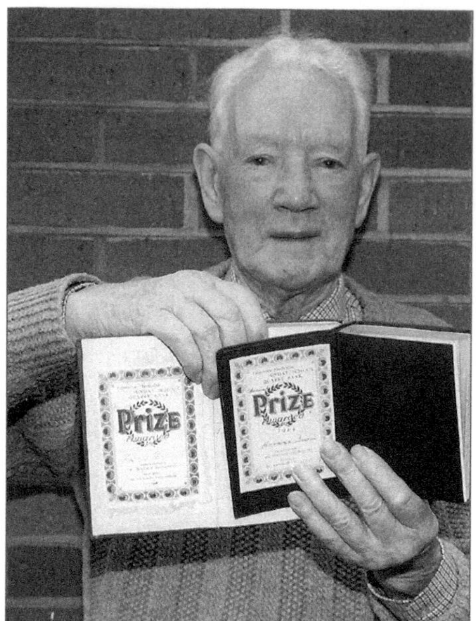

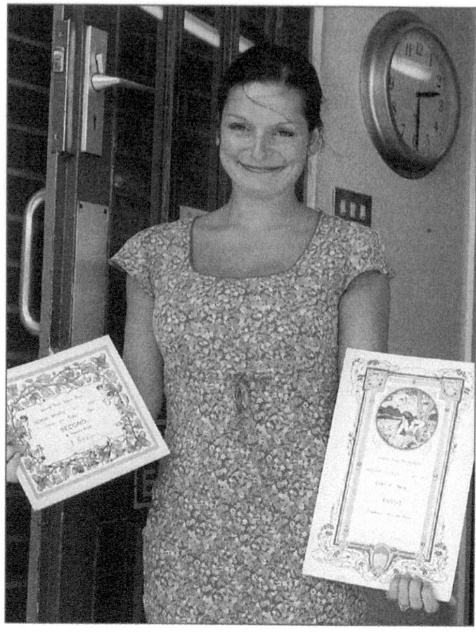

Above left: Horace Dunn shows a couple of books presented to him as attendance prizes at New Street Methodist Sunday School, *c.* 1925. Many schools and Sunday schools gave prizes of this sort containing nicely produced certificates stuck on the inside covers. *Right*: Jeanette Parsons displays ornate certificates once given out at Quarry Bank Primary School. (*Ned Williams*)

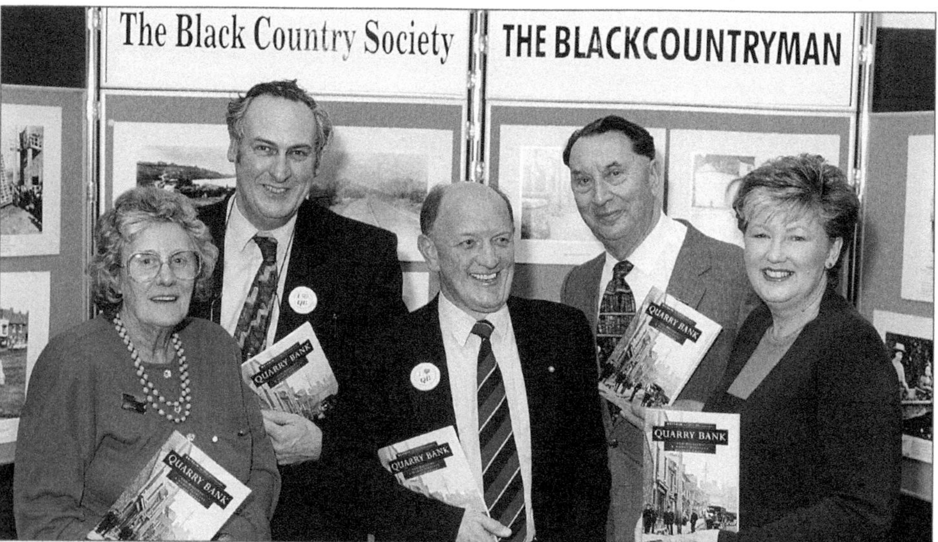

The publication of *Quarry Bank in Old Photographs* on 13 November 1998 marked the arrival of the first book ever entirely devoted to Quarry Bank. Left to right: Vi Whetton, president of the Black Country Society, Ned Williams, Dr John Woodhouse, Stan Hill, editor of the *Blackcountryman*, and Gail Bedford, head teacher at Mount Pleasant Primary School, home of the Local History Group. (*Graham Beckley*)

ACKNOWLEDGEMENTS

This book is compiled by the members of the Mount Pleasant Local History Group, all of whom have made a valuable contribution to the 'group effort'. The group is grateful to Mrs Gail Bedford, head teacher of Mount Pleasant Primary School, for making it possible for the group to be based in her school, and to the Workers' Educational Association, which continues to support the group's work.

Members of the group are grateful to all their friends and contacts who maintain a supply of photographs and information to the group. Those who have specifically contributed the photographs used in this venture include:

Mrs Askins, Graham Beckley, June Bowen, Marilyn Bullock, Julie Bird, Marjorie Blanshed, Liz Cullinane, Kathleen Day, Jabe Edwards, Margaret Price, Sybil Genner, Vera Greatorex, Brian Harris, Keith Hodgkins, Geoff Price, June Price, Ken Rock, Dawn Shaw, John Shaw, Nancy Marchant, Hazel Payne, Roger Pirie, Betty Priest, Mary Roussell, Derek Siviter, Dave Whyley, Norman Williams – all the way from California, Rose Williams, Janine Willetts, Marie Willetts, Shirley Winwood and Margaret Yates.

Over the last few years many people have contributed to the group's knowledge by correspondence or by visiting the group and passing on information. It is impossible to list all these people, but we acknowledge their help and appreciate the existence of a worldwide interest in Quarry Bank.

Help has been forthcoming from the Black Country Society, the shopkeepers, schools and churches of Quarry Bank, staff at Stourbridge Library and the Stourbridge News. All four schools have been particularly helpful in trying to make archive photographs available. The editor of the *Express & Star* has allowed us to use press photographs where these have been found among local people's collections.

Each photograph has been credited, but often the name given is the source of the photograph we have used. This is not necessarily the name of the photographer or the owner of the copyright. Every effort is made to ascertain the name of the copyright holder of a photograph but in some cases this remains obscure.

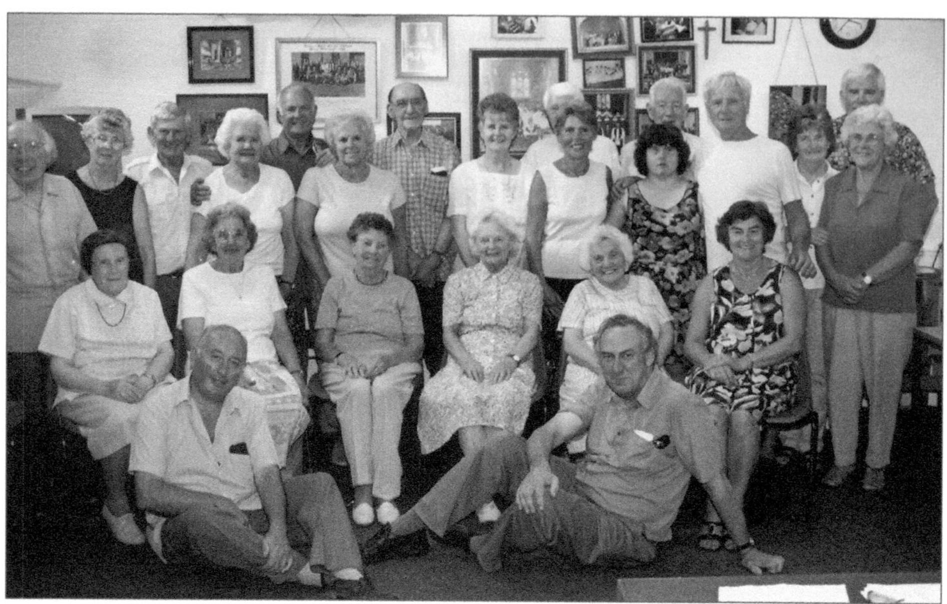

Members of the Mount Pleasant Local History Group meet in the vestry of Christ Church, Quarry Bank, in August 2003 while checking progress on this book. (*Photo by group member John James, who couldn't be in the photo and take it at the same time!*)

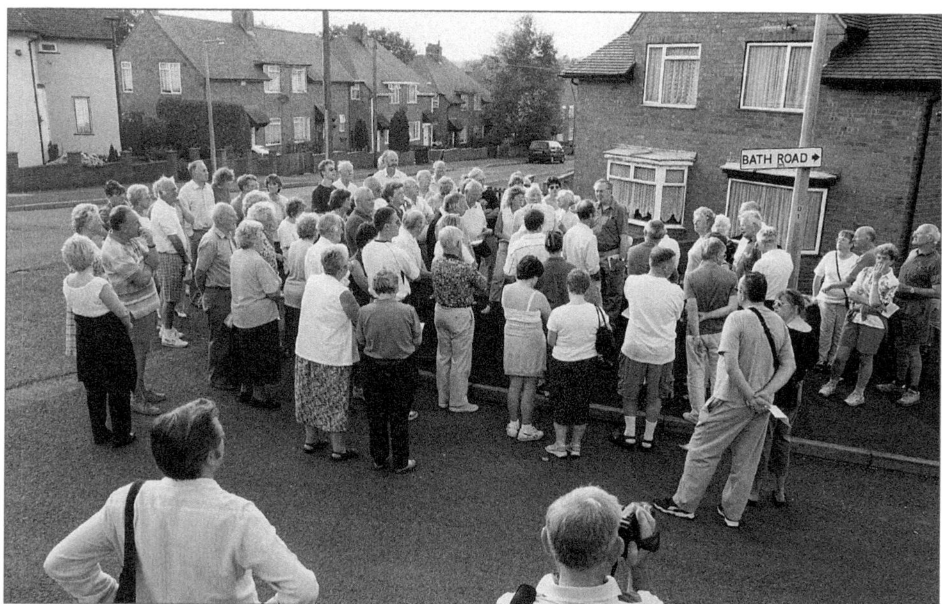

The History Group leads an exploratory walk round Quarry Bank for the Black Country Society in June 2001. The group has paused here on the corner of Birch Avenue and Bath Road to discuss the shop that once occupied the house in the background, and the origins of the name of Bath Road. (*Graham Beckley*)